Black Ducks and
AN ETHNOGRAPHY OF OL,
AND OUZINKIE, ALASKA

This publication was supported in part by a grant from the Alaska Humanities Forum and the National Endowment for the Humanities, a federal agency. The author gratefully acknowledges matching funds from the Old Harbor Tribal Council, the Old Harbor Native Corporation, the Ouzinkie Tribal Council, and the Alutiiq Museum and Archaeological Repository.

Occasional Paper Series Volume Two
The Alutiiq Museum and Archaeological Repository Occasional Paper Series is dedicated to documenting Alutiiq lifeways and traditions. Over the past two centuries many facets of Alutiiq culture have been researched and published. However, much of this valuable information continues to be inaccessible or out-of-print. Our goal is to change this by helping authors reach a wider reading audience, including the Alutiiq people themselves. With authorization from the Alaska Department of Fish and Game, the Alutiiq Museum is pleased to republish this ethnography.

—Sven Haakanson Jr., *Director*
alutiiqmuseum.com

ALUTIIQ MUSEUM AND ARCHAEOLOGICAL REPOSITORY
211 MISSION ROAD, SUITE 101, KODIAK, ALASKA 99615. (907) 486-7004

Black Ducks & Salmon Bellies

THE DONNING COMPANY PUBLISHERS

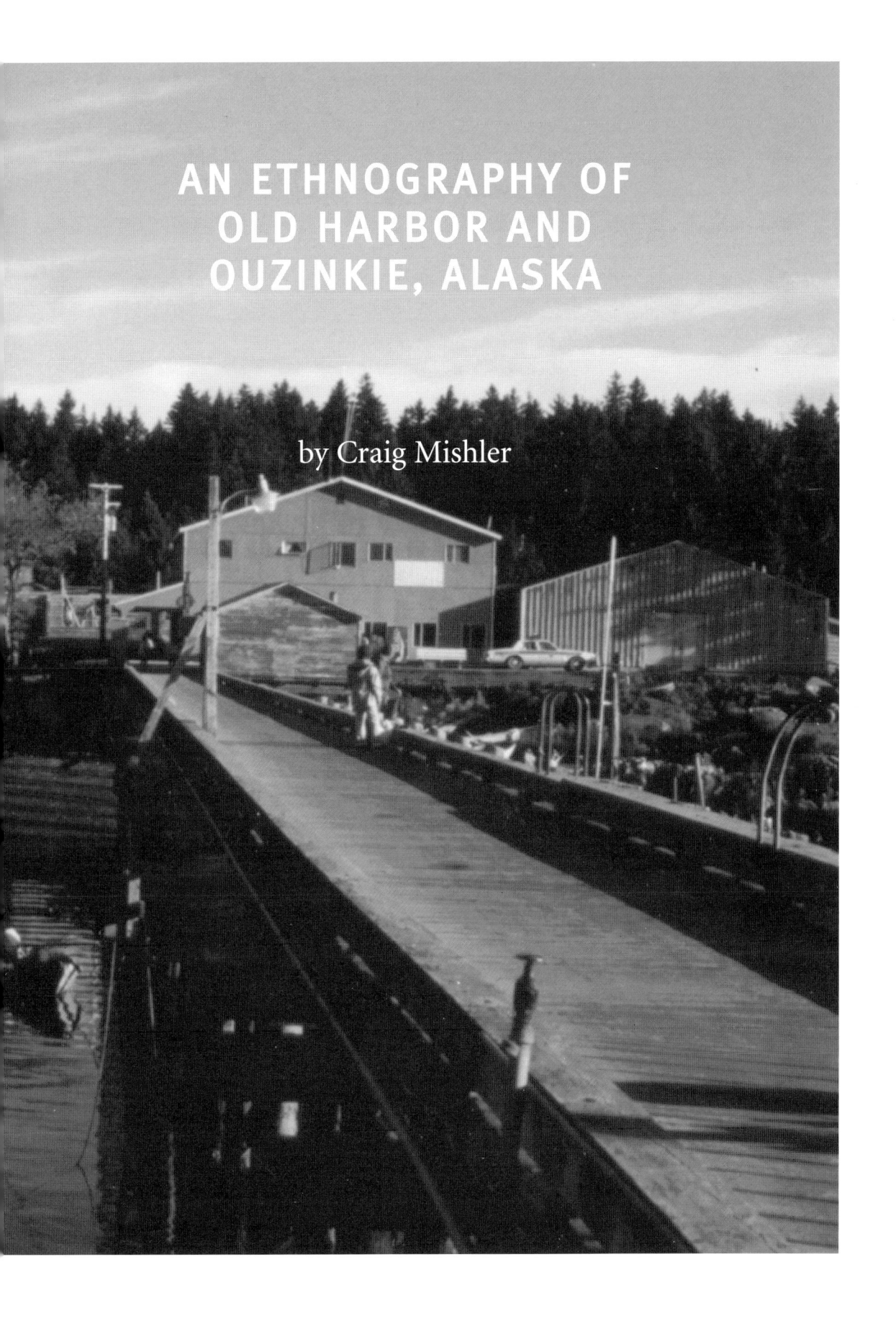

AN ETHNOGRAPHY OF OLD HARBOR AND OUZINKIE, ALASKA

by Craig Mishler

Black Ducks and Salmon Bellies was originally prepared in 2001 by the Alaska Department of Fish and Game, Division of Subsistence, for the U.S. Department of the Interior, Minerals Management Service, Cooperative Agreement Number 14-35-0001-30788, as Technical Memorandum No. 7. The report was reviewed by the Minerals Management Service and approved for publication. Approval does not signify that the contents necessarily reflect the views and policies of the Service, nor does mention of trade names or commercial products or services constitute endorsement or recommendation for use.

Copyright© 2001, 2003 by The Alaska Department of Fish and Game

All rights reserved, including the right to reproduce this work in any form whatsoever without permission in writing from the publisher, except for brief passages in connection with a review. For information, please write:

The Donning Company Publishers, 184 Business Park Drive, Suite 206, Virginia Beach, VA 23462

Steve Mull, General Manager
Barbara B. Buchanan, Office Manager
Marshall McClure, Design Production Coordinator
Richard A. Horwege, Senior Editor
Sarah Elizabeth Cardenas, Graphic Designer
Mary Ellen Wheeler, Proofreader/Editorial Assistant
Julia Kilmer, Imaging Technician
Barbara Bolton, Project Director
Anne Cordray, Project Research Coordinator
Scott Rule, Director of Marketing
Travis Gallup, Marketing Coordinator

Library of Congress Cataloging-in-Publication Data

Mishler, Craig.
  Black ducks and salmon bellies : an ethnography of Old Harbor and Ouzinkie, Alaska / Craig Mishler
    p. cm.
  ISBN 1-57864-218-3 (soft cover : alk. paper)
  1. Pacific Gulf Yupik Eskimos—History. 2. Pacific Gulf Yupik Eskimos—Folklore. 3. Pacific Gulf Yupik Eskimos—Social life and customs. 4. Spruce Island (Alaska)—History. 5. Spruce Island (Alaska)—Social life and customs. 6. Kodiak Island (Alaska)—History. 7. Kodiak Island (Alaska)—Social life and customs. I. Title

E99.E7M662 2003
979.8'4—dc21

2003055062

Printed in the United States of America

CONTENTS

Illustrations. 8

Acknowledgments. 12
    Key Respondents. 13

Introduction. 22
    Religion. 24
    Methodology. 24
    Fieldwork. 25

CHAPTER ONE
Community Histories. 28
    Old Harbor. 28
    Ouzinkie. 48
    Alaska Native Claims Settlement Act. 65
    The *Exxon Valdez* Oil Spill. 66
    Summary. 66

CHAPTER TWO
Demography. 68
    Ethnonyms. 68
    Immigration and Ethnic Identity. 68
    Regional Migrations. 72
    Family Territories. 74
    Population Trends. 75
    Social Mobility: Some Case Studies. 76
    Mortality. 77

CHAPTER THREE
Political Organization. 80
    The Native Village of Old Harbor and Its Traditional Government
        by Laurie Mulcahy. 80
        Village Governance. 80
            Overview. 80
            Meetings. 82
            Court. 82
            Positions. 84
            Toyuq. 84
            Sukashiq. 86
            Staristaq (Lay Reader and Church Warden). 86
            Elders. 88
            Summary. 89
    Old Harbor and Ouzinkie Governance Today
        by Craig Mishler. 89

CHAPTER FOUR
Kinship and Social Organization. 94
    Introduction. 94
    Kinship Terms. 96
    Kinship and Fishing. 96
    Hierarchy and Stratification. 101
    Descent. 102
    Gender Relations. 104
    Marriage and Separation: Some Case Studies. 108
    Other Social Groups. 110

CHAPTER FIVE
Expressive Culture. 112
    Holiday Festivals and Rituals. 112
        Russian Christmas. 112
        Russian New Year's (*Praznik*). 116
        Mazhlinik and Lent. 120
        Russian Easter (*Pascha*). 121
        Memorial Day. 122
        The Fourth of July. 122
        The Pilgrimage to Monk's Lagoon. 124
        Veterans Day. 125
        Thanksgiving. 125
    Music and Dance. 125
        Aboriginal-Style Music and Dance. 125
        Popular Music and Dance. 126
    Stories. 129
        Toshwak. 131
        The Battle in Fox Lagoon. 132
        The Haunted House. 133
    Basketry. 133
    Games. 135
        Traditional Games. 135
        Contemporary Games. 138
            Bingo. 138
            Card Games. 139
    Folk Speech. 140
    Banyas. 141
        Banya Construction. 142
        The Banya Experience. 144
        Banya Testimonies. 145
        A Reflective Note. 147
    Grave Iconography. 148
    Conclusion. 153

CHAPTER SIX
Subsistence and "Food for the Day". 154
    Fall and Winter. 155
    Spring and Summer. 172
        Salmon Gear Types. 178
        Salmon Processing. 181
        Other Fish. 186
        Plants and Berries. 191
    Conclusion. 191

CHAPTER SEVEN
Social and Cultural Change Since the Oil Spill. 194
    The Changing Economy. 194
    Land Buybacks: The Large-Parcel Program. 209
    The Small-Parcel Program. 213
    Corporation Dividends. 214
    The New Affluence. 215
    Enculturation of Youth. 216
    The Monk's Lagoon Controversy. 222
    Conclusion. 223

Appendix A
    Arthur Haakanson's Oral History of
    Commercial Fisheries in the Kodiak Region. 225

Appendix B
    Barabara Cove Oil Spill Journal
        by Theodore Squartsoff. 232

References Cited. 240

Index. 252

About the Author. 256

ILLUSTRATIONS

Front cover   George Inga Sr. with his great-grandson, Michael Inga

Figure 0.1.   Ouzinkie men, May 1939. 11

Figure Ackn. 1.   Sven Haakanson Sr. 14
Figure Ackn. 2.   George Inga Sr. 15
Figure Ackn. 3.   Walt Erickson. 15
Figure Ackn. 4.   Paul Kahutak (Abalik). 16
Figure Ackn. 5.   Anakenti Zeedar. 17
Figure Ackn. 6.   Nick Pestrikoff Sr. 18
Figure Ackn. 7.   Arthur Haakanson. 18
Figure Ackn. 8.   Theodore Squartsoff Sr. 19
Figure Ackn. 9.   Christine Kvasnikoff. 19
Figure Ackn. 10.   Mike Chernikoff. 21

Figure Intro. 1.   Old Harbor school, circa 1940s. 27

Figure 1.1.   Old Harbor small boat harbor, 1998. 29
Figure 1.2.   Barabaras with fish rack and cabin at Old Harbor, 1888. 30
Figure 1.3.   Old Harbor Native family in front of barabara with
                     crew members of the *Albatross*, 1888. 32
Figure 1.4.   Old Harbor Native family in front of barabara, 1888. 33
Figure 1.5.   Old Harbor Natives with skin gut parkas and kayak, 1888.   34
Figure 1.6.   *The Duchess* tender, which carried Old Harbor
                     families to the cannery at Shearwater Bay. 36
Figure 1.7.   Arthur Haakanson Sr. 37
Figure 1.8.   Rolf Christiansen holding the bow of an old kayak. 37
Figure 1.9.   Old Harbor's Three Saints Russian Orthodox Church
                     and village in the 1940s. 39
Figure 1.10.   Old Harbor in the 1940s. 39
Figure 1.11.   Old Harbor aerial photo eight months after the
                     tidal wave, November 24, 1964. 43
Figure 1.12.   Old Harbor houses under construction, with tent
                     frames in the background, November 24, 1964. 43
Figure 1.13.   Ouzinkie waterfront, as seen from the village
                     boardwalk, 1991. 46
Figure 1.14.   Ouzinkie dock and waterfront in the 1940s. 52
Figure 1.15.   SS *Denali* steamship. 53
Figure 1.16.   Mike Chernikoff with seines, circa 1940s. 54
Figure 1.17.   Women processing crab at the Ouzinkie cannery in the
                     late 1950s. 55
Figure 1.18.   Father Gerasim Schmaltz, circa 1940s. 55
Figure 1.19.   Baker House, Ouzinkie Baptist Mission, circa 1940s. 56
Figure 1.20.   Ouzinkie boat builder Wassily Squartsoff with
                     Sergei Panamarioff. 58
Figure 1.21.   Ed Opheim's handmade skiffs at Pleasant Harbor,
                     Spruce Island. 59
Figure 1.22.   Cannery mess hall washed into the sea by the tidal
                     wave, 1964. 61

Figure 1.23.	Closeup of cannery superintendent's house washed into the sea as a result of the 1964 earthquake and tsunami.	61
Figure 1.24.	Ouzinkie waterfront, 1989, shortly after the *Exxon Valdez* oil spill.	63
Figure 1.25.	Ouzinkie community hall, 1997.	64
Figure 2.1.	Kodiak Alutiiq Band Designations.	69
Figure 2.2.	Old Harbor Native Families, 1990s.	70
Figure 2.3.	Ouzinkie Native Families, 1990s.	71
Figure 2.4.	120-Year Population History.	76
Figure 2.5.	Recent Population Figures.	77
Figure 3.1.	Russian Orthodox Church and village of Old Harbor, 1997.	87
Figure 4.1.	Three generations of Haakansons.	95
Figure 4.2.	Kodiak Alutiiq Kinship Terms.	97–99
Figure 4.3.	Marriage Patterns by Ethnicity: Ouzinkie 1993.	105
Figure 4.4.	Marriage Patterns by Ethnicity: Old Harbor 1991.	106
Figure 4.5.	Eagle in the Rigging, Old Harbor, 1997.	111
Figure 5.1.	Ouzinkie masqarataqs, 1946.	117
Figure 5.2.	Masqarataq whistle made by Thomas Ignatin, Old Harbor.	117
Figure 5.3.	Colored Easter eggs with *kulich* (Easter bread) and tea at the home of George and Sophie Inga, 1998.	121
Figure 5.4.	Larry Matfay, Old Harbor, 1996.	126
Figure 5.5.	Arthur Matfay, Old Harbor, 1998.	127
Figure 5.6.	Fedosia Inga, June 1970.	134
Figure 5.7.	Aurcaq dart set made by Thomas Ignatin, Old Harbor.	136
Figure 5.8.	Loptuq playing field.	138
Figure 5.9.	Anakenti Zeedar's banya, Old Harbor, 1997.	142
Figure 5.10.	Old Harbor child's grave with toy boat.	148
Figure 5.11.	Old Harbor elder's grave, 1997.	149
Figure 5.12.	Old Harbor grave with blue cross and old rubber boot.	150
Figure 5.13.	Old Harbor fisherman's grave overlooking Sitkalidak Strait.	150
Figure 5.14.	Ouzinkie grave with miniature chapel containing icon and Easter eggs.	151
Figure 5.15.	Closeup of Ouzinkie miniature grave chapel with Orthodox onion dome.	152
Figure 5.16.	Ouzinkie grave with raised box.	152
Figure 5.17.	Ouzinkie grave with red, white, and blue ribbon on the cross.	152
Figure 6.0.	Seasonal Resource Use in Old Harbor and Ouzinkie, 1990s.	155
Figure 6.1	Theodore Squartsoff Sr. and Theodore Jr. plucking ducks at Barabara Cove, October 1996.	158
Figure 6.2.	Theodore Squartsoff Sr. singeing a duck at his camp in Barabara Cove, October 1996.	159
Figure 6.3.	Theodore Squartsoff's scrubbed mallard duck.	163
Figure 6.4.	Theodore Squartsoff with live octopus near Ouzinkie in May 1990.	167

Figure 6.5.	Ivan Karakin and his wife Keratina, better known as Mashataq.	168
Figure 6.6.	Theodore Squartsoff's aluminum skiff.	179
Figure 6.7.	Paul Kahutak (Abalik) at his smokehouse in Old harbor, 1996.	183
Figure 6.8.	Page from author's field notes on cutting a salmon for salt bellies.	184
Figure 6.9.	Walt Erickson salting salmon in Old Harbor, 1997.	185
Figure 6.10.	Anakenti Zeedar holding cod and halibut jigging gear in Old Harbor, 1990.	187
Figure 6.11.	Toni Squartsoff making pirok with a Russian Orthodox cross in the top crust, Ouzinkie, 1997.	189
Figure 7.1.	Ouzinkie houses with rooftop satellite TV dishes, 1996.	195
Figure 7.2.	Old Harbor purse seiner, the *Carla Rae C.*	196
Figure 7.3.	Kodiak Commercial Salmon Ex-Vessel Prices, 1987–1996.	197
Figure 7.3A.	Kodiak Commercial Salmon Ex-Vessel Prices, 1987–1996.	197
Figure 7.4.	Kodiak Commercial Salmon Ex-Vessel Values, 1987–1996.	198
Figure 7.4A.	Kodiak Commerical Salmon Ex-Vessel Values (in Millions), 1987–1996.	198
Figure 7.5.	Japanese logging ship in Danger Bay, 1994.	201
Figure 7.6.	Transportation Old Harbor style: the purse seiner *Glennette C.*	202
Figure 7.7.	Old Harbor sport fish and touring boat, the *Sitkalidak Strait*, 1997.	205
Figure 7.8.	The Sitkalidak Lodge in Old Harbor, 1997.	205
Figure 7.9.	Magazine display ads for Old Harbor Guides and Outfitters.	206
Figure 7.10.	Jeff Peterson dressing out halibut caught by his sports fishing clients, Old Harbor, September 1999.	207
Figure 7.11.	Herman Squartsoff's charter skiff display ad.	208
Figure 7.12.	Old Harbor Native Corporation office.	211
Figure 7.13.	New barabara in Old Harbor, built in 1997.	218
Figure 7.14.	Ed Gregorieff of Tatitlek and George Inga Sr. of Old Harbor in Cordova for the Youth-Elders Conference, August 1998.	221
Figure App. A.1.	Crab pots and buoys, Old Harbor lagoon, 1993.	231
Figure App. B.1.	Squartsoff family cabins at Barabara Cove, Kizhuyak Bay, October 1996.	232
Author bio.	Craig Mishler with silver salmon in Old Harbor, 1998.	256
Back Cover	Skiff windshield splashed by salt water and sunshine near Old Harbor, 1999.	

MAPS

Map 1.	Twentieth Century Kodiak Communities.	23
Map 2.	Old Harbor.	45
Map 3.	Ouzinkie.	49
Map 4.	Large Parcel Land Buybacks, Kodiak Archipelago, 1990s.	212

Fig. 0.1. *Ouzinkie men, May 1939. Father Gerasim is second from right and Kolya (Nick) Pestrikoff, third from right. Peter Pestrikoff is front row left with hands in pockets. Herman Anderson is back row, fifth from left. Philip Katelnikoff is back row, seventh from left, with string tie. Freddy Katelnikoff is behind Philip. Vinokouroff Collection, Alaska State Library, Juneau, PCA-243-2-189.*

ACKNOWLEDGMENTS

It would be impossible to list all of the individuals I have worked with in Old Harbor and Ouzinkie over the past ten years, but there are many, both living and dead, who informed my field notes and shaped my thinking. If their names have been overlooked, the oversight is unintentional.

In addition to all the key respondents listed below, I would especially like to thank the community leaders in Old Harbor and Ouzinkie who gave me the necessary permission to undertake the research and thought it would be beneficial to their communities. In Old Harbor, Emil Christiansen of the Old Harbor Native Corporation, Mayor Rick Berns and members of the Old Harbor City Council, and Tony Azuyak, Al Cratty Jr., Jeff Peterson, and other past and present members of the Old Harbor Tribal Council were all very supportive, along with the late Larry Matfay. In Ouzinkie, I am grateful to have had the encouragement of Andy Anderson of the Ouzinkie Native Corporation, Mayor Zack Chichenoff and members of the Ouzinkie City Council, and Alex Ambrosia, Mike Boskofsky, Paul Panamarioff, Angeline Campfield, and other past and present members of the Ouzinkie Tribal Council.

Other persons who assisted in my research are Bruce Parham of the National Archives in Anchorage, Amy Steffian of the Alutiiq Museum in Kodiak, Alice Ryser of the Kodiak Historical Society and Baranov Museum in Kodiak, Marti Murray in Phoenix, and Ann Elizabeth Williams in Anchorage. Jim Fall of the Alaska Department of Fish and Game, Division of Subsistence, and Don Callaway of the National Park Service (on behalf of the Minerals Management Service) provided lots of guidance in the shaping of the ethnography and supplied numerous comments on early and later drafts. Jim Fall deserves special mention for his support and encouragement over my ten years at the Division of Subsistence and for helping to get this book republished. I shall not forget the cordial assistance of two cartographers, Carol Barnhill at the Department of Fish and Game, who composed the two area maps, and Carol Belenski of the Bureau of Land Management, who created the community maps. I am also grateful to my daughter Susanna for accompanying me twice to Old

Harbor. On one trip she helped me collect biological samples, and on a later visit operated the video camera while I did oral interviews. I wish to thank my cousin Clark Mishler for his fetching photo of my Aurcaq dart game set, and Janet Cohen, my dedicated field work assistant.

Naomi Klouda, a freelance journalist who worked as my local assistant doing subsistence harvest surveys in Old Harbor in the fall of 1998, has shared with me many of her keenly perceptive observations and has aided substantially in helping me revise the manuscript, imparting to it some much-needed rigor. As a resident of Old Harbor, Naomi has given me a much better grasp of the profound changes tourism has had on the people and economy of that community in the 1990s.

I am especially grateful to Laurie Mulcahy for allowing me to include her well-researched essay on Old Harbor's political organization in Chapter 3. This paper, written under a Bureau of Indian Affairs grant to the Kodiak Area Native Association in 1987, was never published but remains on file at the Alutiiq Museum in Kodiak. I have made a few minor edits to bring it to its present form. Its original title was, "The History of the Traditional Native Village of Old Harbor and Its Government."

My other longtime colleagues in Kodiak ethnographic research, Nancy Yaw Davis and Rachel Mason, both took an early critical look at the manuscript and shared with me their wealth of field experience in these communities. Both Nancy and Rachel continue to inspire and enlighten with their abundant energy, careful thinking, endless good humor, and love for the people. Finally, I owe much in the way of appreciation to Sven Haakanson Jr., director of the Alutiiq Museum, for coordinating the republication of this volume and helping me find the financial support to make it go forward.

KEY RESPONDENTS

Old Harbor

Mary and Sven Haakanson Sr.
This couple is rather unique in that both are the children of Scandinavian men who married local Alutiiq women. Sven's father was Danish and Mary's father was Norwegian. Sven served with Paul Kahutak in the U.S. Army in the 1950s, and for twenty-three years, from 1968 until 1991, he was the mayor of Old Harbor. A distinguished community leader, he sat on the Old Harbor Native Corporation Board of Directors and also served many years on the Board of Directors for the Kodiak Area Native Association and the Koniag Corporation. Sven had his own purse seiner and for many years made a living commercial fishing for salmon. Up until his death in November 2002, Sven worked seasonally as a construction camp cook, and he and Mary continued to cook for special events in the community such as the Alutiiq Heritage Week at the Old Harbor school. In

Fig. Ackn. 1. *Sven Haakanson Sr. Photo by Craig Mishler.*

1998 Sven and Mary worked as cooks at Dig Afognak, an archaeological site and culture camp on Afognak Island. Their son, Sven Haakanson Jr., now director of the Alutiiq Museum, graduated from Harvard University graduate school in anthropology and has spent several years doing ethnographic fieldwork among the Nenets reindeer herders on Russia's Yamal Peninsula. Subsistence foods form a substantial part of the Haakansons' diet. Mary, a fluent speaker of Alutiiq, is very active in processing subsistence foods, and her favorites are fish, fish eggs, and seal. In her own words, "I crave for fish, mainly salmon."

Ron Bernsten

Ron Bernsten was born in King Cove on the Alaska Peninsula in 1943 and moved to Kodiak in 1960. He has a twin brother in False Pass and an older brother in King Cove. He came to Old Harbor from Kodiak in 1965 and married Betty Alexanderoff, an Old Harbor woman, in 1970. They have several children. In the 1990s Ron was elected president of the Old Harbor School Board and he has also served on the Kodiak Regional Fish and Game Advisory Committee. He made his living crewing as a commercial fisherman until forced to retire for health reasons. In 1990 he sold his limited entry permit and all his gear to his son Darryl for a two-dollar bill. Built like an offensive tackle, Ron says his favorite football team is the Oakland Raiders, and he usually wears his Raiders jacket as he drives around the village on his four-wheeler.

Ron has taken an active role in local and regional politics. He frequently testifies at public hearings and considers deepwater trawlers or "draggers" to be a detriment to the marine environment. At a public hearing held in Old Harbor in November 1991, Ron made a speech in which he described God's creation of the earth and all its animals and concluded that God put them all here under the trust and care of the Native people. This speech was later published in the *Tundra Times* (Berntsen 1991).

George Inga Sr.

Born in 1925, George Inga Sr. is one of the most respected elders in Old Harbor and comes from one of the oldest Old Harbor Alutiiq families.

Having served in the Aleutian Islands as part of the Eleventh Air Force, "Papa George" is a veteran of World War II. For many years he was the owner and captain of a salmon purse seiner but finally gave up his boat after commercial fishing was closed for the season following the *Exxon Valdez* oil spill. After that, he crewed for several years with his friend Walt Erickson and has now retired from a lifetime of fishing, but he still gets out now and again in his aluminum skiff.

From 1989 until 1996 he conducted numerous community harvest surveys working for the Division of Subsistence at the Alaska Department of Fish and Game was awarded a certificate of appreciation for his outstanding service. George is a fluent speaker of Alutiiq and teaches the language to children in the elementary grades at the Old Harbor school.

After the tragic loss of his granddaughter to chicken pox in the early 1990s, George and his wife Sophie decided to adopt and raise their great-grandson Michael. George is a member of the Board of Directors of the Old Harbor Native Corporation and serves on the church committee of the Old Harbor Russian Orthodox Church. Two of his favorite activities are playing bingo and listening to country music. His favorite Native foods are fish, clams, and brown bear meat, but he also goes wild for salmon berries.

Fig. Ackn. 2. *George Inga Sr. Photo by Craig Mishler.*

Walt Erickson

Walt was born in the Chigniks in 1924 and moved to Kodiak in 1941. His father was a Swedish Finn. Walt entered the Army during World War II, and after the war he worked for several years as a baker in Kodiak. He came to Old Harbor in 1960,

Fig. Ackn. 3. *Walt Erickson. Photo by Craig Mishler.*

married a local woman, Jennie Inga, and turned to commercial salmon fishing and trapping to make a living. He and his wife adopted three children. In 1996 he sold his boat, *The Merganser,* to his son-in-law's son-in-law and retired from commercial fishing. He remained active by operating a small grocery store in the village, which he first opened in 1968, until his death in March 2000 (see Rostad 2000). Walt served on the Board of Directors of the Old Harbor Native Corporation. He was also a member of the Kodiak Elders Advisory Group for the Alaska Rural Systemic Initiative, a group dedicated to improving the state's rural education curriculum. By generously extending credit at his store, Walt was praised for carrying many people through hard times (Klouda 2000).

Paul Kahutak (Abalik)

Paul is an elder who was born on Woody Island in 1933. His father was from Eagle Harbor, and his mother, who died when he was six years old, was from Carmel (Halibut Bay) on the west side of Kodiak Island. After being widowed, Paul's father moved with the children to Rolling Bay, on the south end of Sitkalidak Island near Old Harbor. Paul briefly attended Mt. Edgecumbe High School in Sitka where he was an amateur boxer but has spent most of his life as a subsistence bear hunter, commercial fisherman, and trapper. He was drafted and served in the U.S. Army in Fairbanks and Anchorage for two years during the mid-1950s. Because of her medical condition, Paul's wife Martha must remain in Anchorage most of the time, so he travels back and forth, spending about half of the year with her and half of the year with his daughter and son-in-law and their children in Old Harbor. He is a *staristaq* or church warden in the Russian Orthodox Church and a fluent speaker of Alutiiq. Though largely inactive in recent years, Abalik is also a skilled musician, playing accordion, guitar, and piano.

Fig. Ackn. 4. *Paul Kahutak (Abalik). Photo by Craig Mishler.*

Freddy Christiansen

Freddy was born and raised in Old Harbor. He is a young commercial fisherman and seine boat captain. A former president of the Old Harbor Tribal Council, Freddy now serves on the Board of Directors of the Alaska Federation of Natives. In 1989 Freddy and Rick Berns, another boat captain, invested in a lodge and cafe, the first ever built in Old Harbor. After several years, Freddy bought out his partner, and since then has developed a tourist business based on the lodge and an excursion boat, the *Sitkalidak Straits*. Freddy is a visionary, leading the way in developing ecotourism in the community. These leadership qualities have led to his election to the Board of Directors of the Koniag Corporation. Freddy is married to Glenna, has two daughters, and his fishing boat, the *Tarissa Jean C*, is named after his oldest daughter.

Anakenti Zeedar
The late Anakenti Zeedar, who passed away on February 18, 1996, at the age of seventy-seven, was a genuinely friendly elder who took me and my daughter out to collect oil spill samples of cod, salmon, butter clams, and chitons. He was largely monolingual in Alutiiq, and I usually had to use a translator (George Inga Sr.) to interview him, but he was extremely knowledgeable about traditional ways of harvesting and using wild foods. Anakenti and his wife Nina spoke Alutiiq almost exclusively in their home. He lived a subsistence lifestyle and served as a *staristaq* in the Old Harbor Russian Orthodox Church. We always had an ongoing joke about his becoming a millionaire at my expense.

Fig. Ackn. 5. *Anakenti Zeedar. Photo by Craig Mishler.*

Ouzinkie

Martha Anderson
Martha Anderson (*née* Katelnikoff) was born in Ouzinkie in 1920 and raised in a log cabin. Her father spoke fluent Russian. In 1940 she married Herman Anderson, and they had ten children. During the 1940s she worked summers processing salmon at the Grimes Packing Company cannery. After World War II she commercially fished with her husband and sons and was the first woman in the village to do so. Their seine boats were called the *Fortune* and the *Fawn*. Now widowed, Martha generally spends her summers in Ouzinkie and her winters in Anchorage. Although raised as a Russian Orthodox, she and two of her daughters have since converted to become Jehovah's Witnesses.

Nick Pestrikoff Sr.

Nick was born in Ouzinkie in 1935, one of thirteen children in the family. After his father passed away in 1943, he was raised at the Kodiak Baptist Mission. Nick was hired to work as a deck hand on a purse seiner for the first time in 1950. After that he worked his way up to skiff man, then skipper, and boat owner. Nick married Lilly Ellanak from Karluk, and they have five children. For over twenty years, off and on, Nick worked in Anchorage bingo halls, popular gathering places for Alaska Natives, but he was never a bingo player. Now semiretired, Nick and his family returned to live in Ouzinkie in the mid-1990s. Along with Walt Erickson, he is a member of the Kodiak Elders Advisory Group for the Alaska Rural Systemic Initiative, a group dedicated to improving the state's rural education curriculum.

Fig. Ackn. 6. *Nick Pestrikoff Sr. Photo by Craig Mishler.*

Arthur Haakanson

Arthur was born in Deadman's Bay near Akhiok in 1931 and was named after his father, a Danish immigrant. His mother was from Eagle Harbor. He was raised in Old Harbor with his brothers, Sven and Herman, before moving to Ouzinkie while he was still a child. Arthur worked for many years with his father gill-netting and hand purse-seining as a commercial fisherman. He is a former mayor of Ouzinkie, and a founding member of the Ouzinkie Native Corporation. Sometime around 1970 he went to Washington, D.C., to lobby for Alaska Native land claims. From 1978 to 1985 he lived in Old Harbor before returning to Ouzinkie. Most recently he has worked as the land manager for the Ouzinkie Native Corporation.

Fig. Ackn. 7. *Arthur Haakanson. Photo by Craig Mishler.*

Theodore Squartsoff Sr.

Born in 1943, Theodore was raised in a large Alutiiq family and has himself raised a large family of five girls and one boy. He is an active commercial gill-net salmon fisherman and each summer oversees a crew of four college students. Theodore and two of his brothers, Pete and Martin, spend each fall hunting ducks and deer at their family's traditional camp at Barabara Cove in upper Kazhuyak Bay near Port Lions, where they each have a cabin. Theodore probably spends more time out on his skiff doing subsistence than anyone else in Ouzinkie and seldom comes home empty-handed. Always on the go, he keeps a watchful eye on all the birds, animals, fish, and shellfish in and around Marmot Bay, Kizhuyak Bay, and the straits between Spruce Island and Kodiak Island.

Fig. Ackn. 8. Theodore Squartsoff Sr. Photo by Craig Mishler.

Although he says he is not a political man and not a religious man, Theodore is seldom short on opinions. Prosperous from their years of hard work as a fishing family, Theodore and his wife Toni recently built a five-thousand-square-foot house with a magnificent view of the ocean where they now run a bed and breakfast. In March 1994, I watched Theodore's three grandchildren playing in a giant playpen he built out of plastic water pipe and recycled gill net. I was amused to see him enjoying his grandchildren as if they were little fish that he had caught. For the first time anywhere, Theodore shares here the unique and timely journal he kept during the 1989 oil spill (see Appendix B).

Christine Kvasnikoff

Christine was born October 26, 1928. Her father was Trafeme or Trefim Shanigan, who came from the village of Katmai, and her mother was Verna Squartsoff. They had six children, and Christine was the only girl. Her father trapped in Seal Bay and Perenosa Bay on Afognak Island. Christine only went as

Fig. Ackn. 9. Christine Kvasnikoff. Photo by Craig Mishler.

far as the eighth grade because her father could not afford to send her to Mt. Edgecumbe, the Native high school in Sitka. Christine was first married to Peter Wolkoff, who drowned on a crab boat tender in 1950. She was later remarried to Ponto Kvasnikoff from Ninilchik.

Ed Opheim Sr.
Born in the Shumagin Islands in 1910, Ed is the son of an Aleut woman who married a Norwegian immigrant. He spent part of his youth in Seattle and arrived in Ouzinkie from Seattle in 1923 with his brothers and his father Chris Opheim. For the next ten years he became a cod fisherman. The family acquired land on Spruce Island at nearby Sunny Cove and started a small saltery. Right after World War II, Ed bought and operated Ouzinkie's first pool hall and dance hall. In 1945 he settled in at Pleasant Harbor, located on Spruce Island about five miles from Ouzinkie, and became one of Alaska's most famous fox farmers and small boat builders. He is also a prolific writer, having published several books and numerous articles on skiff and dory building in the *Alaska Sportsman* magazine. A widower twice over, he now spends his summers in Pleasant Harbor and his winters in Kodiak. His favorite hobby is writing letters to the editor of the *Kodiak Mirror* newspaper.

Reed Oswalt
Reed is a non-Native who worked at the Grimes Packing Company cannery in Ouzinkie with his father, Marion "Jake" Oswalt, from the 1940s through the 1960s. Reed took many quality photographs of village life and has a large personal photograph collection which he shared with me for this project. His photographic memory is just as good as his prints. Reed and his wife now live in Kodiak.

Hender Toms
Hender was the business manager and bookkeeper at the Grimes Packing Company cannery in Ouzinkie from 1936 to 1951 and has an excellent memory of labor and management relations during those years. He is retired and living in Seattle.

Joyce Smith
Joyce is a Baptist missionary who first came to Ouzinkie in the early 1950s with her husband Norman Smith. She worked for many years as the community's public health aide, a position from which she retired in the early 1990s. Widowed in 1996, Joyce continues to run a preschool and teaches Sunday school to children in the community. She provided me with copies of some missionary letters and two issues of *The Spruce Bough*, an Ouzinkie school newspaper mimeographed in 1946 and 1947. Joyce and Norman kindly supplied us with a place to stay when we first arrived in Ouzinkie shortly after the *Exxon Valdez* oil spill in 1989.

Mike and Jenny Chernikoff

The late Mike and Jenny Chernikoff were very knowledgeable about Alutiiq place names around Spruce Island and Afognak, and they freely shared with me a lot of their stories and experiences. This elderly couple was amusing because they would argue and debate small facts with great passion. Once when I complained about the intensity of these debates, Jenny said, "If you don't argue, it's a sign of a sick mind." When I walked into the Chernikoffs' house, it was like turning the clock back to the 1940s. Except for their television set, none of their furnishings had changed in fifty years. They still cooked and heated the house with a wood stove, preferring it to a more convenient oil stove. Mike was a fluent speaker of Alutiiq and English, and Jenny was fluent in Russian and English.

Fig. Ackn. 10. *Mike Chernikoff. Photo by Craig Mishler.*

Esther and Fred Chernikoff Sr.

Fred Chernikoff is the son of Mike and Jenny Chernikoff, and he grew up in Ouzinkie with his wife Esther, whose family is originally from Carlsen Point (Larsen Bay). Fred and Esther are avid social dancers and provided a wealth of information about the old Ouzinkie dance halls, musicians, and holiday celebrations. Now retired, they divide their time between Ouzinkie and Anchorage.

INTRODUCTION

Old Harbor and Ouzinkie (locally pronounced "Yu-zink-ee") are located at opposite ends of the Kodiak Island archipelago on the northern Gulf Coast of Alaska (see Map 1). Along with Akhiok, Karluk, Larsen Bay, and Port Lions, they are two of the six Kodiak area Alaska Native villages impacted by the *Exxon Valdez* oil spill of 1989. I have paired Ouzinkie and Old Harbor together because they are communities with strikingly similar histories, economies, and climates, and because I have spent an extensive amount of time in each village. I would be less than honest, however, if I did not admit that I also selected these communities because of the continued hospitality and friendship of their residents and their zest for living a subsistence way of life. In a very real sense they selected me by encouraging me to come back again and again.

An ethnography is an anthropological description of many facets of cultural life. It includes such topics as local history, demography, political organization, kinship and social organization, expressive culture, subsistence, and social change, all of which are treated here in depth. An ethnography also illuminates the grain and texture and vibrancy of life as it exists in the present day. For the purposes of this book, the "present day" encompasses a ten-year time window beginning in June 1989, when I first discovered these two communities, through September 1999. The challenge of writing this ethnography has been to record what is traditional and constant along with what is changing and flowing.

One subject which needs some preliminary clarification is the ethnic background of the people who dwell in these communities. As I go on to demonstrate in Chapter 2, ethnicity has become rather complex during the historic period due to waves of intermarriage, even though the "core population" consisted of aboriginals often identified in the literature as Sugpiaq or Pacific Eskimo (Davis 1984, Clark 1984b), according to their linguistic affiliation with Central Yup'ik. More recently, the term *Alutiiq* has been used in place of *Sugpiaq* in linguistic accounts (Leer 1989, 1990) and has found increasing acceptance within the scholarly community (Pullar 1992; Mishler and Mason 1996; Mishler 1997). The term *Koniag* also retains some currency and is found in many historic sources. The regional for-profit Native corporation for Kodiak communities is called Koniag Inc.

Map 1. Twentieth Century Kodiak Communities

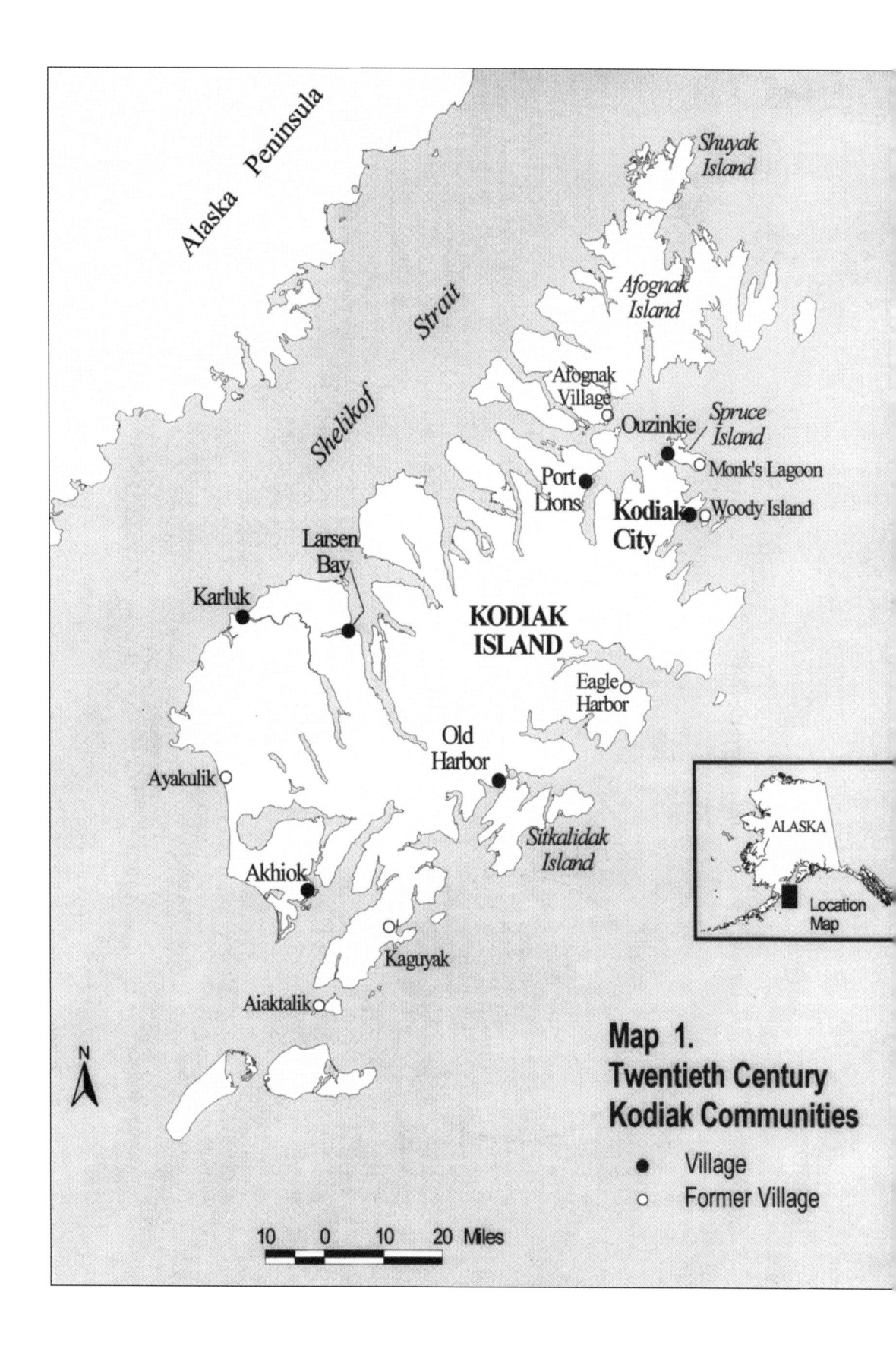

- ● Village
- ○ Former Village

Introduction

Ironically, the people of Ouzinkie and Old Harbor insist on calling themselves "Aleut," even though they have no linguistic or ethnic affiliation with the Aleut language spoken in the Aleutian Islands. This is because the word *Aleut* was used by Russian fur traders in the late eighteenth and early nineteenth centuries to lump together all of the coastal peoples they encountered except the Tlingit and Dena'ina, in a fashion very similar to the way *Native* is used by Anglo-Americans today.

In the chapters that follow, I generally employ the term *Alutiiq*, though sometimes *Koniag* occasionally seems more appropriate because it is more regionally specific and relates better to the early historic period. *Alutiiq*, on the other hand, may refer to the entire culture area where the Alutiiq language is spoken. This includes not only the communities of Old Harbor, Ouzinkie, Akhiok, Karluk, Larsen Bay, Port Lions, and Kodiak City within the Kodiak archipelago, but also the lower Cook Inlet communities of Nanwalek and Port Graham, the Prince William Sound communities of Tatitlek and Chenega Bay, and the Alaska Peninsula communities of Chignik Bay, Chignik Lake, Chignik Lagoon, Perryville, Ivanof Bay, Port Heiden, Pilot Point, and Egegik.

Religion

An overwhelming majority of the Native residents of Old Harbor and Ouzinkie are Russian Orthodox Christians. I have written about some historical aspects of Russian Orthodoxy in Chapter 1, about various forms of religious expression in Chapter 6, and about recent religious controversy in Chapter 7. Nevertheless, I have not included any extended discussion of contemporary Koniag religious belief and practice. This omission is not due to any lack of interest in the subject on my part but comes in deference to the many scholarly sources already available on this subject. Robert Rathburn (1981), for example, interprets Russian Orthodoxy as a uniquely Alaska Native institution and feels that the adjective *Russian* is very misleading, even though the faith was originally introduced by Russians. Other good sources dealing with Orthodoxy in the Kodiak area are Davis (1970), Williams (1993), and Mousalimas (1995). Golder (1968) and Eliel (1989) have written biographies of church leaders, Gregory (1977) and Oleksa (1990) have compiled church missionary histories, and Smith et al. (1994) provide a visual feast illustrating Orthodox religious art.

Methodology

The principal source of information used in the research and writing of this monograph was the systematic recording of events in my own field notes, supplemented by oral interviews with key respondents, mostly elders. One of the conscious and reflexive methods I have used in the writing of the ethnography is to transcribe substantial portions of my interviews with the elders so that readers can "hear" Alutiiq voices and recognize them within the context of dialogues. Consequently, I have edited the syntax and phrasing of their speech as little as possible to preserve their identity and authenticity. To the extent that many elders in each community contributed stories, opinions, thoughts, and observations to this ethnography, the result is at once multivocal and polyphonic.

As often as possible, I tried to participate in subsistence hunting and fishing and other social activities such as bingo, seniors dinners, wrestling meets, basketball games, and council meetings. In many cases my travel to these communities was prompted by other projects only distantly related to the ethnography. Over the years, one of my duties as a Subsistence Resource Specialist was to collect household harvest data through structured questionnaires. Immediately following the *Exxon Valdez* oil spill it was my responsibility to collect samples of subsistence foods for chemical testing to determine whether they were contaminated or safe to eat. Still another duty, since 1992, was to recruit and train local hires and administer bi-annual harvest surveys on the subsistence taking of harbor seals and Steller sea lions. All of these tasks have led to opportunities to observe and participate in village life, even though the idea of writing an ethnography was not conceived until late in 1995.

In working with elders, it was my consistent practice to compensate them at the rate of $30/hour, paid by check. When tape recordings were made, signed releases were obtained so that the information, after being transcribed, could be used in print. Besides my field notes and oral interviews, I also took a large number of still photographs of these communities and found many others in archives and museums. Repositories for photographs included the National Archives in College Park, Maryland, and Anchorage, the Erskine House Museum in Kodiak, as well as several private collections, including those of Reed Oswalt, Nick Pestrikoff Sr., and Ed Opheim Sr. I also shot many reels of videotape documenting social events and subsistence activities. In addition, I was fortunate to find transcripts of taped interviews done by Laurie Mulcahy of the Kodiak Area Native Association with village elders during the mid-1980s. These have been digested and edited (Mulcahy 1987) and are now housed at the Alutiiq Museum in Kodiak City.

Fieldwork

I flew to Old Harbor for the first time for a community meeting about the impact of the *Exxon Valdez* oil spill on July 21, 1989. I returned again that year on September 28 and once more on November 29–30. In 1990 I was in the village on January 9, February 6, May 7–10, August 6, and October 2–3. In 1991 I was in the village for Russian Christmas from January 8 to 10, for the Fourth of July celebration on July 3–4, from September 17 to 20, and once again from November 12 to 13. In 1992 I traveled to be in the community from March 13 to 16, from April 6 to 14 for a major harvest survey, and from September 11 to 13 for a Russian Orthodox wedding. In 1993 I was in the village for only two days, April 1–2, and I did not visit the community at all in 1994. In 1995 I was there from February 15 to 18. In 1996 I traveled to Old Harbor in the company of my daughter Susan from September 8 to 12. In 1997, I was there on February 6–8 to introduce the community ethnographies project, and I returned again September 9–12. In 1998, I visited the community from April 21 to 23, September 23–24, and October 1–5. Once again I returned to the village from September 15 to 17, 1999. The total number of field days I spent in Old Harbor was sixty-nine.

My first trip to Ouzinkie was on June 27, 1989, for a community meeting about the impact of the *Exxon Valdez* oil spill. I returned again that year on July 18, September 14–15, September 27, and November 27. In 1990 I was there on March 13–14, May 22, September 17–18, and November 14–15. In 1991 I spent time in the village from April 16 to 20 doing a major harvest survey and returned once again on May 26–28. In 1992 I was there from February 26 to 28 and May 18–22. I did not visit Ouzinkie at all in 1993 or 1995. In 1994, I was there only for a few hours on March 18. In 1996 I stopped in the village to visit from July 29–August 2, and from Otober 24 to 26 of that year I stayed with Theodore Squartsoff at his family homestead at Barabara Cove, in upper Kazhuyak Bay. In 1997 I traveled to Ouzinkie from January 21 to 23 to introduce the community ethnographies project and returned again from May 13 to 15. In 1998, I again made four trips to Ouzinkie, first on February 2, again May 25–27, on September 23, and from October 6 to 9. The total number of field days I spent in Ouzinkie was fifty-two.

In addition to these Old Harbor and Ouzinkie visits, I have also made numerous visits since 1989 to other Kodiak communities: Karluk, Akhiok, Larsen Bay, Port Lions, and Kodiak City. For this project I spent several additional days in 1997 and 1998 interviewing Ed Opheim Sr. and Reed Oswalt, both former residents of Ouzinkie, at their homes in Kodiak City. On March 9, 1997, I spent part of a day interviewing Hender Toms, another former resident of Ouzinkie, in Seattle, Washington.

Fig. Intro. 1. *Old Harbor school, circa 1940s. Photo courtesy of Old Harbor Seniors Center.*

Chapter One

Community Histories

I begin this ethnography by providing brief narrative histories of the two study communities. There are two important and practical reasons for doing so. First, local history provides a texture and a context for the matrix of present-day life, vividly illustrating how things came to be the way they are. Second, there simply are no comprehensive written histories for these communities, and it is necessary to establish some basic reference points and timelines. In the words of Alutiiq scholar Gordon Pullar (1992:189), "As Alutiiq people, we owe it to ourselves to learn our histories, both cultural and familial."

OLD HARBOR

Old Harbor, called *Staraia Gavan* in Russian and *Nunyuq* in Alutiiq, is located in the well-protected waters of Sitkalidak Strait, on the southeast end of Kodiak Island. In contrast to Ouzinkie, Old Harbor is relatively treeless, but high mountains and snow-capped peaks behind the village enhance its spectacular natural setting. The climate is mild and rainy, with temperatures that only occasionally drop below freezing or rise above sixty-five degrees Fahrenheit.

An abundance of archaeological evidence indicates that the region around Old Harbor has been occupied by a series of prehistoric populations over several thousands of years (see Clark 1984a; Fitzhugh 1998). Although no direct continuity has yet been demonstrated, it is entirely possible that these ancient peoples were the direct ancestors of Alutiiq-speaking Koniags living in the area today.

The English place name *Old Harbor* is derived from the early Russian settlement days when a small colony at Three Saints Bay was moved to the present site of Kodiak City to be closer to timber. Kodiak City in turn became the "New Harbor" for Russian ships. The original *artel* or sea otter trading post at Three Saints Bay, founded in 1784 by Gregorii

Fig. 1.1. *Old Harbor small boat harbor, 1998. Photo by Craig Mishler.*

Shelikhov, was one of the first Russian colonial outposts established in North America, and it lies only about eight miles south of Old Harbor. It is possible that some of Old Harbor's current residents have ancestors who lived and worked at the Russian colony in nearby Three Saints Bay. The post was active for seven years until it was abandoned in 1791.

The Russian *artel* at Three Saints Bay consisted of living quarters for the Russian manager, barracks for ten families (which must have consisted of Alutiiq households or Russians with Alutiiq wives), a blacksmith shop, a whale and seal oil–rendering station, and three storage barabaras (Black 1977:89). In 1786 the *artel* supported a population of 113 Russians (Gibson 1976:6) and an undetermined number of Alutiiqs. Recent archaeological investigations at Three Saints Bay have helped to unravel much about Russian and Native life at the time of historic contact (Crowell 1994a, 1997).

As late as 1804 many Alutiiqs were still residing in Kiliuda Bay, on the north side of Old Harbor, where 177 men and 173 women were counted (Langsdorff 1993:30). In 1805 the Russian explorer Lisianskii paddled a kayak down the eastern side of Kodiak Island and found seven Alutiiq communities within fifteen miles of Old Harbor and another ten communities along the coast between Kiliuda Bay and Ugak Bay (Clark 1987:106). Archaeological surveys done by Ben Fitzhugh during the mid-1990s have resulted in the discovery of 152 sites on Sitkalidak Island alone, with the oldest ones dated at six thousand to seven thousand years before the present (Fitzhugh 1998). At the time of historic contact there was apparently no settlement at Old Harbor itself, but it is clear that the southeast side of Kodiak Island was the most heavily populated part of the archipelago at the time.

The Russians treated the Alutiiqs shamefully and quickly forced the men to become slaves in the sea otter fur trade, sending them away from their families in kayaks for as long as six months at a time. In the meantime, Russian men took Alutiiq women as their wives and mistresses. A German explorer, Georg Langsdorff, watched Alutiiq men in Kodiak harnessed to plows and lamented that: "The conquered and suppressed Aleuts are badly fed, badly clothed, and subjected daily to danger. They have had all of their possessions confiscated. They are mostly ruled by *promyshlenniks* [fur hunters], some of whom are Siberian criminals. Under these conditions, depopulation becomes more noticeable with each passing year" (Langsdorff 1993:135). Archaeologist Donald Clark (1987:123) estimates that the Koniag population was cut in half from over eight thousand people down to about four thousand during the first three decades of Russian colonization, between 1784 and 1814. By the 1830s sea otters around Kodiak became depleted through overhunting (Gibson 1976:34), but when this happened, the Russians simply encouraged local hunters to exploit other far more abundant bearers such as fox, land otter, and weasel.

The Russians' worst atrocity occurred at a place called Refuge Rock, located on the Pacific Ocean side of Sitkalidak Island near the head of McDonald Lagoon (locally known as *Awa'aq* or Fox Lagoon), only a few miles distant from Old Harbor. In 1851 an old Alutiiq man named Arsentii

Fig. 1.2. Barabaras with fish rack and cabin at Old Harbor, 1888. **Albatross** *Collection, 22-FA-264, National Archives, Washington, D.C.*

Aminak (Kuspuq) told how the Russians, led by Grigorri Shelikhov, attacked this settlement across a portage at low tide and shot three hundred men and women, taking their children as hostages (see Holmberg 1985:59). Russian accounts of this 1784 massacre (summarized in Black 1992) indicate that muskets and cannon fire were used to storm the rock. Using this history for topographic clues, archaeologists rediscovered Refuge Rock during an archaeological survey following the 1989 oil spill. Some excavations have since taken place there, and it is now regarded as a sacred site by the people of Old Harbor.

The heaviest damage and bloodiest fighting was done between 1784 and 1786, when Shelikhov sent armed parties all over the island to crush every pocket of local resistance (Black 1992:173–177). Although greatly outnumbered, the Russians prevailed with their superior weapons. Some of their cruelties were halted or at least lessened, after the arrival of the first Russian Orthodox priests, but that did not happen until much harm had been done and many lives had been lost. A ship named the *Three Saints*, carrying eight Russian Orthodox monks and two novices arrived in St. Paul Harbor, Kodiak, on September 24, 1794. These monks, especially Fathers Juvenali and Makarii, wasted no time paddling around Kodiak Island in small *baidarkas*, and within just a few years they made over seven thousand converts to Christianity. Also among this group was Father Herman, who became a special friend of the Alutiiq people and who is still widely revered in all the Kodiak villages today (Gregory 1977:25–27).

A smallpox epidemic that lasted from 1837 to 1839 killed another 736 Kodiak Alutiiqs and prompted the Russians to provide emergency provisions to the widows and orphans. In their attempt to make the Alutiiqs more self-sufficient and to cope better administratively with the settlements depopulated by the smallpox, the Russians forced the people to consolidate from sixty-five communities into seven. By 1844 Chief Manager Etholin of the Russian-American Company had supplied the villagers with frame houses, clothing, sheep, and cattle, and had tried to turn them into farmers (Fortuine 1989:237). Old Harbor was clearly not one of these seven, but it would seem as though Three Saints Bay and either Ouzinkie or Monk's Lagoon were. The others, apparently, were Igatsk/Orlov (in Ugak Bay across from Eagle Harbor), Afognak, Karluk, either Akhiok (formerly known as Alitak) or Kaguyak, and Woody Island (see Tikhmenev 1978:200).

While the present Old Harbor village site was not actively used when the Russians first arrived, it seems to have been well established by 1868, one year after the American purchase of Alaska (Clark 1987:121). Some recent excavations done just above the Old Harbor Narrows, at the lighthouse site, have resulted in the identification of two Russian-period houses dating from 1855 to 1865 (Fitzhugh 1998).

After Alaska was sold by Russia to the United States in 1867, sea otter hunting continued to be lucrative and was sponsored by the Alaska Commercial Company, which established stores in such places as Ouzinkie and Kaguyak. Recognizing that sea otters were an important part of the Alaska Native economy, the federal government banned white men from hunting and killing sea otters, although they were still allowed to take Natives out on hunting expeditions. Alutiiq men hunted sea otters from their *baidarkas* (i.e., kayaks), and they were frequently organized into hunting parties and hauled to the sea otter hunting grounds on large schooners (see Gibbs 1968). Federal revenue cutters inspected the schooners and enforced this law. When they caught a ship hunting sea otters without any Natives aboard, they would seize the ship and confiscate the skins (Roscoe: 1992:50–53).

Even at remote places such as Kaguyak sailing ships came and went every few days. On May 30, 1881, for example, as many as fifteen hunters and their *baidarkas* were loaded on the sixty-nine-ton schooner *Pauline Collins*, which stopped and picked up men at Afognak and then took on additional men at Kaguyak (Alaska Commercial Company 1881). From Kaguyak the schooners sailed to such places as the Trinity Islands where sea otters were still relatively abundant. After several weeks, the schooners brought the hunters and their *baidarkas* back home.

Fig. 1.3. *Old Harbor Native family in front of barabara with crew members of the* Albatross, *1888.* Albatross *Collection, National Archives, Washington, D.C.*

Fig. 1.4. *Old Harbor Native family in front of barabara, 1888.* **Albatross Collection, 22-FA-265, National Archives, Washington, D.C.**

Alutiiq hunters were not always dependent on the schooners, however, and sometimes worked independently. On July 2, 1881, nine Old Harbor *baidarkas* arrived in Kaguyak en route to Tugidak Island. They returned to Kaguyak on July 29 and traded their catch (which may have included sea otter and harbor seal) at the Kaguyak store (Alaska Commercial Company 1881). This was a very long way to paddle, but it was presumably profitable for the hunters to travel such distances.

Account books indicate that in 1885 the Kodiak District included six sea otter hunting parties, organized by community. Eagle Harbor had twelve baidarkas, Ouzinkie had eight, Woody Island eighteen, Kiliuda five, Afognak fifteen, and Chiniak two, for a total of sixty. Old Harbor, Kaguyak, and Karluk are not listed but may have been part of a separate district. The 1884 "Ousinkie party" consisted of just two *baidarkas*: one was a two-hatch craft manned by John Squartsoff and Mechila, and the other was a three-hatch manned by Peter Squartsoff, Paul Katelnikoff, and Ivan Squartsoff. Each *baidarka* was supplied with three sacks of white flour, three pounds of tea, five pounds of sugar, one pound of tobacco, five bars of soap, and matches. The following year the parties began to receive an abundance of additional things in their outfit such as salt, rice, pilot bread, candles, axes, spools of thread, needles, rifles and shotguns,

Fig. 1.5. *Old Harbor Natives with skin gut parkas and kayak, 1888.* Albatross *Collection, 22-FA-268, National Archives, Washington, D.C.*

tea kettles, fry pans, iron pots, and shirts and pants. These additional goods must have provided great incentive, for the 1885 "Ousinkie party" swelled to eight kayaks (Alaska Commercial Company 1884–1885). With the Company paying prices of $80 to $100 per skin, presumably paid in trade goods, some Natives killed as many as fifteen or twenty sea otters on each trip (Roscoe 1992:19).

According to Katherine Arndt (personal communication), there was no attempt by the American government to manage commercial sea otter harvests during the late nineteenth century, and in this free-for-all atmosphere, stocks were pretty well depleted by the 1890s. Also, by this time the gold rush diverted the Alaskan economy away from fur and toward minerals. Since gold was never discovered in Kodiak, the number of sailing ships calling on Kodiak harbor declined radically.

Members of the first American scientific expedition to the area arrived in Old Harbor on the ship *Albatross* in early August 1888, and probably took the first photographs of the community, which show only a handful of sod houses (barabaras) and one log structure. Scientists onboard the *Albatross* were on a mission to collect species of fish in the North Pacific but also took an interest in local Native settlements. Four photographs of Old Harbor taken by the *Albatross* expedition have great lasting value and provide strong insights into what life was like in the community 112 years ago (Figures 1.2–1.5).

George Inga Sr., in looking at these old photos, observed that the log structure with the unfinished roof in Figure 12 was where he was raised. Sometime after this photo was taken, it belonged to his father, Sasha Inga.

While their ship was anchored in front of the village, whose population was estimated at "some 250 souls," members of the *Albatross* crew met the writer Ivan Petroff, who was running a salmon saltery at a small lake some fifteen miles distant (perhaps in Three Saints Bay). Petroff (who may be one of the men in the photos) reported eighteen white men and a few "Indians" (i.e., Alutiiqs) putting up salmon in barrels and moving the barrels via a "horse railroad" from the lake to salt water. These fish were then shipped to San Francisco for sale (Anonymous 1888).

Long before salmon ever became the big money fish for Kodiak commercial fisheries, however, cod and herring were king. The first Pacific (gray) cod saltery was built on Sitkalidak Island across from Old Harbor in 1883, although it took another thirty years for markets to develop (Johnson 1979:78–79). In the mid-1920s Karl Armstrong built a herring saltery in Three Saints Bay, and Kadiak Fisheries built a salmon cannery at Shearwater Bay (inside Kaliuda Bay) to process pink salmon (Roppel 1994:57–58; 269–270).

During the 1920s, 1930s, and 1940s, a whaling station at Port Hobron on Sitkalidak Island provided employment for some Old Harbor people, who were hired to cut up the blubber when whales were brought in (Reeves et al. 1985). Jack McCord, who had a grazing lease for a ranch farther inside Port Hobron, raised sheep and cattle there and generously shared his beef with Old Harbor residents because they kept an eye on the herds and reported poachers to him. All of the cattle, over three hundred head, were finally killed and shipped out after McCord sold the ranch in the 1960s.

During these years commercial salmon fishing was largely done through the use of fish traps and beach seines. Fish traps were built in Kiliuda Bay and also in Sitkalidak Strait, near Old Harbor. Although some Old Harbor people found seasonal work at the fish traps, they also found summer jobs beach seining and working in the Shearwater Bay cannery. Both men and women began working for wages or a percentage of the catch. Commercial beach seines were adapted for use in subsistence fishing, with the result that many people in Old Harbor today get their fish from beach seines.

Although the Shearwater Bay cannery collapsed from a windstorm in the fall of 1926, it was rebuilt and continued to be operated by Kadiak Fisheries intermittently over the next thirty-eight years. George Inga Sr. (1996), who was born in 1925 and grew up in Old Harbor, remembers what it was like living at the cannery during the summer:

CM: *So in the summertime you went up to Shearwater, when you got a little bit older?*
GI: *Yeah. Every time my mom and dad go, you know, there used to be*

Fig. 1.6. The Duchess *tender, which carried Old Harbor families to the cannery at Shearwater Bay. Photo courtesy of Old Harbor Seniors Center.*

a tender come and pick up everybody from here. Take them to the cannery.

CM: So [Old Harbor] would be like a ghost town in the summer?

GI: Yeah. Well sometimes there would be one family or a couple [of] families left behind. It was pretty small then, you know. It was real small. And we'd stay in Shearwater until August month when the canneries closed down. You know before, the fisheries would open up in June 15 and close in August 15, instead of closing one area at a time, you know. They opened the whole island June 15, and they don't close it. They leave it open until August 15. Fishing was from Monday at 6 o'clock to Saturday 6 o'clock evening. That was it. No closing one area and open another. The whole island would be open all summer.

CM: What did they have up at Shearwater? Was there a bunkhouse, or what did you stay in?

GI: Well, first they had bunkhouses, yeah. Like you say, bunkhouses. Then they had a fire, and it burned up. And then we lived in tents, all summer. Lived in tents, and that was bad. When it rains, you know, it used to be bad, leak. And then later on they brought up quonset huts. They were

Fig. 1.7. Arthur Haakanson Sr. Photo courtesy of Sven and Mary Haakanson Sr.

good. They were good. At least they didn't leak anyway. And lot of room. They lived in them tents, not very big.

. . .

We used to get our fish from cannery. They give you fish, enough to eat. You know, they give you all kinds of [fish] heads. They give you fish. And there was fish in the creeks. We'd go up and get them. Like in Shearwater there was about three or four creeks, instead of one, now. Like I said the beavers closed them up. I was pretty young then; when I was only about ten or twelve, I used to go up the creek and get them with a hook for eat, you know.

It was about this time, during the early 1930s, that two Scandinavian immigrants, Rolf Christiansen, a Norwegian, and Arthur Haakanson Sr., a Dane, arrived on sailing ships. The ships anchored inside Sitkalidak Strait, and the men rowed skiffs to Old Harbor for social dances. A post office was established in 1931, and by 1934 Old Harbor had twenty houses, all made of frame or log construction (BIA 1934). Rolf and Arthur both ended up marrying local Alutiiq women and stayed in the region for the rest of their lives. Arthur Haakanson Sr. married Roselissa Shugak, and Rolf Christiansen, whose nickname was "Nookin," married Sasha Kelly. Rolf and Sasha produced nineteen children, fourteen of whom survived. Today the Christiansens and Haakansons are two of the largest families in Old Harbor. Arthur Haakanson Sr. lived and worked both in Old Harbor and Ouzinkie and has descendants in both communities.

During the Great Depression of the mid-1930s, the people of Old Harbor went through tremendous suffering due to a collapse of salmon

Fig. 1.8. Rolf Christiansen holding the bow of an old kayak. Photo by Dr. William Laughlin, courtesy of Sven and Mary Haakanson Sr.

Community Histories

runs. George Inga Sr. (1998), who was still only ten years old at the time, talks about it:

In 1935 and 1936 we went through a couple years of really hard times because there was no salmon. We were so poor then that we couldn't even buy shells for our rifles. We couldn't even afford salt. No kidding! All we lived on that winter was codfish. Morning, noon, and night we ate codfish. I don't know how my father did it, we had such a big family. But someone showed us how to jig for codfish right from the shoreline by throwing out a line with a small stick on it. That stick floated, and when it bobbed under the water then we knew we had a fish on.

Yeah, there were lots of codfish that time, and the codfish saved us from starvation. Then the next year the BIA helped us out. They paid us to build a trail from Barling Bay to Big Creek using axes and shovels. It's mostly overgrown now, but just a few years ago you could still see that trail clearly behind the lagoon. They didn't pay us cash. They paid us with coupons that we could turn in for groceries.

The 1930s and 1940s were also characterized by widespread attacks of the lung disease, tuberculosis. Many people in Old Harbor acquired TB and suffered and died from it before a reliable treatment was ever found. In 1944 the antibiotics streptomycin and para-aminosalicylic acid were isolated and used to treat the disease, and in 1952 the drug isoniazid provided an effective popular cure, but even as late as 1950 the only thing doctors could do is recommend prolonged bed rest. The nearest sanitorium for TB patients living on Kodiak was in Seward.

During the 1930s and 1940s commercial fishing was the principal activity in the summer months, while winter was devoted to fur trapping. Fox, land otter, and weasel were the three targeted species, and fur trapping lasted as a way of life up until the mid-1950s. Each trapper had his own territory. As George Inga Sr. (1996) recalls:

Most of the time we used to go [out] about the fifteenth or sixteenth of November. Come back just before Christmas. About a month anyway. You know, like if a guy have a barabara or what you call, and the next one would have one not too far from him. When they go hunt, they tell each other how far he could hunt, you know. Don't bother the other one. So that other one could have his own place to hunt. Not go close to other guy's cabin, whatever. 'Cause after they come back around December, then anybody could hunt and use that land. That's the way they used to work, pretty good, you know.

When the Japanese attacked Pearl Harbor in 1941 and began invading the Aleutians, Kodiak Natives were afraid of being attacked by the Japanese. At the peak of World War II, in 1943, over eleven thousand U.S. troops were stationed on Kodiak Island (Anonymous 1992: 45–47). The

Fig. 1.9. *Top: Old Harbor's Three Saints Russian Orthodox Church and village in the 1940s. Alaska Nurses Collection, Rasmuson Library, University of Alaska, Fairbanks.*

Fig. 1.10. *Above: Old Harbor waterfront in the 1940s. Alaska Nurses Collection, Rasmuson Library, University of Alaska, Fairbanks.*

Army built gun batteries, searchlights, fire control, and radar installations all along the northeast and southwest coasts of Kodiak Island, and a large Naval base was constructed in Women's Bay just outside of Kodiak City. However, zealous American soldiers sometimes proved to be nearly as terrifying to the locals as the Japanese. In the words of Sven Haakanson Sr. (1997):

SH: When the Japs hit down at Unalaska and Shemya and Attu, everybody thought they were, you know, island hopping all the way up to Kodiak, and it was known that Kodiak was one of the main targets. To control the Pacific Ocean here in Alaska was to get a hold of Kodiak. And we were all scared, so you had to have blackouts and stuff. And I was gill netting with my Dad. It was 1942, I think, and we had a tent and we were at the gill net camp.

CM: This was at Soldier's Bay?

SH: No. This was at Kasanof, which is known as Deadman's Bay. Way up in the head of the bay they were building a lumber mill for the Army that supplied wood for most all the bases up and down the Chain. Anyway, when we were in our tent, it was either '41 or '42 when we still had to fish, and we had just a kerosene lamp, but at night, you know, in white tents, how they glow? And I don't know, about midnight people come running up the beach. We heard clickety-clack and everything, and my Dad opened the tent, and there was soldiers with bayonets challenging him. And he told them, "We're gill netters." And they said, "Douse that light! After this don't keep your light on at night."

They told him they thought we were a Japanese advance party coming in ahead for a Japanese landing. They were afraid they were coming to Kodiak. So those spotter planes or reconnaissance planes would fly real high, and if they see any light, they'd send a craft, PT boats, crash boats, in there with soldiers to see who was there. And that was quite scary.

Six young men from Old Harbor served in the armed forces during the war, and all returned home safely, although Mike Inga, the village chief, was wounded in the leg in Attu. The others were William Hansen Jr., Edward Pestrikoff Sr., George Inga Sr., Nickolai Ignatin, and Sergei Pestrikoff (Bailey 1949).

The year 1941 was a significant one for Old Harbor, not only for marking the beginning of the war, but also because it was the year that the 1.8-million-acre Kodiak National Wildlife Refuge was created to protect brown bear habitat. The Refuge today comprises approximately two-thirds of Kodiak Island, including nearly all of the area around Old Harbor except Sitkalidak Island and other lands later selected by the Old Harbor Native Corporation during the 1970s. With the creation of the Refuge, land development around Old Harbor came to a virtual standstill, and today the Federal Subsistence Management Program, for which the U.S. Fish and Wildlife Service is the lead agency, oversees the subsistence take of game animals on Refuge lands.

The strong economy of the postwar era allowed many Alutiiqs to acquire their own fishing boats, although many still fished on cannery-owned vessels. As canneries around Kodiak Island began to proliferate and new technologies entered the workplace, the old small-scale hand pack salteries began to disappear. In 1948, for example, a halibut cold storage plant was built at Port Otto across from Old Harbor by Raymond Krautter and Nels Christiansen (Bailey 1949:10), but the power went out and all the fish spoiled. It was during these years that most of the villages around the island began to get electric generators. With electricity came shortwave radios and sustained contact with the outside world. Several photographs of Old Harbor taken during the 1940s show a fairly small community with most of the houses strung out along the waterfront like a string of pearls.

In 1947 Old Harbor suffered a severe flu epidemic, which was complicated and intensified by pneumonia and tuberculosis. Virtually the whole village was coughing, and an emergency radio message sent to Kodiak by the storekeeper or schoolteacher brought the services of Marion Curtis, a public health nurse who later wrote in detail about her experience (Curtis 1948). Curtis flew into the village on a amphibious seaplane known as a PBY. Although there were eight deaths, primarily to elders and small children, Curtis's diligent administration of penicillin shots saved the lives of many others. She set up a makeshift hospital in the old school, and then made the rounds to every house three or four times a day until she was completely exhausted.

Paul Kahutak, who was just fourteen at the time, remembers Curtis's heroic efforts and credits her with saving the village. As one of the few who was not sick, Paul was called on to cut firewood, haul water, and dig graves. It was one of the worst experiences of his life, and it occurred right around Easter (Kahutak 1987):

We'd go up [to the cemetery] and bury their dead, you know. Bury their dead. And we'd come down from the cemetery, somebody else is dead too. That's first time I went there, there was two buried. And eight [people] died then. And we'd come down from cemetery and somebody else said, "Somebody else is dead."

During the 1940s and 1950s communication and transportation between villages were improved through the establishment of a mail boat which made a circuit around Kodiak Island twice a month. The *Ruf Ryder*, and its successors, the *Charlotte B.*, the *Phyllis S.*, and the *Shuyak*, all operated by Robert von Scheele of Afognak, would go clockwise around the island on one trip, and the next time would go counterclockwise, making stops in each community and carrying passengers as well as mail, groceries, and lumber (for details see Harvey 1991). People would place their orders on one trip and receive their goods on the return trip. The mail boat era came to an end in the early 1960s, following von Scheele's death, at a time when airstrips were being built in the villages. Sven Haakanson Sr. (1997), who once worked on the mail boat, remembered that when the mail boat came in, people usually celebrated with a dance:

It was amazing when I worked on the mail boat coming around. Also my Dad told me every village had their own band. There was guys that played guitar, accordion, violin, mandolin, you name it. They'd play them. Like Ouzinkie had four or five accordion players. One got tired and another one would take over. Same way here [in Old Harbor]. And the mail boat used to sail twice a month. One month it went around the east side [of Kodiak Island], well for first two weeks went the east side, then go back to Kodiak and then go on the west side. Just unwind and go back and forth that way, twice a month all year round. But we'd bring the supplies and everything, and it seemed like every village we went, they'd have a dance when the mail boat came in, every two weeks. And it would take maybe a week or sometimes two weeks to go clean around the Island because of weather. They had no radar or nothing, just a compass and a steering wheel and a clock, and that's how they went, by dead reckoning.

One of the benchmark events in the history of Old Harbor and Ouzinkie came on March 27, 1964, the date of the Great Alaskan Earthquake, which registered between 8.4 and 8.6 on the Richter scale. Old Harbor was all but destroyed by the earthquake and accompanying tsunami, which forced residents to evacuate to Anchorage for several months until conditions were safe and decisions made for rebuilding (for details see Davis 1970 and 1986b). The Three Saints Russian Orthodox Church survived the tsunami without extensive damage, and local residents took this as a symbolic, prophetic event. Although the villages of Kaguyak and Afognak were destroyed and Ouzinkie was badly damaged by the earthquake and tsunami, the other Alutiiq communities of Akhiok, Karluk, and Larsen Bay were left virtually untouched.

The Great Alaskan Earthquake and tsunami washed out the Shearwater cannery and brought an end to its operations. In addition to the processing plant, many boats were also lost, and Old Harbor was economically devastated. Sven Haakanson Sr. (1997) talked about how this disaster led to a long-term dependence on welfare:

Before the tidal wave, people were embarrassed to get welfare. It was only for crippled people, or people that were devastated, or you know, widows. They're the only ones the village would allow to get welfare. Everybody got along without it.

And after the tidal wave, once we built the community back, everybody worked together, from kids to older people did something. Then there was a fellow named James or Jim Dayton, was the BIA welfare person, came around, sent down by the BIA, to put everybody on welfare because at that time, sure, people did need it, you know. Because they lost everything.

Fig. 1.11. *Old Harbor aerial photo eight months after the tidal wave, November 24, 1964. GSA RG 269, National Archives, Anchorage.*

Fig. 1.12. *Old Harbor houses under construction, with tent frames in the background, November 24, 1964. GSA RG 269, National Archives, Anchorage.*

Community Histories

So what the Council did at that time, and George Inga [Sr.] was with me, Alfred Naumoff he's gone, and I forget the rest, but we made sure that everybody that got welfare went to work. And this worked good. Everybody painted their houses, cleaned up the scaffolding, and made the village look good, because when the newspaper people came here, said one of the cleanest, nicest towns that they went and seen. We had trash receptacles, you know, we did everything we could for our community. And this even hit the papers, and I was proud to tell them what we were doing. That anybody drawing welfare would do something in the community, so many hours [of] work. And old people that couldn't finish their houses up, their tiles on the floor or paint their houses, everybody helped and we did it all, and the system was working good.

Everybody was happy, and then Jim Dayton came back. He was real sad. He got bawled out by his superiors in Anchorage or Juneau, and said they have to tell the people down here that they don't have to work. And we still had a lot more work, landscaping and stuff we were planning to do, but they said, "No. It's unconstitutional." That the city will have to pay people back. Then the going rate was $2 an hour, you know.

But I had a big meeting with all the people, and I told them, "Look. How would the village look if we didn't all get together and work and paint all the houses and clean up the roads, pile the lumber, and take care of all that?" So nobody pursued the city to collect back the $2 an hour. I'm glad because I think we had like $700 in the city budget at that time. But I remember Alfred was upset. Everybody was upset because they told the people they didn't have to work any more. And that's what spoiled the people.

All residents returned to Old Harbor by the first week in May, but were forced to live in tents. A freighter ship from Seattle brought building supplies for new houses. Because they were easy to build, over forty new houses were completed between August and November 1964. These houses were all prefabricated units with oil stoves, and they were all completely identical inside and out except that some had two bedrooms and some had four bedrooms. Today these houses are painted different colors, but they still look very much alike. During the first year of resettlement people frequently got mixed up about which house belonged to which family because they had no paint or nameplates to distinguish them, and they were all built in symmetrical rows and columns. This confusion led to some comical arguments and attempted evictions. Paul Kahutak (1997) recalls:

PK: *Everybody, every time somebody start a movie theater, you know, Carl [Christiansen] or somebody, Larry [Matfay]. And we used to go [to the] movies. We'd come back and find the houses. They're all the same, you know. Walked into somebody else's house! [laughs] You know, they all looked same.*
CM: *You got mixed up, huh?*
PK: *Yeah. All mixed up. This one guy, you know, he's Dimitri. That old*

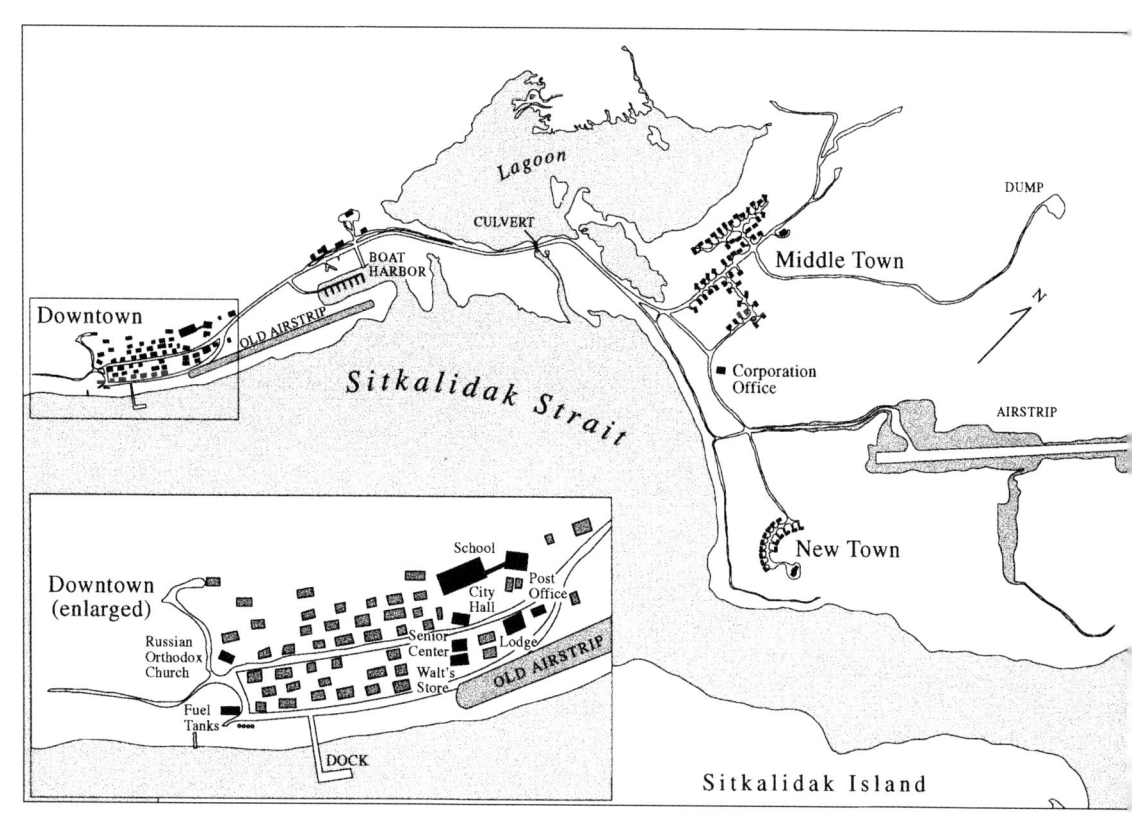

Map 2. Old Harbor.

man. He used to walk back and forth. I asked him, "What's wrong?" "I can't find my house." [laughs] So I'd have to bring him home, you know.

CM: *Were they all painted one color too?*

PK: *No, they weren't even painted.*

So this guy, you know George [Inga Sr.]'s mom. When Albert [Adonga] was alive. So Albert was half-drunk or something. So they had movies or something. George's mom went home. "Holy Smokes! Somebody's in my bed." And Albert opened his eyes. "You're in my house!" "No, I'm in my house." "No way! You get out of here! Get up! You're in the wrong house!"

So in my house there was . . . Jenny [Erickson]'s dad. Kept coming in the back door, you know. One time Jenny's mom come in, and he came in the back door. [S]he said, his [her] husband, you know, Costia Inga, hollering. Me and Martha were there, and hollering like: "How come you moved the furniture?" And Martha said, "Oh, you're in the wrong house!" "How come you moved the furniture?" [laughs] He said, "Oh! I'm in the wrong house!"

As a result of the 1964 earthquake and tsunami, Old Harbor also acquired two new families, the Zeedars and the Melovedoffs, from the destroyed village of Kaguyak. This made Old Harbor the only remaining Native settlement on the east side of Kodiak Island, and it experienced considerable growth. In the late 1960s and early 1970s, a salmon processing ship, the *Sonja*, docked at Old Harbor and provided the village with electrical power. The processing plant on the *Sonja*, however, burned in March 1975, putting many people out of work.

Since the earthquake, the population of Old Harbor has grown rapidly and expanded into three distinct neighborhoods—Downtown (the original townsite rebuilt after the earthquake), Middle Town (also known as "Uptown"), and New Town (See Map 2). Middle Town and New Town were built through federal HUD housing grants between 1978 and 1984. Each of the three neighborhoods is dedicated to the memory of one of three Orthodox saints: Downtown is associated with St. Basel, Middle Town with St. Gregory, and New Town with St. John. With the development of Middle Town and New Town, Old Harbor acquired a gravel road system which extends approximately four miles from the downtown area.

Periodically, since the early 1970s, Old Harbor has had a temporary Russian Orthodox priest or clergyman, but in the late 1970s, the community built a new rectory next to the church and requested and received its own year-round resident priest. Father Sergio Gerken was one of the first to arrive, followed by Father Wasilly Askoak, and most recently by Father Gerasim. Father Michael Oleksa has also served there and continues to make frequent visits. The Orthodox Church serves as a focal point for the entire community and is involved in virtually every aspect of

Fig. 1.13. *Ouzinkie waterfront, as seen from the village boardwalk, 1991. Photo by Craig Mishler.*

public life. This reflects a change from the period just before the earthquake, when some villagers were drawn away from traditional Orthodoxy by Protestant missionaries.

After the earthquake, a protected small boat harbor was constructed for the community's fleet of purse seiners and skiffs. Centrally located, the boat harbor provides moorage for about twenty-five resident purse seiners and several larger boats. Seiners come and go at all hours of the day and night, and there is usually a truck or two parked nearby that belong to fishermen working on their boats.

A gravel airstrip was constructed along the waterfront in the downtown area, built right on top of the old village. Due to the strip's shortness and exposure to winds, however, it has been replaced by a new longer and safer airstrip near Middle Town in the early 1990s. Today Old Harbor receives scheduled commercial air service about five times daily year round, and many additional charter flights also come in. The flight from Kodiak City takes approximately twenty-five minutes.

In the fall of 1989, two local commercial fishermen and their wives formed a partnership and opened a modern lodge facility conveniently located right next to the old air strip. The lodge also housed a cafe with a full-time cook and waitress, and the cafe became a very popular community social center until closing during the winter of 1997–1998. In the summer of 1991 the village received a new health clinic, which is staffed by a local community health aide and visiting nurses from Kodiak.

Unlike Ouzinkie, where everyone lives fairly close to the center of the village, Old Harbor has gradually stretched itself out over a four-mile-long road system.

The community's three neighborhoods of Downtown, Middle Town, and New Town are distinct geographically but not socially, because most families have cars or trucks to get around easily, and young people get about on four-wheelers. Most of the elders and single men live Downtown in the small older houses built right after the earthquake, and beside or behind most of the Downtown houses there is a *banya* or steam bath.

Downtown provides the social center of Old Harbor, and all of the public buildings are located there except the clinic and the corporation office. The school, the city and tribal offices, the senior/teen center, Walt Erickson's grocery store, the Sitkalidak Lodge, and the Three Saints Russian Orthodox Church are all located Downtown. A big deepwater dock for large ships is also located downtown next to the old airstrip. Heating fuel and gasoline are stored here. Gasoline for cars and trucks and boats is only sold on certain days of the week at certain hours.

Old Harbor features several recreational facilities. One is a bingo hall located upstairs above the city offices. Bingo is played two or three nights a week and attracts a steady following. The senior center also doubles as a teen center. Seniors gather there three times a week in the late afternoon for a hot meal, and teens use the building for Friday and Saturday night dances. A third facility is the school gym, which opens evenings for volleyball and basketball. When the gym is closed and the weather is fair, teens often gather around the outdoor basketball court and play under the street lights.

OUZINKIE

Ouzinkie, formerly spelled *uzinki* after the Russian word for "narrows," is located in a small picturesque cove on the north end of Spruce Island adjacent to the Narrows between Kodiak Island and Spruce Island. The village is arranged in a semicircle around this cove and extends up the hillside (Map 3). In contrast to Old Harbor, Ouzinkie is surrounded by a mature black spruce forest. On one side of the cove a boardwalk extends along the waterfront to the mouth of Katmai Creek, a salmon-spawning stream which empties from two small lakes. The community shares the relatively mild climate of the Kodiak archipelago, characterized by substantial amounts of rain and fog during the summer months and frequent high winds but only occasional freezing temperatures during the winter. Precipitation is moderately heavy. The village averages about seventy-eight inches of rain and about twenty-seven inches of snow each year. Of all the Kodiak area villages, Ouzinkie is the closest in distance to Kodiak City, just ten miles away.

The earliest history of Ouzinkie has yet to be researched and written, and in contrast to Old Harbor, little or no archaeology has been undertaken on Spruce Island. We do know that a temporary shipbuilding community was established somewhere on Spruce Island (known in Russian as *Yelovoi* or *Elovoi*), possibly at Monk's Lagoon. Under the supervision of a Mr. Shields, an English navigator and shipbuilder employed by Alexander Baranof of the Russian-American Company, two sailing ships named the *Delphin* [i.e. *Dolphin*] and the *Olga* were built in 1795 (Khlebnikov 1835:9).

Like the nearby community of Afognak, Ouzinkie was founded in the early to mid-nineteenth century as a retirement community for employees of the Russian-American Company, and the pensioners (called "colonial citizens" and "colonial settlers") lived off cattle herding and small-scale agriculture (Tikhmenev 1978:346). Unfortunately, there is little documentation of Ouzinkie community history during the Russian period. We do know that a small community grew up in Monk's Lagoon, which probably preceded the one in Ouzinkie, and it is known that a total of fourteen families were living on Spruce Island in 1847 (Gibson 1976:108). The Monk's Lagoon community was apparently known as Yealovnie (Kozely 1963:8).

One early event of note, nevertheless, was the arrival of the monk Herman to Kodiak Island in 1794. Twenty-four years later, in 1818, Herman retreated to Monk's Lagoon, located at the south end of Spruce Island, about two miles from Kodiak. In a letter composed the following year, Herman refers to three families of "Americans" [i.e. Alaska Natives or Russian Creoles] living just "two versts" or a little more than a mile away from him (Herman 1989:166). It is not clear whether these families preceded him or followed him to Spruce Island, but Herman was apparently motivated to move to the Monk's Lagoon site due to political persecution from his fellow Russians in Kodiak.

After moving to Spruce Island, Herman established a school, an orphanage, and a garden and is believed to have performed several miracles there. Herman, also remembered as the Elder, lived very simply and remained at Monk's Lagoon until his death in 1837. On August 9, 1970, he was glorified and canonized by the Orthodox Church of America and became known as Saint Herman (Kreta 1983).

One of the earliest descriptions of Ouzinkie comes from Eli Huggins, an American Army officer who visited there in 1868, one year after the United States purchased Alaska from Russia. Huggins stopped for the night and observed there was one large house occupied by a Russian named Vasilli, and a dozen smaller houses. "The people, with the exception of the Russian," he wrote, "are Creoles. They speak Russian quite brokenly for the most part, using the native language [i.e. Alutiiq] at home." By chance, Huggins and his companions arrived at 8 p.m. just in time for a big social dance at Vasilli's house, with music provided by "a string band of three, one seven-stringed guitar and two balalaikas. . . . The dance

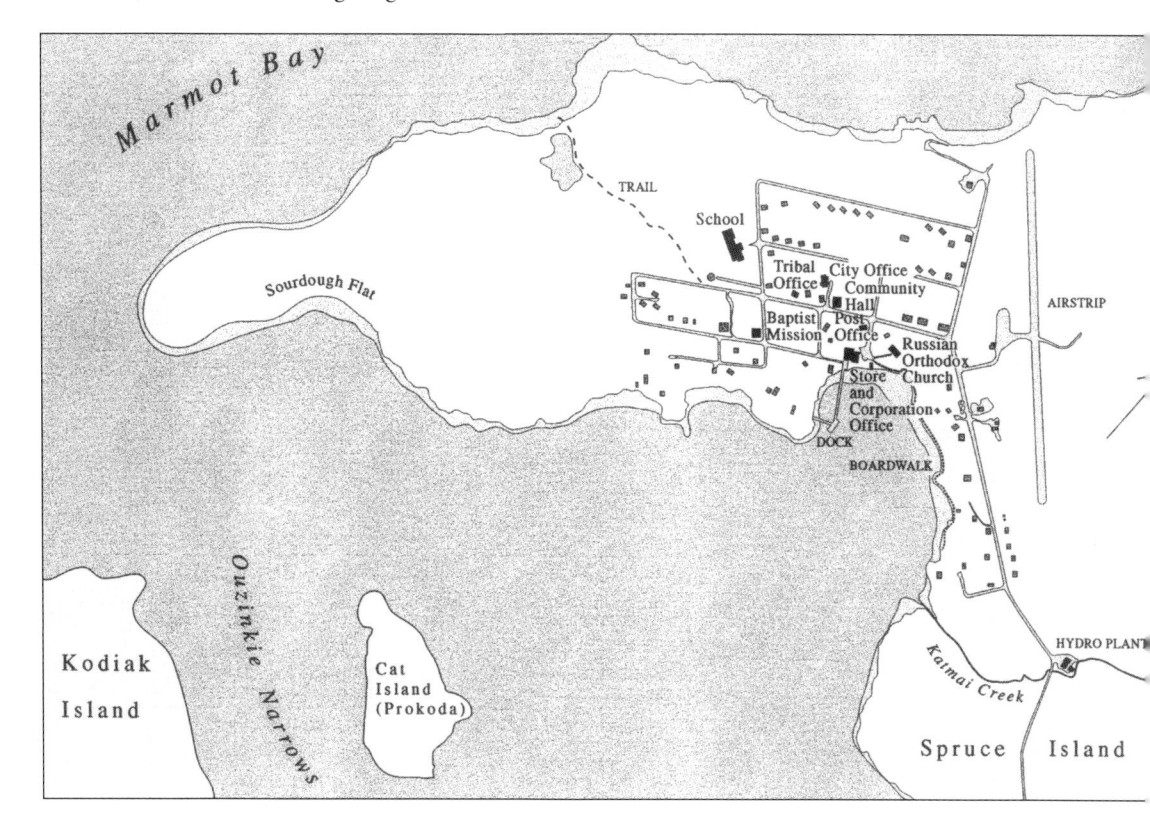

Map 3. Ouzinkie.

closed at midnight with a rollicking drinking song and chorus from the musicians, which seemed to produce a great effect, and was loudly applauded" (Huggins 1981:33-34).

The late Jenny Chernikoff (nee Torsen), the oldest woman in Ouzinkie at the time of the *Exxon Valdez* oil spill, was born in 1906, the same year the dome was added to the present Nativity of Our Lord Russian Orthodox Church. Jenny remembered that her grandparents were the first residents of Ouzinkie, having moved there from Monk's Lagoon. "Since my family was here first," she once joked to me, "this whole island is mine!" Her mother's father's name was Vasilli Pestrikoff, and he lived in a big two-family log house. Vasilli married a woman named Pareskeva and was sixty-nine years old in 1905 (Russian Orthodox Church Confession Records). During an interview, Jenny remembered her grandfather (Mulcahy 1987:2):

Vasilli. Yeah, that was his name. Yeah, a big fellow, kind of hunched over like that. So they moved here [to Ouzinkie] and then they built a church, a new log church, and that's all gone. My papa and mama lived on Woody Island after they got married, but these Pestrikoffs, they lived in Sitka. From Sitka they moved to Monk's Lagoon, and Monk's Lagoon got so crowded they moved to Pestrikoff Beach. That's how that name, Pestrikoff Beach [came to be]. They moved here. No one lived here before. So that's how it was. And from then on people started moving and coming in. There used to be quite a few people here before, but they died off during that terrible [flu] epidemic, 1918, 1919.

This must have been the very same Vasilli whom Eli Huggins (1981) met in Ouzinkie in 1868.

Although subsistence was the most important part of the Ouzinkie economy during the nineteenth century, subsistence hunters quickly adapted to the commercial market for marine mammals. At the Ouzinkie Alaska Commercial Company store, for example, Wasily Squartsoff was credited in 1898 with bringing in forty-five seal throats, 1.5 gallons of [seal] oil, one luftas [seal skin], 2.25 pounds of sinew, and one-half pound of twine (for sewing baidarka skins).

Historical accounts of Ouzinkie during the first two decades of the twentieth century are very thin indeed, but one event which seems to have devastated them and is recorded in oral history was the eruption of Mt. Katmai on the Alaska Peninsula in June 1912. According to Larry Ellanak (1982:32-35), the west side of Kodiak Island around Karluk and Larsen Bay escaped the heavy ash fall which subsequently fell on the north end of Kodiak Island and Afognak Island. The entire region was affected for three days, however, by the constant rumbling and earthquakes generated by the Mt. Katmai volcano. Afterwards, there was a massive fish die-off as the ash fall got into their gills (Chernikoff 1982:36–37; Muller 1982:37–38).

Another disaster which affected Ouzinkie and other communities in the region was the Spanish flu epidemic of 1917–1918. We do not have many firsthand accounts of the suffering caused by this worldwide epidemic, but it seems safe to assume that Ouzinkie was affected in much the same way as nearby Afognak village, where there were numerous cases of chills, fever, and exhaustion, leading to death (Harvey 1991:149–150). And it would seem that Old Harbor must have been affected in much the same way as nearby Akhiok, where there were many deaths to children and elders (Rostad 1988:68–69).

But long before the residents of Spruce Island turned to commercial fishing and fish processing, Ouzinkie was distinctive for its cattle, its chickens, its gardens, and its log cabin architecture. It closely resembled a European peasant community, and in this respect it was quite different from Old Harbor. There are a number of Ouzinkie elders who still recall those days. Martha Anderson (1997), for one, talks about her early life:

I was born in Ouzinkie in 1920. My father was Nick Katelnikoff and my mother was Irene Katelnikoff. I was raised in a log cabin, and my father spoke fluent Russian. He fished with skiffs and beach seines using my brothers as his crew—John, Aleck, and Nick Jr. They would just "swamp" the cannery with fish. Besides my three brothers I had one sister.

My grandfather (my father's father) was named John, and my grandmother (my father's mother) was named Froxia. My mother's father was Nick Shisharemkin, and my grandmother (my mother's mother) was named Olga.

My father trapped foxes and land otter on Afognak Island. We had thirty heads of cattle. When the wind blew hard we would go across to Camel's Rock and cut grass and build haystacks. The reason we went when it was windy was so the grass would dry out fast. We would haul the haystacks back to Ouzinkie in our skiff. We also kept chickens.

At Garden Point we had a big garden where we raised potatoes, rutabagas, turnips, beets, carrots, and lettuce. The garden was fertilized with kelp hauled in buckets, and we watered with water buckets too. My mother would pack her baby and take seed potatoes in a sack from the village to Garden Point. Sometimes she made four trips in a single day. We had root cellars with ladders going underground to store the vegetables. The Squartsoffs, Chernikoffs, and Andersons all had gardens. There were three or four gardens at Sourdough Flats; even Cat Island had a garden.

The cattle stayed out on North Cape all summer. They were never corralled. Our milk cows stayed right around the village, and we had barns for them too. We had a lot of milk, and my mother churned her own butter.

Although the cows were never corralled, people did build fences to keep them out of their yards and their gardens. Christine Kvasnikoff (1997) remembers that the women would cook on the beach while men were tilling and hoeing gardens. Ed Opheim Sr. (1997) remembers the Ouzinkie landscape dotted with small peak-roofed storage sheds called

Fig. 1.14. *Ouzinkie dock and waterfront in the 1940s. In the background are the first Territorial School and the Grimes store (center). The skiffs in the foreground belonged to the Grimes Packing Company. Reed Oswalt Collection, Kodiak Historical Society.*

soriahs. Dry fish were hung in the top of the soriahs, while hay was stored in the bottom. They also had root cellars and covered their potatoes with hay. The gardens had carrots, lettuce, cabbages, radishes, turnips, and rutabagas. Reed Oswalt (1997) recalls how the vegetables were stored:

> *Each garden usually had a little building. They called it the "potato house" that was dug down, and then they would have about three layers in it. Your bottom layer would be where they would store the potatoes, and then they'd come up and they'd have hay over the top of that for insulation, and then you'd have another opening and another layer of hay on top of that. And they were able to keep like potatoes and rutabagas, big rutabagas, and turnips through the winter, and it was another way of life.*

Nick Pestrikoff Sr. (1996) reminisced about living conditions in the late 1930s and early 1940s when he was a child and all six children in the family slept on one bed in a small hand-hewn log cabin with an attached lean-to. The cabin was divided into two main rooms: a kitchen and dining room area and a living room that doubled as a bedroom.

Today Ouzinkie no longer has any barns, cows, big vegetable gardens, soriahs, or potato houses. Only one log cabin is still being lived in, and only one person keeps chickens. In this respect its present cultural landscape bears little or no resemblance to the Ouzinkie of the 1920s and 1930s in which Martha Anderson, Nick Pestrikoff, and Christine Kvasnikoff grew up, a landscape that had largely disappeared by the early 1960s (Kozely 1963:9). One vestige of the old days, however, is that Paul Panamarioff still keeps a horse, which grazes freely in the Sourdough Flats area.

Ed Opheim Sr., whose father was a Norwegian immigrant and whose mother was Aleut, came to Ouzinkie in 1923. He recalls how his father bred dairy cows so they would have milk and butter and kept a fox farm. The Opheims, like most Norwegians, always put up a little pickled herring. He recalls several herring salteries in the area, including one at Port Williams and another started at Sunny Cove by his father Chris Opheim and by Charlie Svendsen, but the Natives were not involved in fishing or processing cod. In his words (Opheim 1997):

EO: As far back as I can remember, we used to go catch herring with a little salmon seine, fine-webbed salmon seine, in the spring, to catch herring for codfish bait. So we'd eat that fresh, but we never salted it until after July or August, and then the herring got fat.
CM: Would you pickle too?
EO: Oh yeah, we always had a barrel or two of herring that we'd use during the winter, you know, take out enough and soak it out and pickle it. Yeah. That was one thing we always had a big crock full of pickled herring.

Fig. 1.15. *SS Denali steamship. Reed Oswalt private collection.*

Fig. 1.16. *Mike Chernikoff with seines, circa 1940s. Reed Oswalt private collection.*

My father and Fred Sargent, they got the title to Shuyak Island, to raise foxes on there. We went over there, and also they salted salmon, and us boys worked with them. In fact, we were there ten years [from 1923 to 1933].

Although canneries were built on nearby Afognak Island in the late 1880s (Roppel 1994:7), most commercial fishing was done on a fairly small scale for hand-pack salteries, and for the residents of Ouzinkie commercial fishing was still a distant second to subsistence. The Opheims, like others in the area, smoked and salted salmon and salmon bellies, packed them into wooden boxes, and shipped them directly to Seattle.

But by the mid-1920s Ouzinkie began to emerge as a center for commercial fisheries. The first Ouzinkie processing plant, called the Katmai Packing Company, was built at the mouth of Katmai Creek in 1922. Ouzinkie Natives and Filipinos were hired to work as herring gibbers. Gibbers gutted and beheaded the herring brought in by the fishermen.

In 1927 a Texas lawyer named Oscar Grimes, who had a part-interest in the Katmai Cannery, built the Grimes Packing Company across the bay near where the public dock is today. Grimes was a striking character who chewed tobacco and generally wore a black hat and a suit coat and a tie over a pair of bib overalls. Ella Grimes, his wife, always wore a pair of white gloves with the finger tips cut off. In this same year the first Ouzinkie post office was established.

Grimes owned and managed the company, employing many local people, as well as Chinese and Filipinos. Many of the cannery workers and cannery equipment arrived aboard a large steamer ship, the SS *Denali*, which made one round trip from Seattle about every two weeks during the summer months. On its return to Seattle, the *Denali* took hundreds of cases of canned herring and salmon.

Grimes owned a fleet of small fishing boats, and Ouzinkie men were hired to run them. Grimes treated the Natives very well, and was well liked by them.

Fig. 1.17. *Women processing crab at the Ouzinkie cannery in the late 1950s. Left to right: Lilly Pestrikoff and Alice Anderson. Photo courtesy of Nick Pestrikoff Sr.*

In some years as many as fifty people worked in the cannery, which kept expanding each year as pilings were brought in to extend the cannery out over the waterfront.

Reed Oswalt, who now lives in Kodiak, worked in the cannery and recalls what the cannery boats were like:

RO: These boats had a little 4-cylinder universal [engine] in them, and there were generally three fellows that worked on the boat, a three-man crew, and these were the ones that Grimes Packing Company had all over the island. These guys would fish anywhere on the island with these little boats that right now make you wonder if you'd go across the channel in one, but at that time they were fearless and would go anywhere.

And there was no power as far as winches or anything else; everything was done by hand power is what it amounts to. When bringing in the seine everything was pulled up over the stern or pulled up over the side. And these fellows went out, and they would sneer if they didn't catch at least ten thousand fish with one of these little boats.

CM: What would they bring in a day?

RO: Oh, it would vary. Some days they'd have some real heavy fishing, and they'd load these things up maybe once or twice a day. These little boats were out, but the tenders were always fairly close. There was no communication as far as radio or anything else. As I say, some of these didn't even

Fig. 1.18. *Father Gerasim Schmaltz, circa 1940s. Hank Eaton Collection, Kodiak Historical Society.*

have a compass. Everything was general knowledge, is what it amounts to, as far as their maneuvering.

CM: And there wasn't any specific name for this kind of boat, huh?

RO: Well, they called them "power dories." But they were really a little power seiner is what it was. Because everything else up to that point was done by rowing with a big skiff and a small skiff, is what it amounts to, and this was a jump ahead. This was a big move. This had an engine [laughs]. This was a lot of excitement, and of course, they could really travel fast, maybe four or five knots.

CM: And they came in about what time?

RO: In the '30s. Yeah. They always traveled with a skiff behind because that was a safety factor. They could always hop in it and row ashore if the motor quit or something else.

CM: And you were telling me the nets were cotton?

RO: These were all cotton nets, about 100 fathom, about 600 feet long or thereabouts, one strip. They were fairly shallow, and these were not pursed like we purse these now. They were siwashed, where they pulled the lead line in first and then pulled the corks in after.

Local men also rose to positions of high responsibility at the cannery. Mike Chernikoff, who was born in Little Afognak, was one of them. Hender Toms (1997), the cannery bookkeeper, remembers that Mike was "very competent, and he did things right when he did them." And as Reed Oswalt (1997) recalls:

Mike was the foreman down there. And he worked at the cannery. He didn't fish at that particular time at all. He worked in the cannery always.

Fig. 1.19. *Baker House, Ouzinkie Baptist Mission, circa 1940s. From* The Spruce Bough, *1946, Ouzinkie High School yearbook. Photo courtesy of Joyce Smith, Ouzinkie.*

And he took care of the cannery in the winter time, so he was kind of the winter watchman there also. And a very dependable person. He worked there at the cannery for years and years, and always did a good job, and tried to keep it running and keep it going. He took care of the filling machine always, and the can line.

For over thirty-seven years, from 1927 to 1964, the Grimes Packing Company was the economic focal point of the entire community. Aside from management, three different labor groups were involved: the fishermen, the local women, and the Filipinos, and each group had its own contract. According to Hender Toms (1997), Ouzinkie men (except for Mike Chernikoff and maybe one or two others) refused to work in the cannery because they could make much better money fishing. Ouzinkie women were recruited to work at the cannery alongside the Filipinos but worked on a different union contract and wage scale. Some Native women came all the way from Afognak to work in the cannery.

Martha Anderson (1997), a young mother at the time, was one of the local employees at the cannery:

I started working at the Grimes Cannery in 1945, when I was about twenty-five. I used to slime fish. At that time they still had an "iron chink."

Community Histories   57

Fig. 1.20. *Ouzinkie boat builder Wassily Squartsoff (right) with Sergei Panamarioff (left). Hank Eaton Collection, Kodiak Historical Society.*

Fig. 1.21. *Ed Opheim's handmade skiffs at Pleasant Harbor, Spruce Island. Photos courtesy of Ed Opheim Sr.*

Almost everybody in the community worked in the cannery. We would get paid $1/hour, or later on $2/hour. A. L. Rogers took over the cannery operation after Grimes died [in 1945].

In the mid-1930s Father Gerasim Schmaltz of the Russian Orthodox Church moved to Monk's Lagoon from Afognak and built a small chapel there. Father Gerasim, like Father Herman before him, was much loved by the people of Ouzinkie. Each summer he would spend at Monk's Lagoon, returning to Ouzinkie during the winter months. Father Gerasim, who died in 1969, led the effort to canonize Father Herman. Herman became venerated as a saint in 1970 and remains highly revered by Natives throughout the Kodiak archipelago (Morrison 1981).

In 1937 the Baptist Mission and Orphanage on Woody Island, which began operations in 1893, was destroyed by fire and was relocated to Kodiak City. But at the same time the Baptist Church also built a large new Mission House in Ouzinkie and sent in two women, Miss Setsicorn and Miss Scroll. Some Ouzinkie children, such as Nick Pestrikoff and his brother David, were sent to the new Mission in Kodiak. There was little or no conflict between the Baptists and the Russian Orthodox, at least according to Joyce Smith (1997), who arrived at the Baptist Mission with her husband Norman and three children in 1951, spent one year in Larsen Bay, and returned to Ouzinkie, where she has remained ever since.

The Japanese attack on Pearl Harbor in 1941 and the beginning of World War II brought about sudden changes in Ouzinkie. After the Japanese invaded the Aleutians, the Ouzinkie Narrows were considered important to defend militarily since they provided an open gateway to Kodiak

City from the other islands to the north. To prepare for a possible Japanese attack, the U.S. Navy Seabees built a large camp in Soldier's Bay, only about a mile from Ouzinkie, and another one on Afognak Island in Danger Bay. Another military camp was built at the East Cape of Spruce Island and foxholes were dug at Monk's Lagoon. At the same time they built a road connecting the two camps along the south end of Spruce Island (Ed Opheim Sr., personal communication).

In Soldier's Bay there were two to three hundred men stationed with 40 mm guns. In Danger Bay there was a big steam sawmill which cut 12 million feet of lumber. Reed Oswalt (1997) recalls that about five to six hundred men worked there. Kazhuyak Point (aka "Rubber Boot Point," a place where fishermen traditionally leave their rubber boots outdoors on trees at the end of each fishing season) had 150 men and an observation tower. The military also appropriated a large number of local fishing boats, and many areas were closed off to local boats for security reasons. Even the Ouzinkie school was shut down, and blackouts were strictly enforced at night (Llanos 1981:23).

Arthur Haakanson (1997), the brother of Sven Haakanson Sr., also remembered what it was like:

AH: I was nine years old, and yeah, I remember going to school, and the teachers and everybody was all excited and running around. The Japs had bombed Pearl Harbor. It was December 7, 1941, and things started changing then.

It wasn't long before a Seabee engineer camp, military camp, was built in Soldier's Bay right across from Ouzinkie. And they had a single float plane that used to fly over the village towing an orange target way behind them for practice for the small anti-aircraft gun that the Seabees had at their outpost in Soldier's Bay.

CM: Did you guys get kind of scared when they started firing?

AH: No. And we had a good relationship with the Seabees. They were actually Naval people, but they used to bring their movies over to Ouzinkie and show them in the old dance hall here, and it was the first people had ever seen of movies, and their seaplane, I think, was the first plane we here ever seen too. And it was a novelty whenever one of them landed on our beach. The whole village would go down to look at it. Now we have planes all day long, and nobody even gives them a second thought. I guess that's called progress too. [laughs]

CM: And how many years were they active over there. Till the end of the war, till '45 or '46?

AH: Yeah. They were very active there until around '45 and '46 when there was no more threat of a Japanese invasion. We even had blackouts once when Japs in that earlier time bombed Dutch Harbor. . . .

CM: And then Nick Pestrikoff told me they started scavenging some of the buildings over there and brought them to Ouzinkie after the war.

AH: True. Some families they brought over Quonset huts. Grimes Pack-

Fig. 1.22. *Top: Cannery mess hall washed into the sea by the tidal wave, 1964. Photo courtesy of Nick Pestrikoff Sr.*

Fig. 1.23. *Above: Closeup of cannery superintendent's house washed into the sea as a result of the 1964 earthquake and tsunami. Photo courtesy of Nick Pestrikoff Sr.*

ing Company brought them over and just more or less gave them to the people. They used their own tenders and their barges and everything that people didn't have, and they brought them over and just helped the Ouzinkie people out. So there were Quonset huts here too in the village, and they lasted until the 1960s even. They were still in use to some families. No sign of them now. In fact, Theodore [Squartsoff] grew up in one of them, with his dad and mom.

As in Old Harbor, Ouzinkie men joined in the war effort. Veterans from Ouzinkie who served during World War II were Nick Katelnikoff Sr., Fred Katelnikoff, Fred Chernikoff, Doc Chernikoff, Stan Panamarioff, Peter Pestrikoff, Johnny Pestrikoff, Jacob Yakoff, Pete Wolkoff Sr., Herman Anderson Sr., Fred Squartsoff, and Billy Squartsoff.

The postwar period, from 1945 to 1955, brought relative prosperity to Ouzinkie as more local women found employment in the local cannery and more and more families got involved in commercial fishing and acquired their own boats. In 1950 Oscar Grimes made a million dollars from the salmon pack, and by 1951 the Grimes Packing Company had six tenders and twenty-six seine boats. Boat building during the winter months became a profitable cottage industry. Men such as Phillip Katelnikoff, Wasilly Squartsoff, Nick Pestrikoff Sr., Fred Torsen, Waska Boskofsky, and Ed Opheim Sr. began to build skiffs, dories, and purse seiners using local spruce trees, and they became very good at it (Chernikoff 1982; Oswalt 1997).

As late as 1963, most houses in Ouzinkie lacked running water, sewers, or electricity, and there were no telephones. At that time the only communication with Kodiak City and the outside world was through a radio at the Ouzinkie Trading Company and another at the Baptist Mission (Kozely 1963:27).

The March 1964 earthquake was nearly as devastating to Ouzinkie as it was to Old Harbor. The tsunami which followed the quake took out the entire Ouzinkie Packing Company cannery. Several buildings were left floating around out in the harbor, including the superintendent's house. Boats were used to tow some of the houses back to shore. The worst thing was that six or seven men lost their lives on the boat *Spruce Cape*, which got caught in the tsunami and sank at Spruce Cape. Two young men from Ouzinkie, Teddy Panamarioff and Alfred Reft, were among them. For safety, villagers camped out on top of the mountain, fearing another big wave which never came. At least two Ouzinkie residents have told lengthy hair-raising stories about their experiences during the earthquake and tsunami (see Panamarioff 1982 and Muller 1982).

Without the Grimes cannery, Ouzinkie fishermen and cannery workers alike lost their livelihood. Columbia Ward rebuilt the store and the dock, but not the cannery. It was very similar to what happened in Old Harbor when the nearby Shearwater cannery was destroyed. In the late 1960s the Ouzinkie Seafoods cannery was constructed, but it mysteriously

Fig. 1.24. *Ouzinkie waterfront, 1989, shortly after the* Exxon Valdez *oil spill. Photo by Craig Mishler.*

burned down in 1976 shortly after it was sold. For a short period, a floating processor, the *Kalakala*, tied up at Ouzinkie and carried on the work. The *Kalakala* was a surplused Washington state ferry that later ended up as a cannery in Kodiak City. No canneries have operated in Ouzinkie since that time.

Sometimes disasters bring unexpected benefits. After the tidal wave, everybody who had a boat in Ouzinkie claimed insurance damages. The insurance companies paid off and gave everyone a new boat, whether their old one had been damaged or not, but only on the condition that the old boats be destroyed. Nick Pestrikoff Sr. remembers that if people wanted a new boat, all they had to do was take a chain saw and cut a hole in the bottom of their old one. As soon as the new boats arrived, the old ones were taken down to the beach and burned.

After the tidal wave there was a long period of rebuilding. One central feature of Ouzinkie's contemporary cultural landscape is the large central dock facility, built close to where the old Grimes Packing Com-

Community Histories

Fig. 1.25. *Ouzinkie Community Hall, 1997. Photo by Craig Mishler.*

pany cannery was. The dock sits up on high pilings and extends way out into the water to accommodate large oceangoing ships at low tide. These ships arrive periodically to deliver building supplies, fuel, and groceries for the village store.

The store, a two-story building, is located at the foot of the Ouzinkie dock and is a central gathering place for those wishing to socialize (Figure 34). The Ouzinkie Native Corporation has its offices directly above the store. The City of Ouzinkie offices reside in the old elementary school building about one hundred yards away. A large community hall provides facilities for public meetings and is transformed into a bingo parlor two or three nights a week. It is also used for the senior citizens' hot lunch program.

Unique among Kodiak Island communities, Ouzinkie has a state-of-the-art community freezer and smoker facility, which was constructed during the early 1980s under a state grant. This facility, now supported by annual membership fees, is operated by the Ouzinkie Tribal Council. In addition to tribal offices, it contains stainless steel counters and sinks for cleaning fish and game and a vacuum bag sealing machine.

Ouzinkie's large gravel airstrip was not built until the 1980s, fairly late compared to other Kodiak communities. Before that, only float planes could land there. Today flights to and from Kodiak City only take about ten minutes, and the community receives three scheduled flights each day.

Ouzinkie residents also travel back and forth to Kodiak City by boat and skiff. It is also common for Ouzinkie skiff drivers to run across to Anton Larsen Bay to pick up family and friends who have driven cars or taken land taxis across Kodiak Island. This connection is especially popular whenever weather conditions are marginal or poor for flying.

In 1998 a large dredge arrived in the village to begin construction of a long-awaited small boat harbor. Some twenty years in planning, the small boat harbor will spare boat owners from having to get up in the middle of the night during a rainstorm to move their boats simply because the wind changes direction. Over the years many local boats have been damaged by strong winds. When the wind is blowing from the north, northwest, west, and southwest, they have to "tie up" their boats at the dock to avoid being swamped by heavy waves. However, when the wind turns and starts blowing from the south, southeast, east, or northeast, they have to "anchor up" in shallow water away from the dock to prevent their boats from being slammed up against the dock pilings (Mishler 1995).

ALASKA NATIVE CLAIMS SETTLEMENT ACT

Shortly after the discovery of oil on Alaska's arctic coastal plain in 1968, there was an impetus to build an oil pipeline from the North Slope to the ice-free port of Valdez. In order to acquire the right of way to build the pipeline, however, it was imperative that the longstanding land claims of Alaska Native peoples be settled. When the Alaska Native Claims Settlement Act (ANCSA) was passed in 1971, Natives all over the state received title to thousands of acres of aboriginal lands. These lands and millions of dollars in cash were conveyed to Native regional and village corporations, created by the act as profit-making businesses. Out of this legislation the Old Harbor Native Corporation and the Ouzinkie Native Corporation were conceived and born, along with Koniag Inc., the regional corporation representing all Kodiak area Native communities.

But even with this far-reaching settlement, some people recognized a major shortcoming in the terms. Sven Haakanson Sr., for example, observed that the Native people of Kodiak have always focused their lives on the resources of the ocean. Their ancient maritime economies were based on fishing and marine mammal hunting, but under the terms of the ANCSA they were not given a single drop of water. In testimony before the Berger Commission, Sven said:

> *In the digging, archeological diggings, or whatever you call it, they find fish bones, fish tool, hooks . . . and then they take the water away from us*

and give us land. How could we live without the water? . . . If the federal government can't give us title to our waters so we can fish and protect our family from now on, we'd recommend that if they can't do that, that we get a section of the ocean off the three-mile limits (Haakanson 1984:16).

In light of this it is also significant that on February 17, 1950, twenty-one years before the passage of ANCSA, the Ouzinkie Village Council, led by Mike Chernikoff as president and Tim Panamarioff as secretary, held a public meeting and passed a resolution petitioning the U.S. Department of the Interior for recognition of its "exclusive use and occupancy" of lands and waters around Spruce Island and "the eastern shores of Kodiak Island from Monashka Bay to Kizhuyak Bay inclusive" (see copy of document in Kozely 1963:41). This claim, which was apparently rejected, included all of the inshore waters up to three thousand feet from the two islands.

THE *EXXON VALDEZ* OIL SPILL

After the 1964 earthquake, the most traumatic event in the lives of people living in Old Harbor and Ouzinkie was the oil spill. The *Exxon Valdez* oil tanker spill took place at Bligh Reef in Prince William Sound on March 24, 1989. The oil soon began drifting south and west, entering lower Cook Inlet and arriving on the north end of Kodiak Island and Spruce Island, about April 15. It then followed tidal currents and winds through the Ouzinkie Narrows and down the west side of the Island into Shelikof Strait, reaching the vicinity of Larsen Bay and Karluk by the middle of May. By the end of May it had also reached Port Lions and Barabara Cove at the upper end of Kazhuyak Bay (see Appendix B), and the communities of Akhiok and Old Harbor on the southern end of the Island. More oil, much of it in the form of mousse and tarballs, kept arriving throughout June and July. During the summer of 1989, the Department of Fish and Game closed all of the commercial salmon fisheries in the Kodiak area. Division of Subsistence staff members Craig Mishler and James Fall began visiting each of the Kodiak communities and holding public meetings about the impact of the spill on subsistence in June and July 1989.

As a result of our subsistence harvest survey in January 1990, Old Harbor and Ouzinkie, along with Port Lions and Karluk, showed substantial declines in harvest production as a result of the oil spill, and Ouzinkie was the community in which subsistence harvests were curtailed the most severely (Fall and Field 1996). Since Ouzinkie was the first Kodiak area community to see the oil arrive and see it in denser, fresher concentrations than other communities in the region, it is understandable that Ouzinkie residents reacted more strongly to it. A very large proportion of Ouzinkie residents (61 percent of all adults) were employed by VECO and involved in oil spill cleanup, and they saw firsthand the devastating effects of the spill on bird and marine life. The harvesting of butter clams, a favorite wild food resource, came almost to a standstill, and there was a fear not only of contaminated fish but also of deer, which are observed to come down to the ocean beaches to eat kelp.

SUMMARY

Ouzinkie and Old Harbor have distinctive but parallel histories dating back to the mid-nineteenth century. They resemble each other in several respects, especially in their twentieth century commercial fishing and fish processing economies, in their reliance upon subsistence foods, in their strong adherence to Russian Orthodoxy, in their settlement history, and in their ethnic identity.

Today, however, their histories and economies appear to be diverging. While both communities were formerly dominated by the commercial fishing industry, Old Harbor has maintained strong ties to that economy and has also diversified into tourism. Meanwhile, Ouzinkie has moved steadily away from commercial fishing and is becoming more reliant on the logging industry, showing only a modest interest in local tourism. This historical thread is picked up again in Chapter 7.

Chapter Two

Demography

Demography, the study of population dynamics, is a useful tool for examining certain aspects of social structure, social change, and ethnicity. As such it has a natural tie-in with my discussion of kinship and social organization in Chapter 4. The salient topics here are ethnonyms, ethnic identity, regional migrations, family territories, population trends, social mobility, and mortality.

ETHNONYMS

Figure 2.1 illustrates the Alutiiq names for the bands or extended families who resided in each of the modern Kodiak Island communities. These bands obviously represent a "short list" compared to the number of settlements and groups which existed during the early Russian period of the late eighteenth and early nineteenth centuries. Nevertheless, they reflect, at least to some extent, the forced consolidation which took place under Russian rule in the 1840s. A total of ten groups are identified. Although I collected the information from two fluent speakers of Alutiiq in two different communities (reflecting a small dialect difference), the two lists complement each other.

IMMIGRATION AND ETHNIC IDENTITY

Ethnicity in Ouzinkie and Old Harbor resembles the structure of sedimentary rock. There are several genetic layers of it, deposited one upon the other, over a two-hundred-year period, with some percolation and melting between the layers. The bottom layer, of course, consists of the aboriginal Alutiiq or Koniag of the pre-contact period. On top of this base is the group of Russian men who arrived during the commercial sea otter fur hunting era of the late eighteenth and early nineteenth century, and on top of this is a group of Scandinavian men in the early twentieth century. These Scandinavians developed the area's burgeoning cod and herring fisheries, but like the Russians, they also participated heavily in the fur trade. One early source (Porter 1893: 79) suggests that the Scandinavians were motivated to marry Alutiiq women in order to dodge the federal regulation against non-Natives hunting and trapping furbearing animals, especially sea otters. Non-Native husbands of Native women were exempted from this regulation and were treated as though they were Natives.

Anglo-American and other non-Native men and women arriving in the villages during the late twentieth century have added yet another thin layer to

---

Kodiak Alutiiq Band Designations

Alutiiq Ethnonyms: from Ephraim Agnot, Akhiok 12/8/93

Nunyagmiut (Old Harbor people)
Kangniyamiut (Kaguyak people)
Kasuqwaqmiut (Akhiok people)
Iraqmiut (Eagle Harbor people)
Sunaqmiut (Kodiak City people)
Aranaqmiut (Afognak people)
Kaloqmiut (Karluk people)
Uyaksakmiut (Larsen Bay people)

Alutiiq Ethnonyms: from Paul Kahutak, Old Harbor 3/12/97

Nunyuqmiut (Old Harbor people)
Kangiyaqmiut (Kaguyak people)
Arwanmiut (Aiaktalik people)
Kasuqwakmiut (Akhiok people)
Iraqmiut (Eagle Harbor people)
Sunaqmiut (Kodiak City people)
Tamirnaqmiut (Woody Island people)
Arwanaqmiut (Afognak people)
Anwiqmiut (Spruce Island people)

Fig. 2.1.

---

the ethnic mix and have further increased the degree of creolization. A couple of Siberian Eskimo women from St. Lawrence Island, for example, have married into Old Harbor, but after one was widowed in the early 1990s, only one of them remains.

One enduring legacy from the Russian period is the continuation of surnames such as Melovedoff, Larionoff, Pestrikoff, Andrewvitch, and Alexanderoff in Old Harbor, and Chernikoff, Chichenoff, Pestrikoff, Katelnikoff, and Squartsoff in Ouzinkie. Likewise, Scandinavian surnames such as Anderson, Torsen, Skonberg, and Haakanson are as commonplace in Ouzinkie as Christiansen, Haakanson, Johanssen, and Peterson are in Old Harbor.

With Russian surnames, however, there is a caveat. It turns out that not every family with a Russian surname necessarily has Russian blood. Although many Russians in the employ of the Russian-American Company took Alutiiq wives, had families, and remained in Alaska as "colonial citizens" after terminating their employment with the company, it was also a common practice for Alutiiqs to receive the Russian surnames of their godfathers at the time of baptism (Lydia Black, personal communication, August 27, 1998). Because of this, the presumed "Ethnic Heritage" of those families with Russian surnames listed in Figures 2.2 and 2.3 needs to be individually verified through genealogical research. As noted earlier in Chapter 1, there does seem to be genuine Russian blood in the lineage of the Pestrikoffs and Chernikoffs of Ouzinkie, who can all trace their ancestry back to the dance hall impresario, Vasilli Pestrikoff.

Fig. 2.2.

Old Harbor Native Families, 1990s

Surname	First Immigrant or Earliest Ancestor	Ethnic Heritage	Original Community	Year Arrived	Family Married Into
Adonga	Emil Adonga	Alutiiq	Kaguyak		Konduck (Cape Trinity)
Alexanderoff	Peter Alexanderoff	Russian/Alutiiq	Old Harbor		Larson (Unga)
Andrewvitch	Herman Andrewvitch	Russian/Alutiiq	Akhiok	1946	Adonga
Ashowak	Lawrence Ashowak	Alutiiq	Kaguyak	1964	
Azuyak	Gavrilla (Kanga) Azuyak	Alutiiq	Akhiok	1955	Stepan (Akhiok)
Berns	Rick Berns	Anglo-American	Kodiak	1960s	Christiansen
Berntsen	Ron Bernsten	Norwegian/Aleut/Russian	King Cove	1965	Alexanderoff
Capjohn	Feodor (Fred) Capjohn	Russian/Alutiiq	Eagle Harbor		Chokwak
Chokwak*	Boris Chokwak	Alutiiq	Old Harbor		Ashowak (Eagle Harbor)
Christiansen	Rolf Christiansen	Norwegian	Norway	1920s	Kelly (Eagle Harbor)
Chya	Paul Chya	Alutiiq	Kodiak	1940s	Capjohn
Clough	Glen Clough	Anglo-American		1960s	Haakanson
Cratty	Al Cratty Sr.	Scotch-Irish	Kodiak		Christiansen
Erickson	Walt Erickson	Swedish/Finn/Alutiiq	Chigniks	1960	Inga
Gatter	George Gatter Jr.	Alutiiq	Kodiak		Almeter (non-local)
Gregory	Leroy Gregory	Inupiat	Nome	1986	Pestrikoff
Haakanson	Arthur Haakanson Sr.	Danish	Denmark	1920s	Peterochin (Eagle Harbor)
Hansen	Durban Hansen	Norwegian	Norway	1920s	Adonga
Inga*	Alexander (Sashka) Inga	Alutiiq	Old Harbor		Peterochin (Eagle Harbor)
Ignatin	William Ignatin	Alutiiq	Monk's Lagoon		Inga
Johansen	Gene Johansen	Norwegian	Unga	1960s	Matfay
Kahutak	Peter Kahutak	Alutiiq	Eagle Harbor		Peterson (Carmel Bay)
Krumrey	Ray Krumrey	Anglo-American	Idaho	1991	Zeedar
Larionoff	Moses Larionoff	Russian/Alutiiq/Japanese	Aiaktalik Island	1960s	
Lukovitch	Luzon Lukovitch	Russian/Alutiiq	Aiaktalik Island		
Matfay	Larry Matfay	Alutiiq	Akhiok	1951	Naumoff (Karluk)
Melovedoff	Victor Melovedoff	Russian/Alutiiq	Kaguyak	1964	Shugak
Mordhorst	Anne Mordhorst	Alutiiq	Afognak	1960s	(non-local)
Naumoff	Alfred Naumoff	Russian/Alutiiq	Karluk/Akhiok	1950s	Kelly (Eagle Harbor)
Nestic	Jim Nestic	Anglo-American	Pennsylvania	1970s	Capjohn
Pestrikoff	Mike Pestrikoff	Russian/Alutiiq	Woody Island	1940s	Chya (Kodiak)
Peterson	Victor Peterson	Alutiiq%	Akhiok	1949	Inga
Price	Gary Price	Anglo-American	Oregon	1987	Haakanson
Shugak	Innokenty Shugak	Alutiiq	Eagle Harbor		Peninjohn
Stanley	George Stanley	Alutiiq%	Woody Island		Capjohn
Tunohun	Mike Tunohun	Alutiiq	Woody Island	1940s	Inga
Zeedar	Anakenti Zeedar	Alutiiq	Old Harbor		(Kaguyak)

*Signifies one of the original Old Harbor Alutiiq families. % = Mixed
Old Harbor surnames no longer in use: Aquiak, Aloklie, Chokwak, Kaguyak, Karakin, Makrena, Nickeefer, Peninjohn, Peningiak, Shadula.
Compiled from Alaska Village Census Records (BIA), Microfilm P2286, Roll 45, National Archives, Anchorage, and oral interviews.

Fig. 2.3.

Ouzinkie Native Families, 1990s

Surname	First Immigrant or Earliest Ancestor	Ethnic Heritage	Original Community	Year Arrived	Family Married Into
Ambrosia	Alex Ambrosia	Russian/Alutiiq	Karluk	1970	Anderson
Anderson	John W. Anderson	Danish	Afognak		Katelnikoff (Afognak)
Bennett	Bill Bennett		King Cove	n/a	Wolkoff
Boskofsky	Bill Boskofsky	Russian/Alutiiq	Afognak		Katelnikoff
Campfield	Dave Campfield	Anglo-American	California	1990	Ellanak (Karluk)
Chernikoff	Mike Chernikoff	Russian/Alutiiq	Little Afognak	1917	Torsen
Chichenoff	Zack Chichenoff Sr.	Russian/Alutiiq	Afognak		Katelnikoff
Christofferson	Andy Christofferson		Akhiok	1960s	Panamarioff
Clarion	Danny Clarion	Anglo-American	Texas		Chichenoff
Delgado	Duke Delgado	Hispanic	Mexico	1960s	Katelnikoff
	Paul Delgado	Hispanic	Mexico	1960s	Pestrikoff & Squartsoff
Denato	Fred Denato		Kodiak		Boskofsky
Ellanak	Larry Ellanak		Afognak/Karluk	1953	(Katmai)
Garner	Willis Garner	Alutiiq	Afognak/Pt Lions		non-Native
Haakanson	Arthur Haakanson Sr.	Danish	Denmark	1920s	Shugak (Eagle Harbor)
Johnson	Roger Johnson	Swedish/Alutiiq	Larsen Bay	1960s	Panamarioff
Katelnikoff	John Katelnikoff	Russian/Alutiiq	Monk's Lagoon		
Kvasnikoff	Ponto Kvasnikoff	Russian/Alutiiq	Ninilchik		Shanigan
Larionoff	Roger Larionoff	Russian/Alutiiq	Old Harbor		
Llanos	Joe Llanos	Filipino/Tlingit	Southeast Alaska		Smith
Morrison	Don Morrison		Kodiak?	1990s	Panamarioff
Muller	Fred Muller		Afognak	1926	Torsen
	Julian Muller		Afognak		Katelnikoff
Opheim	Chris Opheim	Norwegian/Aleut	Norway	1923	Devine (Unga)
Panamarioff	Sergei Panamarioff	Russian/Alutiiq	Ouzinkie		Toshwak (Afognak)
	Stephan Panamarioff		Monk's Lagoon		Bellavina
Pestrikoff	Vasilii Pestrikoff	Russian	Russia	c 1860s	Pareskeva
Shanigan	Trafeme Shanigan	Russian/Alutiiq	Katmai		Squartsoff (Afognak)
Skonberg	Jim Skonberg	Swedish/Alutiiq	Chigniks	1960s	Chernikoff
Smith	William Smith Sr.	Dutch	Holland		Larionoff
Squartsoff	Peter Squartsoff Sr.	Russian/Alutiiq	Ouzinkie		Yagashoff (Woody Island)
Torsen	Albert Torsen	Norwegian	Norway		Pestrikoff
Totemoff	Wayne Totemoff	Russian/Alutiiq	Tatitlek	1980s	none

Ouzinkie surnames no longer in use: Apalone, Berestoff, Davis, Derinoff, Gugel, Lachinsky, Larsen, Novikoff, Orloff, Sucharemkin, Toshwak, Yagashoff, Yakoff, Wasbrakoff

Compiled from Alaska Village Census Records (BIA), Microfilm, P2286, Roll 46, National Archives, Anchorage and oral interviews.

In Old Harbor there are still a few families which have retained their Alutiiq names, although many have disappeared (see Figure 2.2). The surnames Ashouwak, Azuyak, Inga, Kahutak, and Shugak continue. At least one of these families, the Ingas, appears to be an "original" Old Harbor family although even they recall living for a time in Eagle Harbor before coming back to Old Harbor. In Ouzinkie, all of the Alutiiq names have now disappeared (Figure 2.3). The last one still in use was Ellanak, but all of the descendants from this family are women who have married and adopted their husbands' surnames.

It is generally true that Ouzinkie and Old Harbor people of mixed blood identify themselves first as "Aleuts" or "Natives." No one speaks with any sense of pride about their Russian blood and heritage, and only in a joking kind of way do they call themselves "Danes," "Swedes," or "Norwegians." The late Jenny Chernikoff of Ouzinkie was the only person I met who took pride in being a "Creole," a term which represented her mixed Russian and Alutiiq heritage. Jenny took pride in the fact that she could speak Russian and could call out local Russian place names.

REGIONAL MIGRATIONS

It is a worthwhile exercise to examine the origin of the present-day Old Harbor and Ouzinkie families by looking at their surnames. In Old Harbor, it would seem that the great majority of the men now living there migrated from someplace else, or their fathers did. This process was dictated in part by the Alutiiq traditions of matrilocality and bride service, in which the husband is expected to move into the community of his wife and apprentice himself to his father-in-law. Another factor seems to have been Russian Orthodox restrictions against the marriage of cousins, leading to widespread village exogamy (Mason 1998).

In the 1930s a number of families moved to Old Harbor from the old village of Eagle Harbor (called Orlova by the Russians). Eagle Harbor was located on the southwest shore of Ugak Bay and had a population of sixty to seventy in 1890 (Porter 1893:76). Some people who remember the exodus say it was Eagle Harbor's exposure to storms, particularly southeasterlies, which prompted them to move, but there is also evidence that people left to get away from an unlikable man named Peter Petorochin, also known as Eagle Harbor Pete. George Inga Sr. (1987) says Pete was a big man who was very gentle most of the time but got pretty wild and trigger happy when he was drinking, and they were afraid he might shoot someone. It was simply easier to move away than to kick him out. While some Eagle Harbor families went directly to Old Harbor, others moved to Woody Island for a few years and later on migrated to Old Harbor. Woody Island was a Native village taken over in the early nineteenth century by colonial Russians and was later taken over in the twentieth century by Baptist missionaries, who built an orphanage and school there. Woody Island had a population of about 120 persons in 1890 (Porter 1893:75).

After the Great Alaska Earthquake and tsunami of 1964, some more tiles were added to Old Harbor's cultural mosaic when several displaced families from Kaguyak moved in (Figure 2.2). Some Kaguyakers also moved to Akhiok. Yet another group of families including the Larionoffs moved to Old Harbor from the old village on Aiaktalik Island after a short stay in Akhiok, but the reasons and the timing for this migration remain obscure. Aiaktalik seems to have been largely vacated by the mid-1940s, although it had a population of 106 people in 1890 (see Porter 1893:78).

In a similar fashion Ouzinkie grew after the 1964 earthquake due to the destruction of Afognak village (Figure 2.3). Although a majority of the Afognak families moved to Port Lions, several, including the Chichenoffs and the Boskofskys, found their way to Ouzinkie. A much earlier migration to Ouzinkie, which took place in the nineteenth century, came about when the families at Monk's Lagoon, on the south end of Spruce Island, moved away. Like the migration from Eagle Harbor to Old Harbor, the Monk's Lagoon people's move to Ouzinkie may well have been prompted by exposure to severe southeasterly storms from the open ocean. Some residents of Little Afognak moved to Ouzinkie following the 1918 flu epidemic (Oswalt 1997).

Both Old Harbor and Ouzinkie then, retain a core group of "original" Alutiiq families plus a convergence of families, many with Russian blood, who were displaced from the now-abandoned villages of Little Afognak, Afognak, Eagle Harbor, Aiaktalik, and Woody Island. Some of these consolidations occurred as a result of natural disasters such as the Katmai eruption of 1912 and the Great Alaskan Earthquake of 1964. As a result of the development of commercial cod, herring, and salmon fisheries in the late nineteenth and early twentieth centuries, Scandinavian men from Norway, Denmark, and Sweden immigrated to these villages and intermarried with Alutiiq women.

Since the 1960s, Anglo-Americans have begun marrying Ouzinkie and Old Harbor women, and this most recent wave of immigration has further creolized and thickened the existing mix of Russian, Scandinavian, and Alutiiq blood. As discussed below in Chapter 4, village exogamy and matrilocality prevail. There are several marriages or unions between local men and local women but very few between local men and nonlocal women. If the women are nonlocal, they also tend to be non-Native.

To summarize, there are two observable migratory processes going on in these communities. First, there is genetic layering through Alutiiq intermarriage with other Alutiiqs, and with Russian, Scandinavian, and American male immigrants from outside the region. Second, there is geographic convergence and consolidation within the region as whole families from small remote settlements relocated and merged into the larger ones we now call villages, partly as a result of natural disasters and partly as a result of children facing compulsory attendance at territorial schools. And what makes it all interesting and complex is that both processes have been taking place simultaneously over the past two hundred years.

FAMILY TERRITORIES

During the early American period and perhaps even during the Russian period, most Ouzinkie families had their own traditional hunting and trapping territories. Except for the Squartsoff family homestead located at Barabara Cove in Upper Kazhuyak Bay, these family territories have now been largely abandoned although some may well have been claimed through the Bureau of Indian Affairs Native allotment program. Historically, it seems clear that each family had its own proprietary hunting and trapping areas in Kazhuyak Bay and around Spruce Island and Afognak Island. Ed Opheim Sr. says that each family had a cabin which was close to the water and which could be reached in less than a day by rowing a skiff.

According to Reed Oswalt (1997) and Christine Kvasnikoff (1997), the Ouzinkie family territories were defined as follows:

1) Wasilly Squartsoff had the area from Ouzinkie Narrows to Camel's Rock to Shakmanoff Point on the Kodiak Island side.
2) Mike Wasbikoff, who died in the mid-1940s, had the area from Anton Larsen Bay up to Sheratine Bay.
3) Peter Squartsoff Sr. had the area from the head of Kazhuyak Bay to Barabara Cove.
4) Johnny Anderson had the Whale Pass area.
5) Fred Torsen hunted and trapped from Danger Bay to Ban Island.
6) Phillip and Steve Katelnikoff hunted from Tonki Bay through Izhut Bay on Afognak Island.
7) Trefim Shanigan trapped in Seal Bay and Perenosa Bay on Afognak Island.

It seems safe to assume that the families in Afognak Village also had exclusive hunting and trapping territories and that some of these territories were contiguous with those of Ouzinkie families.

Although documentation for the Old Harbor area is less complete, it is clear that similar family territories existed around Old Harbor. Paul Kahutak (1987, 1997), for example, talks at length about his father's cabin and fox and weasel trapping grounds inside Rolling Bay on Sitkalidak Island, recalling that they would go out to their cabin for about a week at a time. Some trappers around Old Harbor, such as the Shugaks, would take their wives and children. George Inga Sr. (1997) remembers traveling in a skiff powered by a three-horsepower kicker all the way to Eagle Harbor with his father and brother. If there was a storm they would stop at barabaras and little cabins along the way, always being careful to respect other families' territories. In George's words:

Most of the time we used to go about the fifteenth or sixteenth of November. Come back just before Christmas. About a month anyway. You know, like if a guy have a barabara or what you call, and the next one would have one not too far from him. When they go hunt, they tell each other how far he could hunt, you know. Don't bother the other one. So that other one could have his own place to hunt. Not go close to other guy's cabin, whatever. 'Cause after they come back around December, then anybody could hunt and use that land. That's the way they used to work, pretty good, you know.

POPULATION TRENDS

Figure 2.4 provides a 110-year timeline of population estimates for Old Harbor and Ouzinkie spanning the years 1880 to 1990. It can be immediately noted that Old Harbor experienced steady declines between 1880 and 1920, only to demonstrate undiminished growth until 1986. Although it probably lost population during the Spanish flu epidemic which swept Alaska in 1918, the reason why Old Harbor experienced a turnaround in growth during the 1920s and 1930s is almost certainly due to the construction of the Kadiak Fisheries salmon cannery at Shearwater Bay. The promise of wage employment and new opportunities for commercial fishing no doubt attracted people from other nearby communities like Aiaktalik Village. Aiaktalik experienced steady declines from 1920 to 1940 and drops out of the census tables completely after 1940. Still, the most surprising thing is that even after the Kadiak Fisheries cannery at Shearwater was destroyed by the 1964 earthquake and tsunami, Old Harbor continued to experience dramatic growth.

Ouzinkie's population, on the other hand, experienced a slow and steady growth until 1940 and then decreased and fluctuated at a reduced level after that. It is not clear why Ouzinkie lost population during the 1940s, although it may well have been as a result of the same 1947 spring flu epidemic that took the lives of so many people in Old Harbor.

The population decline in Ouzinkie between 1960 and 1970 clearly seems to have been related to the 1964 earthquake and tsunami, which removed the community's principal employer, the Grimes Packing Company cannery. Sometime between 1960 and 1970, Old Harbor surpassed Ouzinkie in total number of residents, and it has remained larger ever since.

Figure 2.5 shows more recent population trends in both communities during the 1980s and 1990s. Although Old Harbor lost population in the late 1980s, it has gained some of it back in the 1990s. Meanwhile, Ouzinkie has fluctuated a bit and has gained a little in the 1990s but

120-Year Population History

	1880	1890	1920	1930	1940	1950	1960	1970	1980	1990	2000
Old Harbor	160	86	54	84	109	121	193	290	340	284	237
Ouzinkie	N.A.	74	96	168	253	177	214	160	173	209	225

Source: U.S. Bureau of the Census

Fig. 2.4. overall has remained fairly stable. In 1997 both Old Harbor and Ouzinkie lost about 5 percent of their population, perhaps to some extent as a result of the weakening of commercial fisheries. The *Exxon Valdez* oil spill appears to have had no measurable impact on the population of either community.

SOCIAL MOBILITY: SOME CASE STUDIES

The populations of Old Harbor and Ouzinkie fluctuate seasonally depending on the fishing season. During the summer months nonresidents with kinship and economic ties to year-round residents come back from Kodiak, Anchorage, or from the lower forty-eight states either to participate in commercial salmon fishing or to do subsistence fishing and get back to their roots. With the general decline in fish prices during the 1990s, however, the economic motivations to return are not as great as they were in the 1980s, and there are accordingly fewer seasonal residents.

One seasonal Ouzinkie resident I am familiar with lives in Anchorage during the winter. He was born in Ouzinkie and lives with a much younger Iñupiat woman from the Arctic Slope. They have one young daughter. He was formerly married to a different Iñupiat woman and has a son by her. Neither of these women have liked Ouzinkie well enough to remain more than a few weeks at a time during the summer, so the husband now splits his time between Anchorage and Ouzinkie, while his girlfriend splits her time between Anchorage and Barrow, where her family resides.

Another seasonal Ouzinkie household is a retired couple whose married daughter lives in the village. This couple now summers in Ouzinkie and winters in an Anchorage condo, but they also return during the Russian Christmas holidays to be with their extended family.

Three Old Harbor Native families I am familiar with left the community in the 1990s. One of these was a young couple in their twenties with two young boys who moved to Anchorage to attend college at the University of Alaska. The husband of this couple is a very traditionally minded person who enjoys making kayaks and games such as the dart sets used to play the Alutiiq game Aurcaq (Mishler 1997). He has also

Recent Population Figures

	1982a	1986a	1989a	1990b	1993c	1996c	1997c	2000b
Old Harbor	356	380	279	284	305	316	301	237
Ouzinkie	234	195	219	209	225	259	246	225

a Based upon estimates from ADF&G surveyed households
b U.S. Census
c Alaska Department of Labor estimates

Fig. 2.5.

worked seasonally as a crew member in commercial fishing. It is not clear whether this family will ever return to the community.

The second family, which left Old Harbor in 1997, was a couple in their fifties, whose children are now full-grown and are attending college to become teachers. The husband of this couple commercially fished as a crew member most of his life but became physically unable to do hard manual work and then found himself heavily dependent on welfare. He was extremely active in the community socially and politically and found this dependence demoralizing. Like the husband of the younger couple, this older man also left to attend the University of Alaska in Anchorage. His goal was to acquire the training necessary to become a drug and alcohol counselor so that he could return to Old Harbor and follow a second career.

The third family that left the community was a non-Native woman married to a Native man born and raised in Old Harbor. This man had gone away to college and returned as the principal of the village school. Partly because this couple commercially fishes each summer in Bristol Bay, the husband eventually took a job as principal of the school in Togiak. This man has now moved to become a school principal in Soldotna where he can be near his elderly father and his sister, but his sons still live in Old Harbor.

One Ouzinkie family that left the community and moved to Anchorage in the mid-1990s consisted of a middle-aged Ouzinkie woman married to a Native man from Southeast Alaska. This man was a former president of the Ouzinkie Tribal Council and was also chairman of the Board of Directors of the Kodiak Area Native Association (KANA). During and after the oil spill he was employed by Exxon as their village coordinator. In 1996 he left the village to take a job as executive director of the Alaska Intertribal Council.

MORTALITY

One of the saddest parts of working in Old Harbor and Ouzinkie over ten years is the observance of many deaths, most of them tragic and unnecessary. Some of those who died were key respondents whom I interviewed and became close to. Residents told me of three suicides in the community following the spill but before I arrived in July, but it would be quite a stretch to attribute these three deaths to the spill. Although I am not aware of all of the fatalities and do not know about mortality rates because such statistics are unavailable at the village level, I have noted the following twelve deaths in Old Harbor over a ten-year period between July 1989 and May 1998, drawing upon published obituaries in the *Kodiak Daily Mirror* and fatalities reported to me by word of mouth. All of the deaths were to Natives:

1) A middle-aged woman killed in three-wheeler accident. The accident was drinking-related.

2) A teenage boy who drowned after falling through the ice into the lagoon on his four-wheeler. The accident was said to be drinking-related.

3) A young Native man who was shot and murdered by a white man following a quarrel over drugs and alcohol that the white man was selling. I was in the village the night that it happened.

4) Two commercial fishermen who drowned when their boat, a purse seiner, overturned in rough seas near Kodiak. One of the men left a widow behind.

5) An elderly man who slowly died of stomach cancer at the Alaska Native Hospital in Anchorage. He neither drank nor smoked.

6) A middle-aged man who died of a heart attack in his house. Alcohol was believed to be a factor in his death.

7) A young boy who died of glue sniffing.

8) A teenage girl who died of chicken pox, at least partly because the illness was diagnosed too late for proper treatment. The girl left behind an infant son.

9) A middle-aged woman who died from paralytic shellfish poisoning after eating contaminated mussels.

10) A twenty-five-year-old man who committed suicide with a gunshot wound to the head. This man's father left the community and resided in Kodiak for several months after the death. He was deeply despondent.

11) An elderly man in his nineties, who died of cancer.

12) An elderly man who died from unknown causes.

In Ouzinkie I am aware of eight deaths over the same ten years. In contrast to Old Harbor, the vast majority (six) of those occurring in Ouzinkie were to elders and middle-aged people who died of sickness. One death was a gunshot suicide committed by a Native man in his thirties who was originally from Old Harbor, and the last was to a non-Native man who died in Kodiak City of a drug overdose.

An examination of the cause of death in each case illustrates some of the serious social problems faced by village residents, particularly drugs, alcohol, and suicide. While there are many bright spots, this is the dark side of village life. Substance abuse has taken a heavy toll on both young people and adults (see Pullar 1992).

One of the social forces shaping both the size and the number of households in Old Harbor and Ouzinkie at any given time develops out of the traditional Alutiiq belief that if someone dies in your house, that house carries bad luck to other household members. It is believed that other family members may get sick and die if they continue to stay there. Following a death, therefore, families either move in with other relatives or build a new house. Failing that, they may relocate the old house in the belief that the bad luck is associated with the ground beneath the house rather than with the building itself. Paul Kahutak (1987) remembers at least three different Old Harbor houses being pried up and moved around on rollers because the owners believed the deaths that occurred in these houses were due to the ground beneath them being haunted.

In the late 1980s, just before I first arrived in Old Harbor, there were three suicides over a short period of time, all inflicted by guns. Although Old Harbor apparently had a housing shortage at the time, the three "suicide houses" were deserted because no one wanted to live in them or clean them up after the deaths took place. This certainly has an impact on housing vacancy rates. In 1990, for example, Old Harbor had 112 housing units, but only 87 units or 78 percent of them were occupied (DCRA 1998). That same year Ouzinkie had a total of 82 housing units, but only 68 units or 83 percent of them were occupied.

Finally, one time when I was staying with a family in Ouzinkie, I choked on some salmon and rice at the dinner table and put a scare into everyone there, including myself. The head of the household told me I had better see a doctor pretty quick because he didn't want anybody dying in his house. He didn't want me to come back again until I had a complete check-up. He was very serious and repeated this admonition to me several times over the next twenty-four hours. He even brought it up again a year later, even though I had no recurrences.

Chapter Three

Political Organization

THE NATIVE VILLAGE OF OLD HARBOR AND ITS TRADITIONAL GOVERNMENT
by Laurie Mulcahy

VILLAGE GOVERNANCE

Overview

In former times, before the Great Alaskan Earthquake of 1964, but after Russian contact, traditional village government in the Old Harbor area revolved around the chief, or *toyuq*, and his council: the *sukashiq*, his assistant or second chief(s); the church lay reader; the *staristaq* or church warden; and the village elders. According to those elders I interviewed, including Paul Kahutak, George Inga Sr., Anakenti Zeedar, and Senafont Zeedar in Old Harbor, and Ephraim Agnot Sr. in Akhiok, this system was successful because of the emphasis placed upon an existing cooperative network within the village, which encouraged information-sharing among the people, thus allowing for a greater involvement with actual village operation.

Information was conveyed through a series of meetings in which the entire community was expected to participate. Old Harbor continued with this form of government until 1964, when they elected a mayor and began operating with both a Tribal and City Council. However, it is important to note that the "Tribal Council," established by the tribal constitution to ensure federal recognition of the Native Village of Old Harbor by the U.S. Secretary of the Interior, differs in composition from the "traditional council" that, more informally, advised the *toyuq* in the early days. That "traditional council" consisted of the *sukashiq*, the church lay reader, the *staristaq*, and the elders. By contrast, the new Council comprises seven members of the village, elected to terms of specific length by all the tribal members.

The purpose of my research was to identify those operations present in traditional village government in Old Harbor and to determine who was involved in the decision-making processes. Funding for this oral history project was provided by the Bureau of Indian Affairs. During July and August of 1987, interviews were conducted in Old Harbor and Akhiok. Those who participated shared their knowledge and stories from the following areas: Old Harbor, Kaguyak (now abandoned), Eagle Harbor (now abandoned), Akhiok, Woody Island (now abandoned), and Ouzinkie. The transcripts from those interviews provide the basis for this essay.

It is evident that there is an affinity to the village of one's birthplace but that respect for other villages and chiefs was and continues to be maintained. Kodiak Island area village interaction in the past is not clearcut, but references made by some of those participating in this project indicate that, before, there had been competition between these villages for resources and that there were other sources of conflict that brought about intervillage warfare.

However, when an off-island threat was impending, the villages did band together, and during peacetime periods intervillage feasting did occur, allowing for opportunities to socialize and for trade. In recent times this tradition of village feasts continues on a diminished basis with families and relations traveling to other villages for the holidays.

Each village had control over a certain amount of territory and its associated resources. Operating on a cooperative basis, parcels of land were not allocated to individual families; this was a more recent notion. Utilization by all was the theme. One person said:

Oh, they share the land. They share the land with other families. Not just one family hunt there. Not just one family. They have to share with some other families.

Another person said:

. . . because each person, each household had a certain area where they could hunt foxes or put up fish like that. But they are always cooperative. If someone is not doing so good in certain location, well they help move him to another place.

A subsistence-based lifestyle was and continues to be indicative of Kodiak Island villages; fishing, hunting, and trapping regularly necessitated movement away from the community. Hunting and trapping areas were quite extensive, while fishing sites appeared to be more localized. There is some indication that there were village-controlled territories during earlier times. In Old Harbor as well as Kaguyak, families would leave during the summer months for fishing. Most of Old Harbor would shift to the Kadiak cannery at Shearwater and the Kaguyak people would go to the lagoon located south of their village.

Preceding these shifts, a chief would call for a meeting; his control was maintained over activities in and away from the village. Not only were the chiefs concerned for the welfare of the villagers, but a concern for public safety was evidenced as well. These "pre-season" meetings would allow the chief to assess or determine which individuals/families would be in what areas, utilizing which hunting or fishing barabara, and when they intended to return. For the chief this meeting had a twofold purpose, not only to delineate a certain order in the cooperative venture but also to establish family locations in the event of an emergency. If an occasion should arise that someone was missing, the chief would therefore be able, again through a meeting, to organize and coordinate a search party efficiently.

Meetings

In Old Harbor, meetings were held at the old schoolhouse. However, the chief would meet with his Council before calling a public meeting together, and this would be conducted in his home. Here they would discuss the agenda or other necessary business before presenting it to the villagers. It was after this preliminary meeting that the assistant chief would be sent around in the village to inform everyone of the impending community meeting. In Akhiok, many times the meetings were announced at church and often were held on a Sunday after services.

Anything pertaining to village affairs necessitated a meeting. All village operations were conducted in such a fashion that everyone had an opportunity to participate in the process before a final decision was made by the chief. One major reason for these public meetings was to take everyone's opinion, and, by operating in this fashion, everyone was kept informed.

At the meeting, the chief and Council would present the agenda or a person would request permission for something, the chief would ask for the vote of the people, and then he would voice his final decision on the matter. The examples given that led to these meetings included: an outsider requesting permission to move into the village; moving or building houses; hunting, fishing, or trapping ventures; punishment; and requesting loans.

Court

Villages operated as independent units, preferring to resolve community problems internally. However, the chiefs did engage support from other village chiefs when major decisions were confronted, such as the banishment of an individual from a village, in which case the guilty party was outlawed from all villages on the island.

You see they never invited another chief from another community. It seems like these were done independently to each community. You see, not like, oh, they want people from here to go to Kodiak for meeting and stuff like that and they all discuss something. But each community have their own problems and they solve their own problems. . . . In my younger days, I never see another chief in here [Akhiok], besides our chief.

The chief, along with his Council comprised an effective court system. It seems that, before, there was relatively little crime within the villages; people did not need to worry about locking their doors. Apparently what has been referred to as a "crime prevention" program was well established. Through a series of meetings and close interaction with the elders of the community, people were kept informed. They knew the community traditions and what to expect if they did not conform to them. It does not appear that excessive drinking was a problem in Old Harbor before the 1964 earthquake. Drinking during Lent was prohibited, and breaking that prohibition was dealt with by the chief. During these and other times when celebrating occurred, the chief would dispatch his assistant chiefs, like patrolmen, to watch the community. When the occasion arose that the chief was informed of an offender, the assistant chief would be sent to bring in that individual. Often, as in the case of repeat juvenile offenders, the Council would order a punishment such as chopping wood for the elders or kneeling on rock salt during church services. Warnings were usually issued for first time offenders who would be required to make a public apology during the meetings.

You drinking during the Lent, you [got] punished. . . . pick and shovels. Pascha [Easter]. They got meeting with them first. [The offenders] go to meeting with them too. They've been drinking during the Lent and all that, now they going to do this, they're going to do that. So the third chief, third assistant chief put them up to work.

Well you know how we were when we were sixteen. . . . Sometimes we'd do a little nipping, you know. And when he [Alexis Inga] hears that, boy he used to clamp down on us pretty hard. Held a meeting, public meeting! 'Cause he heard that, "You kids were nipping," and everything. . . . That's how strict they were. And everybody would go. Everybody! . . . At the meeting they let us all bow down, you know, promise that we won't do it again. He called us individually. . . . It was kind of embarrassing.

The Council functioned as judges, along with the chief, to discuss and deliberate the outcome, determining the type of punishment to be administered, varying according to the severity of the crime. This traditional system was phased out when Alaska became a state in 1959 and the centralized jurisdiction of the state's legal and judicial system replaced the judicial systems of the individual island villages.

From what I understand was, if someone was bad, he'd be brought before the Council. . . . They were just a group of elders. Just the older people in the villages were always treated as wise because they lived long. And there was one chief and maybe a second chief and the shaman . . . and from what I heard . . . is when they were real afraid to be brought before. You know, this is like going to court! They were afraid to go before them 'cause they didn't know what punishment they'd give. They might whip them or make them do extra work. Make them get wood for the old people. . . . Yeah, they'd get a bunch of old people. And then they'd argue! . . . They'd argue till late at night and then they'd come out with the decision. They were probably family related or if it was too harsh or something. And then they'd settle on either hard work or banishment or whatever. It's like they had good lawyers or something. . . . It was just certain older people that sat in. Like they say, the young guys would always try to keep, help certain old people. So if he gets in a jam, that guy's going to speak good for him.

Positions

Toyuqs in Old Harbor were Alexis Inga, his son Michael Inga, and Alexis' nephew (Alexis' brother Nick's son), Costia Inga. Herman Andrewvitch, who moved to Old Harbor from Akhiok, was the last chief. Michael Pestrikoff was also a *toyuq* for a brief time. Peter Petorochin was the last chief of Eagle Harbor, but previous chiefs where known to have come from the Tunohun and Shugak families. The *toyuqs* from Akhiok were Pasha Kichak, Anton Yakanak, Simeon Agnot, and Ephraim Agnot Sr. (brother to Miney Agnot, both sons of Simeon Agnot).

Sukashiqs in Old Harbor are known to have included George Stanley, Wilfred Alexanderoff, Simmy Inga, William Ignatin, and Costia Inga. Larry Matfay (grandson of Pasha Kichuk), Evon Farsovitch, Eliza Alokli, Gavrilla Azuyak (Tony Azuyak's father), and Kalumpi Capjohn were *sukashiqs* in Akhiok. No information on the names of *toyugs*, *sukashiqs*, *staristaqs*, or lay readers is available at this time for Aiaktalik or Kaguyak.

For Old Harbor, the *staristaqs* and lay readers were Innokenti Inga, Alexis Inga, Barris Kaguiak, Peter Alexanderoff (father of Wilfred Alexanderoff), and Anakenti Zeedar. In Akhiok they included Jacob Agusha, Polycarp (possibly Alokli), Miney Agnot, and Ephraim Agnot Sr.

Toyuq

Traditionally, the chief had absolute power over any village-related activity but acted with advice from his Council. Without exception, the chief's permission was mandatory for all projects in the village. However, it appears that there were internal influential controls, which included the ever-important kinship network and the election process. As with the positions of *sukashiq* and *staristaq*, the Council voted the *toyuq* into office "by tongue" or general consensus, and they had the prerogative to select a replacement whenever it was deemed necessary.

No, when they older, some people talk too, you know, like they want a new chief, maybe afterwards. It's not a lifetime job, but sometimes they keep him for a long time, reselecting him . . . by tongue, it's always, not by vote of all the people. Well that means, you know, "You be the chief." You know, that's the older people talk and all that.

It is evident that at least in one case, this ousting of a chief did not succeed. The residents of the village of Eagle Harbor opted to abandon their village rather than to vote the chief out of office. This migration was complete by the early 1920s.

Predominantly, the position of chief appeared to follow family lines. A relative or the son of a chief would usually be the assistant and would therefore have the necessary training and experience for the job. The Council would usually consider at least two individuals for the position of chief, and the chosen had the right to decline. The choice, in other words, was not binding. Residency in the village was a mandatory qualification. Additionally, some suggested that a marriage tie was also taken into consideration. But a comment from Akhiok, "I don't remember in Akhiok anybody from other places becoming chief or anything," does convey local preference. There is no indication that there was any rank between the villages' *toyuqs* in earlier times, and at this time it does seem that one could not be both a *toyuq* and a church reader.

See now inheriting position, you see naturally it was common. You see, [if] your dad was a chief, well then they figured, "Well, he's coming from a knowledgeable family." So what they say, "You are going to be qualified too because your dad has been a chief."

It is important here to note that one individual did state that a chief, when retiring, sometimes stepped down to the position of assistant chief. In this account, the roles are reversed because the older ex-chief was training the younger chief. This may reflect an earlier variation of the *toyuq* tradition.

But then I heard where if a chief was bad they'd oust him. Just make somebody else a chief. . . . He just becomes an aide or assistant. Old people get old and couldn't function so they'd make a second chief and third chief and fourth chief. Well I guess, from what someone was telling me, that sometimes the chief would get so old and, he'd have to break in a chief. And he'd not necessarily pick from his family, he'd pick someone that was bright . . . and then he'd train him and stay with him and tell him stories and what's going on. When he'd pass on, that one would be the chief. It would change from one family to another but never dynasty, you know. But usually it was because the chief's sons would learn the chief's abilities and they would become naturally good chiefs because they knew how he make decisions.

Basically, the chief or *toyuq* controlled and supervised the village in economic, political, and, to some degree, social aspects. He was the organizer and made the final decisions, compelling respect and obedience from everyone. This individual was compared by many to be like a president or the chief of police who would delegate orders to the people through his assistant chiefs. Whenever a situation or problem arose in the village it was the chief who called and chaired the meetings. Through these meetings the chief's decrees were made known to the people, and the people, in turn, could make their desires known. None of those interviewed indicated that the chief received any form of compensation for his duties, although there was mention of the chief being wealthy during earlier times.

See, the chief didn't make the decisions himself. He would make the decision with the elder people. He could do it alone. If he didn't like what the other people wanted . . . he could stop it right there. He's the chief and his word is the law. 'Cause they make him the chief and he's right.

Sukashiq

The chief's assistant or second chief was known as the *sukashiq*. Depending on the village or perhaps the chief, the number of assistant chiefs varied. The *sukashiq* was elected by the chief and Council, in a process similar to that for determining a chief. This position involved the following responsibilities: being the acting chief when the *toyuq* was absent, investigating and patrolling of the village, providing counsel to the chief, supervising work and, finally, informing all the villagers by going "door to door" when a meeting was called by the chief.

He's the chief's patrolman. So when something then needs to be done, he tells his second or third chief, he says, "Well, you go and get it. People that needs help, cut wood for them, carry water. People, I need do this."

Staristaq (Lay Reader and Church Warden)

The Russian Orthodox Church was integral to community affairs. The lay reader and the church warden or *staristaq* both worked closely with the chief. While the lay reader was trained and selected by his predecessor or by the priest, the *staristaq* was elected in the same fashion as a chief or assistant chief, by consensus.

[They were] something like a council. . . . A lay reader was included with the chief, and a person, you know what they call the person that takes care of the church and the keys [the staristaq*]? . . . They work with the chief, those two.*

The *staristaq* took care of the church inside and out and arrived early before church services to light the candles. The *staristaq* would build and paint crosses for the graves of the newly deceased and was also responsi-

Fig. 3.1. *Russian Orthodox Church and village of Old Harbor, 1997. Photo by Craig Mishler.*

ble for recording in a log book all of the church's vital statistics: baptisms, marriages, and deaths.

The lay reader, on the other hand, instructed the youngsters in Slavonic and performed certain rites for the church. In the absence of a priest, the reader could conduct only parts of the Orthodox religious service—reading the scriptures, for example—parts which supplement the parts performed by a priest.

These were both influential positions but nevertheless were subjected to the chief's administration. However, it must be remembered that the lay reader was directed by the Kodiak church and therefore had authority appropriated to him from an outside source.

The chief could tell staristaq, *if they want them to clean up. Then the staristaq well, tell the people to clean up. And they used to clean up! They didn't wait for nothing. Especially for Easter. . . . Put new gravel, every year*

Political Organization

they put gravel around the church and then the trail, the road down to the main trail.

In addition, the chief along with the village church, made emergency loans available to the villagers when they were requested. This money was collected from the villagers to support the church but was made available if needed.

And the chief take care of that money and put that church under the chief, whoever is chief. And whatever the church gets, that money amount, he holds it for the people and when they want to borrow money, they have to go see him. And they have to get together with the second chief and the lay reader. . . . That's the way it was run when I first got here. . . . It was in late twenties.

Elders
Elders were considered wise because of their long life and because of their valued knowledge. It was most appropriate that they counsel the chief. These individuals were not elected to their positions but acquired them on the basis of their experience. They were the family heads and probably included many of the village specialists.

But then particular whoever they appoint to be a leader of the community, he's the advisor in everything. But, he's not alone you see. The elders, they talk to each other. They get this, all that they materialize. So, it's not him alone that's working. And so he gets advised from others, elders. So that makes work easier. They put all of their opinions together. It's better to have more than one head to accomplish something.

Respect seems to be the key word applied to the elders who were revered in the village. The villagers did not shirk their responsibilities to provide for them, and it was up to the chief to see that this was so.

And lot of tirades they'd keep the young people busy. Always keeping them busy even up until late times. They'd have all the young people as soon as they were able to work, either pack water or collect berries. . . . Like they'd collect wood for all the old people and help them with their fish and just general every kind of work. Everybody worked together. And the chief would go, say, "Hey, you boys, go." And boy, they ran!

In addition, one of the primary responsibilities of the elders was to instruct the youngsters.

They'd always have a council [composed of elders] . . . once a week or so they'd gather. [At Eagle Harbor] they'd have elders and shamans like or someone tell stories, the history. . . . They'd sit in the evenings and they'd tell them how they hunted, how they fished, who was the great hunters and tell them a lot of stories . . . to teach them. You know, guys that don't listen, what happens to them and stuff like that.

SUMMARY

Many people commented on the involvement of the entire village in the tribal operations, before the earthquake, and on being more active in the decision-making process and more aware and informed of what was affecting their community. Favorable views were expressed about the old system, which incorporated the elders of the community. Decisions, although traditionally finalized by the chief, were made after counsel was sought from others. The control of the village was not necessarily in the hands of the young but was guided through the wisdom and the combined experience of the elders. All agreed that the old form of government was strict and exercised tighter control over the village, but it seemed as though there was a coherent, cooperative undertaking where the chief worked for the benefit of the community and the community worked together to benefit all.

A suggestion made by most was the need for greater involvement of the elders in the current form of village tribal government. People feel that they are losing their young to alcohol and drugs and that they are all losing their heritage. They are also concerned about their economic future. The general consensus is that, before, there was a great deal of respect for the elders because they had lived a long life and that if this reverence could be re-established, perhaps the way of life in the villages would be better.

OLD HARBOR AND OUZINKIE GOVERNANCE TODAY
by Craig Mishler

It is significant that on February 17, 1950, twenty-one years before the passage of the Alaska Native Land Claims Settlement Act (ANCSA) of 1971, the Ouzinkie Village Council, led by Mike Chernikoff as president and Tim Panamarioff as secretary, held a public meeting and passed a resolution petitioning the U.S. Department of the Interior for recognition of its "exclusive use and occupancy" of lands and waters around Spruce Island and "the eastern shores of Kodiak Island from Monashka Bay to Kizhuyak Bay inclusive" (Kozely 1963).

After the Great Alaskan Earthquake of 1964, traditional tribal and church-focused government like that just described for Old Harbor gave way to new institutions which were introduced by forces outside of the villages, namely state and federal agencies. In both Old Harbor and Ouzinkie, tribal governments continued, but at some point chiefs were replaced with Tribal Council presidents.

The shift from chiefs to Council presidents may have been fairly cosmetic, but at the same time there were also some deeper structural changes which fragmented political power and weakened the Tribal Councils. This fragmentation occurred when Tribal Councils were supplanted by state-chartered local governments with mayors and City Councils. The City of Old Harbor was incorporated as a second-class city in 1966, and the City of Ouzinkie was incorporated as a second-class city in 1967.

The advantages to city governments were that they qualified communities to receive state funds for public works and capital improvements. They also received entitlement to a certain amount of land. Ouzinkie, for example, received 840 acres, including almost all of the area known as Sourdough Flats. City governments are organized around mayors and City Councils and hire a small clerical staff. In Old Harbor, Sven Haakanson Sr. served as the mayor for over twenty-three years, and was succeeded by Rick Berns in 1991. In Ouzinkie, Zack Chichenoff has served almost as long as Sven Haakanson. Zack was preceded by Arthur Haakanson Jr., and there was one time when Arthur was mayor of Ouzinkie at the same time that his brother Sven was mayor of Old Harbor and their other brother, Herman Haakanson, was mayor of Port Lions. As small-scale landowners and managers and as beneficiaries of state revenue sharing, city governments have become moderately powerful.

Following passage of the Alaska Native Claims Settlement Act in 1971, yet another layer of leadership and power was added in the form of village profit-making corporations. Although not government bodies in the strictest sense, the Old Harbor Native Corporation and the Ouzinkie Native Corporation (ONC) selected a significant amount of federal land surrounding their communities and have made investments which have turned them into financially powerful organizations. By controlling land use and development and providing job opportunities, the boards of these corporations influence community life in ways that clearly overshadow the tribal governments. It is ironic then that the majority of shareholders in these corporations live outside the communities. In 1993, for example, only 30 percent of the ONC's 339 shareholders lived in Ouzinkie, with 20 percent residing in Anchorage, 15 percent in Kodiak City, and the remaining 35 percent scattered elsewhere across Alaska and the lower 48 states (Berger 1993:26).

With most of the political power concentrated in the corporations and the cities, some residents have sarcastically said that the major function of Tribal Councils is the operation of bingo games. However, Tribal Councils and tribal governments in Alaska today are taking on an increased role in everything from child custody cases to the co-management of subsistence and natural resources, and in some communities the Tribal Councils are more powerful than the cities. The tribes have a special sovereign relationship to the U.S. federal government, which supercedes their relationship to state and borough governments. Consequently, they receive most of their funding from federal agencies.

For the most part, these three entities, the tribal governments, the city governments, and the village corporations in Old Harbor and Ouzinkie all get along quite well. Throughout the 1980s, in fact, the Old Harbor Tribal Council, city, and corporation offices were all located in the same building. In 1996, however, the Old Harbor Native Corporation built its own structure and moved from Downtown to Middle Town. Although the leadership of each entity is different, there is generally some overlapping membership between the two Councils and the corporation Boards of Directors. This is also true in Ouzinkie. In 1998 Paul Panamarioff was serving both as president of the Ouzinkie Tribal Council and as vice mayor of the city.

In Old Harbor, both the city mayor, Rick Berns, and the president of the corporation, Emil Christiansen, are active commercial fishermen. For many years the president of the Ouzinkie Native Corporation was Andy Anderson, and the mayor of Ouzinkie has been Zack Chichenoff. Both are full-time administrators.

On one occasion I observed a direct conflict of interest between the Ouzinkie Tribal Council and the Ouzinkie City Council. I was invited to attend this meeting to announce the research I was doing on this ethnography. However, the main issue of this meeting, which took place on January 22, 1997, was the city's decision to auction off some of its lots. A member of the Tribal Council objected to this, saying they were concerned that outsiders (particularly non-Natives) might buy up these lots and start taking over the community. The mayor's response was that they were obligated to follow a state law of nondiscrimination and equal opportunity. A failure to follow these principles would leave them open to a lawsuit and a loss of revenue sharing. But the Tribal Council felt that these lots were part of their ancestral lands and that once they were sold they might never be recovered. At this writing the issue is still unresolved because only a fraction of the city's lands have been surveyed, mostly in swampy areas unsuited for building, and none of the city lots have yet been sold.

Another difference in the composition of the Tribal and City Councils today is that women are more involved. While under the traditional system, men made all of the key decisions, today a few women take a more active role in both the tribal and city governments. During and shortly after the *Exxon Valdez* oil spill, for example, Angeline Campfield served as president of the Ouzinkie Tribal Council, and Dorothy Pestrikoff served as president of the Old Harbor Tribal Council. This notwithstanding, the corporation Boards of Directors in both Old Harbor and Ouzinkie are still male-dominated. A look at the composition of the City Councils in both communities reveals that in Old Harbor all seven members of the City Council are men (four of them purse seine captains), while in Ouzinkie men occupy five out of the seven seats on the City Council (DCRA 1998).

Women have assumed some leadership roles in the Russian Orthodox Church. In Old Harbor, where there has been a resident Orthodox priest since 1989, Stella Krumrey (daughter of Anakenti Zeedar) is the current lay reader, while Paul Kahutak and Whitey Capjohn are the *staristaqs*. In Ouzinkie the first reader, Herman Squartsoff, still serves an important function as a mediator and messenger between the Corporation, the Orthodox Church, and the local governing bodies. When Herman is away, Angeline Campfield, the second reader, fills in.

Old Harbor and Ouzinkie residents are also shareholders in the regional for-profit Native corporation, Koniag Inc., whose offices are located in Kodiak City, and they receive health, recreation, social services, and public safety services from the Kodiak Area Native Association (KANA), a regional nonprofit organization, also based in Kodiak City.

Law enforcement in each community is concentrated in Village Public Safety Officers (VPSOs) hired by KANA. This is another function that has been taken away from the traditional tribal governments. Due to conflicts of interest and a reluctance by villagers to enforce laws against their own relatives, these VPSO positions have almost always been given to non-Native outsiders, and there is a considerable amount of turnover in personnel. It is noteworthy that Bill Pyles, the VPSO in Ouzinkie during the *Exxon Valdez* oil spill, was pressed into service as the village cleanup coordinator. Pyles later married a Native woman from Ouzinkie and moved to Kodiak City to become a police officer there.

It is worth mentioning that the *Exxon Valdez* oil spill and cleanup put a tremendous amount of stress on local government leaders in both Ouzinkie and Old Harbor. Dorothy Pestrikoff, the Tribal Council president, served as the coordinator for the cleanup effort and had to wear two hats at once. She clearly was facing an overwhelming situation with the telephone ringing off the hook when I arrived on July 21 to set up a community meeting. In spite of these many distractions, Pestrikoff and Vice Mayor Rick Berns contacted seven subsistence fishermen on very short notice, and the meeting was successful.

In Ouzinkie, Andy Anderson, president of the Ouzinkie Native Corporation, took an active role in responding to the spill. Anderson contacted lawyers and consultants during the first few days following the spill and testified at the Coast Guard hearings in Kodiak City. Sven Haakanson Sr. of Old Harbor and Zack Chichenoff of Ouzinkie were two of the "oiled mayors" who commissioned a study of the social and economic impacts of the spill, and they were constantly traveling to attend meetings in Kodiak City and elsewhere. Surprisingly, even amazingly, the mayors' study concluded that "the initial oil spill cleanup had little fiscal effect on Old Harbor or Ouzinkie. Ouzinkie received $6,000 in the fourth quarter of 1989 for rental of space, and Old Harbor received $70,000 from Exxon for winter beach monitoring" (Impact Assessment 1990a:76).

Chapter Four

Kinship and Social Organization

INTRODUCTION

A discussion of kinship ties and social organization is vitally important for understanding how Alutiiq people bond together as families and as communities. Kinship centers around a set of rights and a set of obligations which are obtained through blood or marriage. Marriages between persons from neighboring communities in the same region help to bring those communities together.

When someone has an abundance of food, for example, his or her relatives expect some of that to be shared and distributed. This expectation may occur even if the harvester has not met his own household needs. When persons face a shortage and are in need, especially if those persons are elderly, handicapped, or widowed and are unable to provide for themselves, there is an expectation that they will be given enough fish and game to meet their needs. The distribution of food generally follows along kinship lines from young physically fit persons to elders. Old age is the time when people are paid back for years of sharing during their youth. But the elders are not simply passive consumers. Elders may in turn process the food they receive and redistribute it to their children and grandchildren. In at least two Old Harbor households, fresh fish are brought to elders who hang it, smoke it, and then ship it to their children living outside the village.

In Kodiak Alutiiq village life, where virtually everybody except schoolteachers and transients is related, this ethic results in a kind of leveling which simultaneously reduces both wealth and poverty. Hoarding and selfishness are considered the greatest evils. At the same time, there is considerable economic stratification that works against the ethic of sharing and preserves inequality. The Alutiiq ethic of sharing, for instance, does not hold sway nearly as much with property and material possessions as it does with food.

This social stratification goes back at least to Russian contact, when a class of slaves called *kalgas* was recognized (Davydov 1977:190–191),

Fig. 4.1. *Three generations of Haakansons: Mary and Sven Haakanson Sr. of Old Harbor with daughter Wanda Price and grandson Shawn Michael Price, at the Crab Festival in Kodiak, circa 1993. Photo by Nancy Yaw Davis.*

along with a class of commoners and a class of nobles. While *kalgas* is the Russian word for slave, Kodiak Alutiiqs have a corresponding term, *metqaq* (Leer 1989:97).

Russian Americans had their own system of stratification and hierarchy, which undoubtedly reinforced the Alutiiq one, even though it was not the same system which existed in Russia itself during the nineteenth century. According to Fedorova (1975:15), the Russians were divided into three groups: a) "the honorable ones," which included colonial administrators, naval and army officers, and ship captains, b) "the semi-honorable ones," which were the men of lower rank in the Russian-American Company, sailors, soldiers, and laborers, and c) beginning in 1835, "colonial citizens," Russian men who had married Alaska Native women and raised their families in Alaska. The descendants of "colonial citizens" and Alaska Native women were classified as "Creoles," while the descendants of "colonial citizens" and "Creoles" were given the unique status of "colonial settlers."

KINSHIP TERMS

Although the Alutiiq language is fast disappearing in the Kodiak area and is only spoken by middle-aged and elderly people, a look at Alutiiq kinship terms provides a useful framework for how people in Old Harbor, Ouzinkie, and other communities around Kodiak Island have traditionally interacted. Rachel Mason and I compiled the kinship chart presented below to help understand kinship similarities and differences between Kodiak communities. Although this chart has never before appeared in print, some of my ensuing discussion of it is drawn from our published article, "Alutiiq Vikings: Kinship and Fishing in Old Harbor, Alaska" (Mishler and Mason 1996).

This chart illustrates a number of things. First, it is obvious that in Ouzinkie and to some extent in Afognak/Port Lions, terms such as the Russian words for "aunts" (*tyotya*) and "uncles" (*dyaadya*) as well as "grandmother" (*babushka*) and "grandfather" (*di'edushka*) have to some extent displaced the original Alutiiq, suggesting that perhaps Russian kinship rights and obligations transformed ascending Alutiiq relationships in certain ways. However, since no one except a few elders still speak either Russian or Alutiiq, it may well be that these differences are not as far-reaching as they seem.

Like Kenneth Taylor (1966), who studied kin relations in Karluk, we found church godparents to be a significant extension of the current kinship system. A person's godmother and godfather are not necessarily related to each other, and an individual may be the godparent of more than one child. One Old Harbor woman, who is very fond of children and very popular in the community, is said to be the godmother of ten different children. A literal translation of the kin terms for "godfather" (*taadasinaq*) and "godmother" (*maamasinaq*) indicates that they are "big" or "physically large" fathers and mothers.

Be this as it may, it can still be argued that Alutiiq kinship expectations established hundreds of years ago persist to the present day, regardless of the language spoken to express relationships. In other words, the fabric of kinship rights and obligations is so strong and durable that it transcends the language(s) used to express those rights and obligations.

KINSHIP AND FISHING

Looking at Alutiiq kinship terminology helps us to map the complex network of relationships between seine boat captains and also between seine boat captains and crews as economic production units. It is within the framework of Alutiiq kinship and the Scandinavian Protestant work ethic that Old Harbor residents of Scandinavian descent have attained a high and stable level of material prosperity that is invisible in neighboring Alutiiq communities such as Akhiok and Karluk, where such intermar-

Kodiak Alutiiq Kinship Terms

compiled by Craig Mishler and Rachel Mason

Terms of Reference. First Person Possessive = -ga/-gaa/-gah/-gar. Double vowels indicate stressed syllables. Orthography generally follows that used by the Alaska Native Language Center, University of Alaska (see Leer, 1989; 1990).
* =term of address (R.) = Russian word

English	Old Harbor	Akhiok	Afognak/Port Lions	Ouzinkie
self	ggwiih	ggwiih	ggwiih	
mother	maamagah	aanaga	aanaga/matir (R.)	aanaga
father	taadagah	adaaga	adaaga/atets (R.)	adaaga/taada (R.)
daughter	paniiyagah	paniiyaga	paniiyaga	paniiyaga
son	awaagutaga	awagudaag	awagudaaga	awar udaaga
children	usiranga		challiyaniga	
grandau	elltuwaagah	elltuwaga	Iltuwaaga	Ili'du'aaga
grandau's hus	elltuwama angmuti			
grandson	elltuwagah	elltuwaga	Iltuwaaga	Ili'du'aaga
grandchildren		elltuwangah	Iltuwabuq	
older sis	alugaagah	allgaagah	alugaaga	algaaga
older sis's son	alugaama awaguta		alugaama awaguta	aligaama yaaguta
older sis's dau	alugaama panirah		alugaama paniira	aligaama paniira
younger sis	uyuuwagah	uyuuwagah	wiiyuwaga	uyu'aga
yo sis's son	uyuuwama awaguuta		wiwaamagah awagutah	
you sis's dau	uyuuwama panirah		wiwaamagah paniira	
older bro	anungaga	anungagah	anungaga	aningaagar
older bro's wife	ukwaagah		aningama nuligah	
older bro's son	anungamaa awaguuta			
older bro's dau	anungamaa panirah			
younger bro	uyuwagaa	uyuwaagah	wiiyuwaga	uyu'aga
younger bro's wife	uyuuwama kaiyuurya		wiyuwama nuligah	
younger siblings	uyuwangah	uyuwangah	wiyuwanga	
mo's old bro	mamam anungaa		aanama anungah	
mo's old bro's wife	mamam anungan kaiyuurya			
mo's yo bro	mamam uyurwah		aanama uyurah	
mo's yo bro's wife	mamam uyuran kaiyuurya			
mo's old sis	mamam alukar		anaama alakar	
mo's old sis's hus	mamam alukan angmuti			

Fig. 4.2.

Kinship and Social Organization

Kinship Terms 2, continued

English	Old Harbor	Akhiok	Afognak/Port Lions	Ouzinkie
mo's yo sis	mamam uyurwah		anaama uyurah	
mo's bro	anungah or angaah*	anaagah	dyaadya (R.)	dyaadya (R.)
mo's sis	angagah or anaah*	anaanagah or aanah*	tyotya (R.)	tyotya (R.)
mo's old sis's dau			anaama alakar paniira	
mo's old sis's son			anaama alakar awagutah	
mo's yo sis's dau			anaama uyuran paniira	
mo's yo sis's son			anaama uyuran awagutah	
cousin	ilaaga	iluuwagah	aningagah	ilaaga/rodnya (R.)
mo's mo	umahgah or mamamah mamah* or mamam anii	mmahgah	anaama anii or mmah*	babushka (R.)
mo's fa	apahgah or mamam atii	apahgah or apaah*	anaama atii	di'edushka (R.)
fa's old sis	taadam alukar		adaama alakar	
fa's old sis's hus	taadam alukan angmuti			
fa's yo sis	taadam uyurwah		adaama uyurah	
fa's yo sis's hus	taadam uyurwan angmuti			
fa's old bro	taadam anungah		adaama aningah	
fa's old bro's wife	taadam anungan kaiyuurya			
fa's yo bro	taadam uyurwah		adaama uyurah	
fa's yo bro's wife	taadam uyurwan kaiyuurya			
fa's bro	anungah or angaah*	anaagah	dyaadya (R.)	dyaadya (R.)
fa's sis	angagah or anaah*	anaanagah or aanah*	tyotya (R.)	tyotya (R.)
fa's mo	umahgah or adaama anii	mmahgah or mmah*	adaama anii	babushka (R.)
fa's fa	apahgah or adaama atii or apaah*	apahgah	adaama atii	di'edushka (R.)
wife	aipagaa	nuliiyagar or kayuwigaa	nuliiga	ruliigar

Kinship Terms 3, continued

English	Old Harbor	Akhiok	Afognak/Port Lions	Ouzinkie
wife's mo	kayuwimaa mamah or chakiiga*	chakiigah*	nulima anii	shyaaroq
wife's fa or father-in-law	kayuwimaa atii or chakiiga*	chakiigah*	nulima atii	shyaaroq
wife's old sis	kayuwimaa alukar		nulima alukar	nulima aliiga
wife's yo sis	kayuwimaa uyurwah		nulima uyurah	
wife's old bro	kayuwimaa anungah		nulima anungah	
wife's yo bro	kayuwimaa uyurwah		nulima uyurah	
wife's sis or bro	chakiiga*	chakiigah*		
husband	angmutgah or angmutraagah (when angry)	wiigah	wiigah	wikh
husband's mo	angmutmaa mamah		wima anii	
husband's fa	angmutmaa atii		wima atii	
bro's wife	ukwaagah	chakiigah*	ninaawaq*	sheeya
bro-in-law	nungaugah	chakiigah*	ninaawaq*	
sis's hus	nungaugah			
sis-in-law or grandson's wife	ukwaagah			
dau-in-law	ukwaagah	ukwaagah	ukwaagah	uukwaagah
son-in-law	nungaugah or ninaawaq*	nungaugah	paniiyama winah	awargudargaga
all ancestors	ilengah tugullya or ilarengah	chorlinga	ilengah tugumat	
all living kin	ilengah umurhaut	ilengah	ilengah umurhat	
namesake	adulhutgah	alukaagah	alugaagah	
partner	angaiyugah	angaiyugah or anaiyumah*	anaiyugah	
godfather	taadasinaq*			
godmother	maamasinaq*			
godparent	krasna (R.)*			

Sources: George Inga Sr. and Larry Matfay, Old Harbor
Efraim Agnot Sr., Akhiok
John and Julia Pestrikoff, Afognak/Port Lions
Mike and Jenny Chernikoff, Ouzinkie

riage has not occurred. This is not to imply that Alutiiqs do not have a work ethic, but only that many do not value work for its own sake.

In 1991 I learned that virtually all of the twenty-five seine boat crews in Old Harbor were organized around male kin relations, and that these relations came from almost every imaginable paradigm of male consanguineal and affinal relationships. I found nine instances of fathers fishing with sons, three pairs of uncles fishing with nephews, two pairs of fathers-in-law fishing with sons-in-law, two pairs of brothers fishing together, three pairs of brothers-in-law fishing together, and one pair of cousins fishing together. Two boats had captains and crews whose kin relations were undetermined, and two boats had only nonrelatives working together. More than one kind of kinship relation was represented on several boats.

The occurrence of so many fathers fishing with their sons points to a strong consanguineal bond among Alutiiqs—one which exists between a person and his or her namesake, called an *alukaq* (first person possessive *alukaagah*, see Kinship Chart). This bond, which may occur between a grandparent and grandchild or between a parent and child of the same gender, is an ancient Alutiiq custom manifested in father and son relationships and mirrored in English by the use of identical personal names followed by *Senior* (Sr.) and *Junior* (Jr.). Of the nine Old Harbor boats that had fathers fishing with their sons in 1991, four crews included men and their namesakes.

Because this *Senior* and *Junior* naming tradition is also fairly commonplace among Anglo-Americans, it seems almost totally transparent to non-Natives visiting Alutiiq communities. However, for Alutiiqs the "Junior" or *alukaq* is not necessarily the oldest or first-born in the family, but rather a male child who resembles his father or grandfather either physically or in his behavior. One elder in Akhiok, Ephraim Agnot Sr., said his namesake son was not chosen until after his second marriage, even though he had several sons by his first wife. His namesake son was actually selected and named by his own father, so that even though the son bears both his first and last name, he is really his grandfather's *alukaq* and still bears his grandfather's first name as a nickname.

For women, the same honorary practice is often followed for namesake daughters and granddaughters, although their surnames differ. Thus, the Euro-American and Scandinavian custom of naming a fishing boat after one of the captain's daughters makes good sense to Alutiiqs because the boat becomes her symbolic *alukaq*. In Old Harbor approximately half of the boats in the fleet carry captains' daughters' names (e.g. below, Chapter 7).

The only close male-to-male kin relation I did not discover was that of grandfathers fishing with grandsons, although one man was fishing with his grandson's boat. In 1991 only two Old Harbor boats had women in their crews. One skipper fished with his wife on the crew, while another skipper hired his sister as a crewmember. While it was common for fathers to fish with their sons—who were sometimes their *alukaqs*—no daughters worked on the boats that were their namesakes.

HIERARCHY AND STRATIFICATION

Hierarchy between captain and crew on each boat, and cooperation and competition between captains, illustrate the critical importance of kinship obligations in maintaining the mixed subsistence and cash-based economy. Fishing boats and their location in the small boat harbor, even more so than the captains' homes, are the visible symbols of wealth, rank, and status. Yet class lines are fairly rigid, making it extremely difficult for a man to climb the ladder from deckhand to skiff man to captain, to raise himself up by his own bootstraps through hard work.

Freddy Christiansen (1997), a purse-seine captain, underscores the lack of upward mobility. One day I asked him the following question:

CM: *Is it possible for a young person to start out as a deck hand and then go to a skiff man and then go to a skipper? Can you climb your way up, or do you have to kind of inherit that from your family?*
FC: *The majority of it is your family. You have to inherit it from your family. It's just so economically not feasible to go and buy a commercial fishing boat.*

I asked nearly the same question of Ron Berntsen (1997), a lifelong crewmember in commercial fishing:

CM: *Well, is it possible for a guy or young boy to work his way up by crewing to get enough to buy a permit, or to get a boat?*
RB: *No!*
CM: *You can't do it that way, huh?*
RB: *No. Not unless you have a few big years where you'll be able to save some money. But you can't do it in salmon because of the price, you know. You're working twice as hard for twice as many fish for twice as less money. And as a crewman making 10 to 12 percent, you can't make much, you know.*
CM: *Is that the going rate, 12 percent?*
RB: *Yeah, 10 to 12, whatever. Because now is a bad time of the year. This is a crunch time, real bad. February. Some of the guys will go herring fishing and stuff like that. But between now and the end of summer there's just nothing.*

Well, people can get piecemeal jobs like working for housing [i.e. carpentry] if they have work to do, or something like that, you can get on that. But then by the time the summer ends, and the time you get your check for salmon, you've already spent it. House payments, light payments, and everything else, you know? You get behind on these bills because you only get paid after the seasons done, see? And that comes in too with the lack of hope. A lot of people are moving from these villages.

Shortly after this interview, Berntsen and his family had to leave Old Harbor in order to acquire some new job skills. In addition to the stratification between captains and crewmembers, there are additional levels of social and economic stratification between commercial fishing boat captains and nonfishermen. All of the service businesses in the community are owned by boat captains. Nonfishermen find wage employment through the school, the city, the post office, or the village corporation.

These same hierarchies exist in Ouzinkie as well as in Old Harbor, but in Ouzinkie the lines may be a little less rigid. Nick Pestrikoff (1997) talked about how he started out as a purse-seiner deck hand at the age of fifteen and slowly worked his way up to skiff man, skipper, and boat owner at the age of twenty-nine. According to Nick, however, he was forced to move up the ladder, and it took him fourteen years. His uncle, a highliner, insisted that Nick make the move from deck hand to skiff man, and then later on he was pressured into becoming a skipper:

But I don't think sitting in the skiff, you know, watching the boat at the end of the seine, or whatever, I'd think, "I'd never want the responsibility of being a captain or a boat owner," you know. Then that was more or less forced on me, in a way, because of the death of an older brother, and [I] sort of inherited a boat.

In Ouzinkie, class lines built through commercial fishing are not quite as visible as they are in Old Harbor, since only a few families in Ouzinkie still hold limited entry permits, own their own boats, and actively engage in commercial fishing (see below, Chapter 7). Since commercial fishing in Ouzinkie is rapidly fading, most of the young men in that community find occasional employment as longshoremen, loading logs onto ships in Danger Bay.

DESCENT

Because they are part of the Eskimo language family, one would expect speakers of Alutiiq and those of Alutiiq descent to trace their descent bilaterally, on both the mother's and father's side. This is precisely the case for all of the elders I interviewed in the process of compiling the Kinship Chart. And on paper it would seem that kinship reckoning in Old Harbor and Ouzinkie is genuinely bilateral. There is no evidence at all for the existence of moieties or clans. For example, Alutiiq kin terms for "mother's brother," *anungah* (reference) or *angaah* (address), and "father's brother," are symmetrical and identical, as are the first person possessive terms for "mother's sister" and "father's sister, *angagah* (reference) or *anaah* (address). There is actually a bigger distinction between "mother's older sister" and "mother's younger sister" than there is between the more generalized terms of "mother's sister" and "father's sister." The same is true for "father's older sister" and "father's younger sister." In interviews with seven Alutiiq elders in four Kodiak villages (see Kinship Chart), I found no linguistic evidence to support Leer's (1989:112; 1990:144) conclusion that Kodiak Alutiiqs formerly distinguished between mother's brother and father's brother, at least in terms of address. Such a distinction, if it existed, might point to the presence of matriliny.

It may indeed be the case, however, that the creolized class of Old Harbor and Ouzinkie Natives are matrilineal by default (see Mishler and Mason 1996). With only one exception that I am aware of, the Haakansons in Old Harbor, all of those who are descended from Russian or Scandinavian immigrants are now completely out of touch with their father's, father's father's, father's mother's, and great grandfathers' families in Russia, Norway, and Denmark. Descent for these families must of necessity be reckoned locally on the mother's, mother's mother's, and great-grandmothers' side—the Alutiiq side.

It is nevertheless useful to compile and examine Kodiak Alutiiq kin terms to see which relationships are fundamental to the maintenance of social networks. Because there are so many different permutations and combinations in kin relations, it is difficult to assess which ones are most important. However, in the course of my research in Old Harbor, it was repeatedly brought to my attention that older men place great value on their sons-in-law, and that sons-in-law are expected to serve the nutritional needs of their fathers-in-law by bringing them ducks and other fish and game. When I went sea lion hunting in Old Harbor in 1991, for example, I asked my hunting companion who he would be sharing the meat with, and his immediate response was, "My father-in-law."

Indeed, in subsistence activities, it turns out that the *chakiigah*/ninaawaq** connection is one of the most crucial relationships for maintaining Alutiiq social structure, and it is this relationship that dictates matrilocality. In 1805, the Russian Iosaf Bolotov observed of the Koniags that: "The bride and groom, having met several times by themselves, reach an understanding and then declare their decision to the girl's father. From that time on, the groom must reside with his father-in-law, until such time as the pair acquires its own children" (In Black 1977:85). Another Russian, Gavriil Davydov, noted in 1810 that "the son-in-law becomes virtually a servant of the father-in-law and always brings him the best hunting catch" and furthermore, "Koniags consider themselves luckier having daughters than sons, for the latter leave home when they marry . . ." (Davydov 1977:182).

And lest women be overlooked, it has been pointed out to me that the wife/daughter who stands between this father-in-law and son-in-law relationship is really at the focal point of the relationship. In Old

Harbor, a man's granddaughter's husband *(elltuwama angmuti)* is expected to fill in when his son-in-law is not around, and in this case it is the wife/granddaughter who lies at focal point of the relationship.

GENDER RELATIONS

Although I have not been privileged to know the personal relations between very many Alutiiq couples, the spousal relations which I have observed over the past ten years indicate that women play a greatly subservient role to men and hold a much lower status. This does not mean there is an absence of love and affection between them but only that women's roles in the culture are much more restricted. As a rule, married women are younger than their husbands and do not hold down wage-earning jobs but are expected to stay at home, cook, and raise children.

This pattern of male dominance goes back at least as far as 1930s and perhaps much earlier and certainly has something to do with the age disparity of men and women entering marriage. Not counting the households of single parents, household records from 1934 show that the average age of Old Harbor husbands exceeded the average age of their wives by 11.7 years. For that same year, the average age of Ouzinkie husbands exceeded the average age of their wives by 9 years (BIA 1934). However, by the early 1990s, the averages seem much closer to the norms found elsewhere in the United States. Our household survey data from 1991 shows that on the average, Old Harbor men were just 2.2 years older than their spouses, while Ouzinkie men were 5.5 years older than their spouses (ADF&G Community Profile Database 1991).

It is worthwhile to note that ethnicity plays an important part in the selection of spouses. In Ouzinkie in 1993, 67 percent or two-thirds of all survey-sampled households had spouses who were both Native, and there was very little difference in ethnicity pairings between households if the male partner was under or over fifty years of age. In Old Harbor in 1991 we learned that 64 percent of the sampled households contained spouses who were both Native, but the percentage of households where both spouses were Native was 30 percent higher when the male partner was over fifty years of age.

The table below (Figure 4.4) suggests that younger adults in Old Harbor are more inclined to marry or share a household with non-Native spouses than older adults are and that there appears to be an increasing shift towards interethnic pairings. And since non-Natives are almost *de facto* nonlocals, this means there is a stronger tendency in Old Harbor towards interethnic exogamy. When this interethnic exogamy is coupled with the Alutiiq tradition of matrilocality, the female spouse ostensibly becomes more powerful than the male because the incoming male must live on her turf and serve her father and mother in order to be accepted

Marriage Patterns By Ethnicity:
Ouzinkie 1993 (includes common law marriages)

A. ALL HOUSEHOLDS

		FEMALE NATIVE	FEMALE NON-NATIVE
MALE	NATIVE	30 66.67%	4 8.89%
MALE	NON-NATIVE	6 13.33%	5 11.11%

B. MALES LESS THAN OR EQUAL TO 50 YEARS OF AGE

		FEMALE NATIVE	FEMALE NON-NATIVE
MALE	NATIVE	19 70.37%	2 7.41%
MALE	NON-NATIVE	5 18.52%	1 3.70%

C. MALES GREATER THAN 50 YEARS OF AGE

		FEMALE NATIVE	FEMALE NON-NATIVE
MALE	NATIVE	11 61.11%	2 11.11%
MALE	NON-NATIVE	1 5.56%	4 22.22%

Source: Alaska Department of Fish & Game, Division of Subsistence, Anchorage.

Fig. 4.3.

Marriage Patterns By Ethnicity:
Old Harbor 1991 (includes common law marriages)

A. ALL HOUSEHOLDS

		FEMALE NATIVE	FEMALE NON-NATIVE
MALE	NATIVE	16 64.00%	0 0.00%
MALE	NON-NATIVE	6 24.00%	3 12.00%

B. MALES LESS THAN OR EQUAL TO 50 YEARS OF AGE

		FEMALE NATIVE	FEMALE NON-NATIVE
MALE	NATIVE	10 55.56%	0 0.00%
MALE	NON-NATIVE	5 27.78%	3 16.67%

C. MALES GREATER THAN 50 YEARS OF AGE

		FEMALE NATIVE	FEMALE NON-NATIVE
MALE	NATIVE	6 85.71%	0 0.00%
MALE	NON-NATIVE	1 14.29%	0 0.00%

Source: Alaska Department of Fish & Game, Division of Subsistence, Anchorage.

Fig. 4.4.

in the community. Ouzinkie and Old Harbor each had six households with local female Natives married to male non-Natives, but only one of these non-Native male spouses in each community was over the age of fifty.

While in Old Harbor there were no sampled households in 1991 showing Native males paired up with non-Native females, by 1998 there were four households in which local Native males had paired up with non-Native females. We also encountered four such couples during our Ouzinkie survey in 1993. When a non-local Native woman or a non-Native woman marries into a Native family and bucks the Alutiiq tradition of matrilocality, she does not surrender her power and independence nearly as much as a non-Native man does, but she does run into problems with networking and sharing. One non-Native woman who has been living with a local Native man in Old Harbor for several years told me that she has had a great deal of difficulty making close friends with local women. This is certainly a topic deserving of additional research, for there may be some distinct differences between Alutiiq and Anglo-American ideas of what constitutes a close friendship. At least on the surface, long private discussions, the sensitive sharing of emotions, and exchanges of advice on family problems do not seem to be valued as highly by Alutiiq women as by their non-Native counterparts.

I have observed that some Native husbands boss their Native wives and daughters around and command them to do things at a moment's notice. These men do not request little favors of their spouses but demand them in a loud imperative voice: "Rita, bring us some ice cream!" I have never witnessed or even heard of wives being physically abused by their husbands, but it is only fair to say that in terms of power and important decision-making, many of the families I have come to know in Old Harbor and Ouzinkie are quite patriarchal.

Some of this imperiousness certainly comes from the teachings of the Russian Orthodox Church, which itself is heavily patriarchal. The Orthodox priest, Father Gideon, who lived in Kodiak from 1804 to 1807, observed that gender relations soured during the early Russian period. "Nowadays it happens quite often that husbands chastise their wives for disorderly lives," he wrote, while "in the old days husbands refrained from such actions because wives threatened to run away, and do away with themselves. . ." (in Black 1977:95). Today, women exercise their power by scolding their husbands with a special Alutiiq kinship term, *angmutraagah!* (see Kinship Chart).

Naomi Klouda has noticed that Old Harbor women are heavily involved in food sharing, especially as bread makers. Since the local stores do not carry fresh bread, women take the initiative to bake bread, especially for their mothers-in-law. Like sons-in-law, daughters-in-law are heavily counted on. This is almost the inverse of Anglo-American norms, wherein daughters-in-law often conflict openly with their mothers-in-law or do their best to avoid them.

For myself as both a white man and an outsider, it has been rather difficult to get to know Old Harbor and Ouzinkie women and to interview them. Although I have tried to get to know and understand women better, they have largely remained reticent and aloof. When present in the house with their husbands, women will generally say hello but seldom speak unless spoken to. While my ability to cultivate friendships with only a couple of Alutiiq women could well be the result of my own personal limitations, I have not experienced these same barriers when working with Athabaskan women. It is quite possible that a woman anthropologist would be more successful in eliciting the Alutiiq woman's perspective on gender and the woman's world view. As the black feminist Bell Hooks has persuasively written in her book, *Talking Back* (1989), women who have nothing to say to men usually have a wealth of things to say to each other.

MARRIAGE AND SEPARATION: SOME CASE STUDIES

In nine years of visiting Old Harbor, I was aware of only two formal Orthodox Church weddings and one other wedding. Russian Orthodox weddings are very elegant and require very formal dress, an elaborate and lengthy ritual, and a lavish reception and feast with many gifts. During one part of the ceremony, the best man and best woman hold jeweled crowns suspended over the heads of the betrothed. The one church wedding and reception I saw and documented on videotape was between a local commercial fishing captain and a much younger local woman. It was his second marriage and her first. The Russian Orthodox wedding ceremony appears to have changed very little since it was described in detail in a Sitka newspaper in the late nineteenth century (Anonymous 1887).

The second wedding, which I did not witness, was between a local Native woman and a non-Native outsider now involved in ecotourism and sport fishing. This couple moved away from the community for about a year and then returned. The third wedding took place between a non-local Native man who immigrated into the community and a non-Native woman outsider who came to the community as a Vista volunteer.

Even though many men are away for extended periods of time doing commercial fishing, I have not heard of any infidelities, although I am aware of at least four divorces. In three of the four divorces, at least one of the spouses moved out of the village.

In Ouzinkie I have been aware of three Orthodox Church weddings, though I have not witnessed any of them. One was between an older Native man and a much younger non-Native outsider. Although the husband was away from the community for many years before the wedding, the couple immediately took up residence in Ouzinkie after the wedding. The second wedding was between a local Native woman and a Port Lions Native man. This couple resides most of the time in Port Lions, but when the husband goes commercial fishing, his wife comes back home to Ouzinkie and stays with her parents. The third marriage was between a local Native woman and a non-Native outsider. This couple now resides in Kodiak City.

In Ouzinkie I have observed three marriages that ended in separation. The first marriage was between a local Native man and a non-Native woman from outside the community. The husband of this couple took custody of the three youngest children and is now raising them as a single parent, while the wife took custody of the fourth child, her offspring by a previous marriage, and left the community.

Another marriage between a local Native couple in Ouzinkie ended in a separation. The husband of this couple, a former commercial fisherman, has remarried to a non-Native outsider, while the wife has also remarried to a non-Native outsider. Both of these couples, surprisingly, remain in the community.

A third Ouzinkie couple in their twenties have separated following several years of marriage and after having several children. I found it interesting that after the dissolution, the wife, who was from a Yup'ik community on the lower Kuskokwim River, remained in Ouzinkie with her children, while the husband, who was born and raised in Ouzinkie, left. This woman told me she really liked Ouzinkie because it had a much higher standard of living than her home community on the Kuskokwim. She found running water and flush toilets a great improvement over honey buckets.

As in Old Harbor, I have not heard of any sexual infidelities in Ouzinkie, even though the husbands of many young couples are away doing longshoring work in Danger Bay for weeks at a time. If infidelities do occur, they are not openly talked about.

Before World War II it was a common practice for Alutiiq marriages to be arranged by the parents or godparents of the betrothed, a custom that has now completely disappeared. Apparently the bride-to-be had veto powers, and the prospective groom was grilled at length by the father of the bride (see Rostad 1988:93–101).

In the period from 1989 to 1998, I have knowledge of only a few unmarried couples in each community who have set up housekeeping together, but the relationships appear to be quite stable, and the couples continue to bear children. The Russian Orthodox Church does not condone having children out of wedlock, but some young Ouzinkie and Old Harbor women still have children out of wedlock and set up their own single-parent households. It is also fairly common for these out-of-wedlock children to be taken in and raised by their grandparents.

OTHER SOCIAL GROUPS

In Old Harbor and in Ouzinkie, elders are encouraged to get together over complimentary hot meals. Such gatherings are based not on kinship but on friendship. The meals are served three times a week and are provided by cooks hired by the Kodiak Area Native Association. In Old Harbor the seniors hot meals are served at 4:30 p.m. in the Senior Center, while in Ouzinkie the meals are served at noon in the Community Hall. Wild foods are often featured at these meals, but in addition to hot food, the seniors enjoy the opportunity to get out and socialize. The socializing sustains them emotionally and intellectually just as the food sustains them nutritionally. In Old Harbor, seniors hot meals provide an excellent opportunity to speak Alutiiq. Paying guests, such as itinerant ethnographers, are also allowed to attend these functions.

Fig. 4.5. *Eagle in the Rigging, Old Harbor, 1997.*

Chapter Five

Expressive Culture

The ceremonial, artistic, and playful side of Alutiiq life, which we call expressive culture, can be approached and understood through several traditional forms. One of these forms is the celebration of holiday festivals and rituals. Others are music and dance, storytelling, basketry, games, folk speech, banyas, and grave iconography. Although much of a folk culture's energy goes into subsistence production and other economic pursuits, we would be remiss not to emphasize the artistry which is poured into expressive culture.

HOLIDAY FESTIVALS AND RITUALS

A goodly portion of the calendar year in Old Harbor and Ouzinkie is focused around Russian Orthodox Church holidays. Although some secular American holidays, such as the Fourth of July, are also prominent, they nevertheless contain some religious elements. Holidays are eagerly looked forward to, and the Russian Orthodox Church calendar is loaded with many special religious days every month of the year. In what follows, I will only report on those holidays I have either personally witnessed or received information about.

Russian Christmas

Old Harbor and Ouzinkie, like other Russian Orthodox communities, celebrate what they call "American Christmas" on December 25 as well as "Russian Christmas" on January 7, although in the late nineteenth century it was celebrated on January 6, with New Year's following a week later on the thirteenth (Alaska Commercial Company 1892). This separation of dates between American and Russian Christmas is due to a difference in calendars. The Russian Orthodox Church follows the Julian calendar, while mainstream America follows the Gregorian calendar. American Christmas is celebrated in Kodiak villages pretty much the way it is elsewhere in North America, with the decoration of a tree and an exchange of gifts between family members.

Russian Christmas, however, is observed for three days and nights, from January 7, Christmas day, through January 9. There is no gift giving. Each night, there is a short church service where community members congregate and prepare to form a house-to-house procession. The procession follows a "star" that represents the star of Bethlehem. This star is an elaborate wheel about two feet in diameter that turns on a hand-held shaft, and it is specially made just for this holiday. Although the framework of the star is recycled from year to year, it is always redecorated. The center of the star contains an icon, usually an image of St. Herman, the patron saint of Alaska Natives, and the perimeter is festively adorned with tinsel and sparkling colors.

In Old Harbor, "starring," as it is called, is organized into three nights, and each night a procession of people wends its way through different neighborhoods of the community. On the night of January seventh, the procession visits all the homes in the Downtown area, where the church is located and where most of the elders reside. On the night of the eighth, the procession visits all of the homes in the Midtown or "Uptown" area, and on the night of the ninth, the procession goes to all of the houses in the "New Town" area.

Although I missed the first night of Russian Christmas when the Downtown homes were visited, what took place on the second and third nights of Christmas comes from my field notes for January 1991:

1/8 Arrived in the village at 4 p.m. on Penair. Came to collect subsistence salmon permits but also to witness Russian Christmas. Checked into the Sitkalidak Lodge and met George Inga Sr. passing by in his truck. Starring will start at 6 p.m. from the Church, but George will not go because he doesn't want to get drunk. "They're going to Middle Town tonight, and that's where they really load you up on the booze. You're going to have a hangover tomorrow morning," he warned.

At 5:50 p.m. I arrived at the Church, but it was locked, and there were two other people waiting who were also a little confused. Finally we heard a holler from the rectory, where the resident priest was waving and inviting us in. He promptly put out all kinds of sweetcakes and cookies on a plate for me (more than I could eat) and said: "You'll need to build up your energy." I was welcome to go starring and also encouraged to bring along my video camera.

Other singers arrived, mostly women, but also Wilmer Andrewvitch, who has a very strong voice, and Alex Laetnikoff, the seminary student and VPSO in Akhiok, who starred last night in Akhiok until 3 a.m. In Akhiok they sing in Alutiiq rather than Slavonic, which is used here. Since Akhiok only has a dozen houses, the reason it took so long is that "they have more songs." The atmosphere was jovial, with lots of kidding directed at Father Sergios. Song sheets were produced, but there was a noted shortage of them.

All the lyrics were printed double-spaced in caps in syllables connected by hyphens, with no musical notation.

About 6:15 p.m. we walked over to the Church where three children each held and twirled stars to the accompaniment of the singers. Three stars are used, and those who are twirling the stars stand with their backs to the altar, facing the singers and the front door. Only about three or four songs were sung before we jumped into a caravan of cars and vans and drove up to Midtown. Last night the singers went through the Downtown area only.

At the first house we visited, those holding the stars stood up in the living room, again directly facing the singers. On the song sheets there are about four or five songs, and it appears that any two or three of them are suitable at any given house. The singing concluded with the song Mnoogaya-leta ('God grant you many years'), a kind of coda which virtually everyone knows. The singers generally cross themselves once or twice during the performance of this song. At the conclusion of Mnoogaya-leta, the word "Sprazdnikom!" (lit. 'With the feast!') is shouted. Only the core group of singers seemed to know the Slavonic songs. After the singing we were offered a table of snacks and cans of Olympia beer. . . .

This pattern was repeated about 20–25 times throughout the evening, with small variations in who twirled the star (lots of kids vying for the honor) and in the amount and kind of food put out. The people who put out the most food and drink were the purse seine captains. Some households only put out a small plate of hard candy, and some offered nothing at all. Tony Azuyak put out a couple of plates of homebaked maple bars and sugar doughnuts, and the kids' mouths were watering over these throughout the singing. It is not considered polite to indulge in the treats until after the songs are finished.

Most of the food treats were store-bought items. Very little consisted of homemade or subsistence foods. At the houses with lavish spreads, there was generally a bowl of smoked salmon strips, and Emil Christiansen outdid everybody with a plate of fresh king crab that he caught down at Alitak. For the most part, what was served was chips and dip, vegetables with dip, sliced cheese and sausage plates, tuna fish sandwiches, cookies, and cupcakes. There was little or no coffee, and only an occasional pot of tea available.

The liquor seems to be offered very cautiously and is kept low key. When it is offered, it is often in the form of a spiked punch and kept out of the hands of the kids. But the kids get sugar highs on all the candy. I saw one young boy who got sick to his stomach and had to vomit.

In some of the homes with elders, the Father would ask the head of the household to come forward to the front of the living room, saying "Willie, this is for you." or "Kalumpi, we want you right up front." They seem to relish this attention—a time when Christmas becomes very personal and very communal all at once. Oftentimes people would call their friends elsewhere in the village or perhaps even long distance and hold up the telephone in mid-air for several minutes so these people could hear the singing.

The Father did not go to every house with the stars but frequently leap-frogged, going to one and lining up a third while the singers were at a second house. When the singers emerged from a house, he would often say, "We're going to Christina's now!" or "Whitey's house! Whitey's!" Some houses were uncertain and had to be felt out by the Father, especially if there was very heavy drinking going on. Apparently a few houses simply refused to receive the stars. There were as many as 30–40 people in the procession at any one time, but many more joined in and then dropped out, depending on which house we were at. A lot of young children participated. I got some wonderful footage of the group singing as they were walking down the road in the dark to Rick and Wilma Berns's house. They would not have been visible except for the headlights of trucks and 4-wheelers shining behind them. No one seemed to mind my video camera. In fact, two or three other cameras were also in use.

The accumulation of round after round of singing and visiting began to show about 10:30 p.m., when it seemed as though all of the adults in the group were getting pretty well plastered. The slow accumulation of punch and beer really began to be felt. Some people even carried a six-pack of beer or a bottle with them and drank outside the house where the singers were. I overheard some young adolescent girls several times singing a short ditty outside on the stairwells. The lyrics were in part: "Mary had a baby" and sung to the tune of "Ring Around the Rosie." This ditty was in apparent reference to Mary, the mother of Jesus.

The final house was the only house where we were required to take our shoes off, but it was also the biggest feed (including fresh king crab) and had the most booze. After the required singing was completed, the tape deck came on and there was a general party atmosphere with dancing and lots of drunken revelry. I left to return to the lodge downtown at 12:15 a.m. and don't know how much longer they carried on. One person later said he didn't leave until 2 a.m. and that the starring group always winds up at this same house every year.

1/9 Tonight before the starring began Father Sergios told me the Alutiiq star was built around the old Aleut "rattle," which is photographed in the Crossroads of Continents *book. This "rattle" is circular and allows the star to turn. The original ones had dried puffin beaks attached as noisemakers, but today's stars are completely silent. The ones at Old Harbor have eight points, which refer to eternity.*

Tonight we started again at about 6:15 p.m. but did not begin at the church. We assembled in the rectory and proceeded to the upper or new town. We started with a much smaller group and all fit in one van. Starting at Wanda Haakanson's and going to eight or nine others. The feasting was much more restrained in this neighborhood and not a drop of booze was seen (except for the swig of whiskey offered me outside on the street as "cough syrup"). Only one man was heavily intoxicated, and the Father had to usher him out of one house because he was disrupting the singers.

One interesting variation: at Emily Bigioli's, the singing and star twirling was done outside because, according to Emily, "my husband isn't feeling very well." In this case the star twirlers and the singers all faced in one direction—towards the house windows. Another variation: after all the songs were finished at the Cloughs, Wanda Haakanson held up the telephone from long distance and asked if the singers could sing again for the person on the phone, which they did, even after completing "Noogaiyaa." They cheerfully repeated themselves all over again.

At Sven and Mary Haakanson's our arrival was timed perfectly with a phone call from Sven Jr. who is a student in Providenya, Soviet Union. I was surprised when Sven Sr. said something at length to me in fluent Russian. At one point Sven told Michelle, the new VPSO, to arrest me for "impersonating an Aleut," which I took as a compliment. I took my video camera along again tonight and got some more good footage. This time I tried to record complete songs rather than starting and stopping so much just for the visuals.

The last house was Carl Christiansen's. Staying with Carl was Pete Squartsoff from Port Lions. There were so few houses that we finished up by 8:30 p.m., although a few singers said they wanted to continue starring again Downtown. No big party tonight.

While I have never observed Russian Christmas in Ouzinkie, I am told it is celebrated very much like it is in Old Harbor. In Old Harbor the three stars are cared for year after year by the Haakanson, Erickson, and Bernsten families, but they all travel around together (Murkowski 1990:54). In Ouzinkie there are two stars and two distinct processions which go around the village simultaneously, although back in the mid-1940s there were three (Lund 1946). One Ouzinkie star is called "the church star" and is carried by the church choir, while the other star is called "Waska's star" after the late Waska Boskofsky. It is also known as "the Boskofsky family star."

The two starring groups start at opposite ends of the village and try to visit each house. When they meet about halfway, they stop and exchange songs. Each processional group has its own set of about seven songs, including one called "Many Years" that is known to everyone. Starring is so sacred that it continues even if it snows or rains (Rostad, 1992; Hall 1993). Each starring group tries to visit all of the houses over the course of three nights.

Nick Pestrikoff Sr. says that Christmas treats offered to the starrers should consist of rich foods, so he specially orders several kinds of cheeses, sausages, and crackers to serve to the starrers when they come to his house.

Russian New Year's (Praznik)
In years past Russian New Year's, celebrated annually on January 14, was a great occasion for masking. Similar to starring, masking consisted of

Fig. 5.1. *Ouzinkie* masqarataqs, *1946. From* The Spruce Bough, *Ouzinkie High School yearbook. Courtesy of Joyce Smith.*

going from house to house wearing costumes on three consecutive nights after the conclusion of starring. It is not clear whether masking actually started on the fourteenth or ended on the fourteenth. However, at each house the maskers would be invited in, and if the host family could guess the identity of the maskers, they would have to show their faces. Masks were made of nylon stockings and old stocking caps with holes cut out for the eyes, nose, and mouth. Maskers would often point towards a radio or record player to indicate they wanted to dance, and the host family would oblige by turning on some music. Maskers would not stay very long, however, because they would be very warm and sweaty under their masks and would soon crave the cool night air.

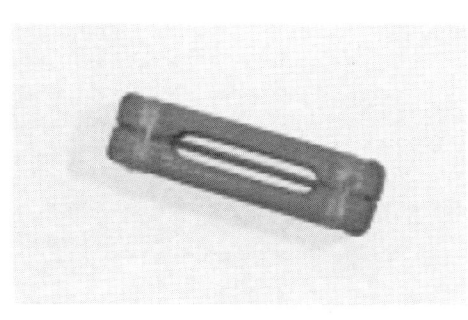

Fig. 5.2. Masqarataq *whistle: Two pieces of wood with rubber band insert. Made by Thomas Ignatin, Old Harbor.*

Costumes were improvised from old rubber boots, rain coats, and other used clothing.

Expressive Culture 117

Oftentimes pillows were stuffed inside pants and coats to distort body shapes. After World War II, oversized soldiers' uniforms were very popular for masking. In the late 1940s, Old Harbor maskers would go around wrapped up in bear skins, fox furs, and even fish nets (Bailey 1949:11). To fool the host families they would either remain totally silent or disguise their voices using small wooden "whistles" made with taut rubber band reeds (Figure 5.2). The low, rasping sounds generated by these whistles are quite unlike the high-frequency sounds of referee whistles commonly used in sporting events.

As in most other Kodiak communities, masking in Old Harbor and Ouzinkie has almost disappeared as a community tradition, and it is not entirely clear why it has disappeared. In the *Spruce Bough* school yearbook for 1946, one student, Zack Katelnikoff, briefly described their New Year's celebration:

On Russian New Year's eve everyone went to church at twelve o'clock. This service lasted until around twelve thirty. Then everyone began shooting skyrockets and guns and making lots of noise. The last night of the masking they had a ladies dance. Lots of people came to this last dance. They served sandwiches, cake, pie, Koolaid, and coffee. They had a Circle Waltz.

Martha Anderson (1997), who grew up in Ouzinkie, recalls some holiday experiences from her youth:

On the third night we started masking from house to house. One old man named John Katelnikoff used to come to the door dressed in rags as the Old Year. I used to be very afraid of him. One time we were dressed up as hula girls, me and my brother, and we went out masking. We used rope to make our wigs, and we made grass skirts. It was really funny because Nick Pestrikoff's cows were following us around and trying to eat our skirts. We had dances almost every night during Russian Christmas—polkas, waltzes, schottisches, jitterbugs, and the circle two-step.

Nick Pestrikoff Sr. remembers that during the big dance held on New Year's Eve, a raggedy and hairy old man would come in to the dance hall. This was the Old Year. At midnight a lot of guns would go off outside, and someone would shoot the Old Year with a BB gun. Then a new masker would enter the dance hall dressed in white bed sheets. This was the New Year. Guns were fired off again all over the village and once again at noon on New Year's Day. Unfortunately, there has been no masking in Ouzinkie since 1995.

The biggest Russian New Year's masking celebration today in the Kodiak area takes place in Kodiak City at the Elks Club, which some villagers also attend. This masquerade ball, sponsored by the St. Herman's Sisterhood of Holy Resurrection Orthodox Church, is a rather formal affair with a live band and prizes awarded for the best costumes. Many participants spend large amounts of money on their costumes.

Variants of one of the old Alutiiq traditions, called the New Year's play or Nuta'aq, was performed all around Kodiak Island. In Karluk it was better known as "The Devil's Dance." Sven Haakanson Sr. (in Simeone 1997) recalled how this play was performed in Old Harbor and Ouzinkie:

The Old Year used to carry a clock, and he would tell people the time. He wore raggedy old clothes and went around saying goodbye to everyone. He knew time was running out. At night the devils came, and they would do away with the Old Year and take him out of the dance hall making way for the New Year. People volunteered to be the Old Year, and sometimes the chief was the Old Year. It was heavy drama and very serious. In the meantime, the New Year was guarded from the Old Year, in case the Old Year tried to do him harm. The Old Year was taken out of the dance hall three times, and the third time he was not allowed to come back.

Compared to the vitality of New Year's masking and the elaborate folk drama done today in Port Graham and Nanwalek (Mishler 1988), New Year's traditions in the Kodiak archipelago appear to be only a shadow of what they formerly were.

It seems clear, nevertheless, that masking at Russian New Year's was largely a syncretic phenomenon, carried over from traditional masking done before Russian contact. Crowell (1992), Liapunova (1994), and Desson (1996) have reconstructed some of the early postcontact winter masked ceremonies and rituals which distinguished Alutiiq life on Kodiak Island in the early nineteenth century. According to Clark (1984b:194), shamans used masks and dolls to make contact with the supernatural. Many of the wooden masks associated with these ceremonies were collected and are now conserved at the National Museum of Natural History in Washington, D.C., and the Peter the Great Museum of Anthropology and Ethnography in St. Petersburg, Russia.

Orthodox missionaries criticized and suppressed Alutiiq rituals and masks, associating these with heathen non-Christian practices. What appears to have happened, however, is that the Alutiiq gave up their masks without giving up the practice of masking. That is, they continued to mask but did so within new, more acceptable contexts, the context of Biblical stories, church holidays, and European secular holidays.

Despite all the fun associated with masking, villagers in Kodiak communities as well as those in Nanwalek and Port Graham firmly believe that those who mask symbolically represent King Herod's soldiers. In the Bible, Herod sent his soldiers out to kill all male babies under the age of two in an attempt to prevent the Christ child from becoming king (see Matthew 2:16). Herod was afraid that the Christ child, who was prophesied to become King of the Jews, would depose him. According to Alutiiq legend, however, Herod's soldiers wore masks and disguised their voices or remained silent so that they would not be recognized later for committing these terrible infant murders. The Bible, nevertheless, says nothing about the soldiers wearing masks or disguising their voices.

Guilty by their association with Herod's soldiers, Ouzinkie maskers were required to attend church and go through a purifying ceremony "so that their evil intents will be washed away and they can once again take communion" (Lund 1946). After masking was over, the maskers also had to take a ceremonial banya to purify themselves (Setzkorn 1945). There was a certain guilt associated with masking which required paying penance. John Pestrikoff of Port Lions (Mulcahy 1986:49) recalls:

When we used to masquerade, they say your mask is there on your face forever if you didn't wash it with seaweed. Cold as it had been, maybe 20 below zero . . . Mom used to tell us, "You better go out to sea." Nighttime, you know. Cold! Ice water! Ice floating in the water. Oh well, what we're told, we have to do. We did that. Mighty cold, I tell you. That's the way you wash your mask off.

Although the Russian Orthodox Church tolerates New Year's masking, it is clear that this practice, contrary to Alutiiq popular belief and legend, is regarded as a totally secular tradition. Kodiak priest Father Joseph Kreta has said that masking "has absolutely no spiritual significance." He adds, "We respect the traditions of people," but they "shouldn't be misconstrued with spirituality or the church" (*Kodiak Daily Mirror*, January 6, 1986, page 6).

Mazhlinik *and Lent*

I asked Sven and Mary Haakanson (1997) how they observed the six weeks of Lent, a time of self-sacrifice and restraint. I was already aware that the Russian Orthodox Church forbids the faithful from hunting or eating meat during Lent.

MH: Three weeks, two weeks before Lent starts we'd have dance every night.

SH: They'd have Mazhlinik, *which means "Mardi Gras," the same way the Catholic is in New Orleans. They have what they called "Crazy Week" Everybody'd like a Mardi Gras. They'd celebrate. . . . And then they go for seven weeks of Lent and fasting, and everybody, you know. Lent was real good because people would take care of their homes and do all the repair work in the whole community, and then when Easter comes, they'd dress up on the holiday. So a lot of life was centered around the church. It was beautiful holidays, you know. Everybody looked forward to them, the baking, the cooking.*

MH: Cleaning up around the church.
SH: The whole town.
MH: Yeah. The whole town used to work together.

SH: You know there was always something to do, and something to look forward to.

Formerly, children were not allowed to run around outdoors or shout in loud voices during Lent. They were supposed to stay at home and be quiet. In Ouzinkie, Orthodox Lent restrictions are no longer observed very strictly. Children are now allowed to run and play all over the village. Bingo, which used to be completely taboo during Lent, is now played in the Ouzinkie Community Hall, though it is still shut down in Old Harbor. Fasting is increasingly rare, and a few people even get drunk during Lent, something unheard of only a decade or two ago.

Russian Easter (Pascha)

I did not witness any celebrations of Russian Easter in Old Harbor or Ouzinkie, although I tried for several years in a row to be there for this holiday. Each time I was kept away by bad weather. Russian Easter is equal in spiritual importance to Russian Christmas. The period of Lent which precedes Easter is a time of sacrifice. One of the things Old Harbor people miss the most during Lent is community bingo, which is normally played two or three nights a week.

In addition to numerous Orthodox Church services just before and on Easter Sunday, it is traditional in Old Harbor to have a children's Easter egg hunt in the graveyard. After gathering their eggs, children go

Fig. 5.3. *Colored Easter eggs with* kulich *(Easter bread) and tea at home of Sophie and George Inga Sr., 1998. Photo by Craig Mishler.*

around from door to door trading eggs, getting one decorated Easter egg for another. At each house the children greet the host family with "Christ Is Risen," and the host family responds with "Indeed he is risen" (Tennessen 1983). Easter eggs symbolize both the resurrection of Christ and the return of spring, when migrating birds return.

On Easter morning after Liturgy the children of the village take turns ringing the church bells all day and all evening until about 10 p.m., and then again for several more hours on Bright Monday and Tuesday (Rostad 1998). This custom of ringing the church bells for three days starting on Easter is also observed today in Ouzinkie. This is because Orthodox Easter, like Orthodox Christmas, is celebrated for three consecutive days.

To celebrate Easter, most Ouzinkie and Old Harbor families also make and eat a special Easter bread called *kulich*. This bread is baked inside of coffee cans so that the loaves have a distinctive cylindrical shape. The bread is laced with raisins or candied fruit to make it festive, and after baking, the top of the loaf is decorated with brightly colored icing and sprinkled with small candies. Formerly, the Ouzinkie village priest, Father Gerasim Schmaltz, would go house to house to bless the *kulich*, but now people take their *kulich* to the church and have it blessed there. It is also customary for families to mail packages containing blessed loaves of *kulich* to their physically distant relatives.

Memorial Day

Although I arrived in Ouzinkie on Memorial Day 1998, I observed no one tending or cleaning graves. After inquiring, I learned that graves are cleaned before Easter. There is no traditional Memorial Day observance, but military veterans continue to be honored on Veterans Day.

The Fourth of July

In 1991 I was present to observe and participate in Old Harbor's Fourth of July celebration. It is interesting that although the Fourth of July is a national political holiday, it has been adapted to become a religious holiday also. Even though I was preoccupied with a video camera, here are my field notes:

7/4 Thursday (Fourth of July)
This morning the first signs of life I observed were Sven Haakanson and a bright young Native man hanging American flag displays in the midway area directly in front of the Old Harbor city office building. This young man turned out to be Phil McCormick, of Larsen Bay and Karluk. Phil had just come in from Three Saints Bay with the archaeology crew of Aron Crowell after a month-long excavation of an early Russian period house pit.
At 11 a.m. the priest led a church service for the benefit of all the fishermen who were going out fishing tonight and tomorrow as the commercial salmon season opens. There were hymns and prayers for the fishermen, and

a short announcement by Sven Haakanson, about the upcoming boat parade and race. Then each fisherman and his children walked through the outer altar area kissing a series of icons and being sprinkled with holy water by the priest.

After church we all trucked down to the boat harbor and clambered aboard purse seiners for the blessing of the fleet. I went aboard Sven's boat, along with Aron Crowell and two of his people. Sven's boat was the lead boat in the parade. First, we passed under the big ship dock where the Father and a small choir of well-wishers sang and sprinkled holy water on each boat as it passed under.

Then all of the seiners (about 15 of them) lined up for a race back to the dock, won by Crimson Beauty, *a big new boat from Port Lions. The end of the race turned into a free-for-all of fast criss-crossing boats, each one trying to rock and swamp the others with big wakes and near-collisions. There was much screaming and laughter by Sven's daughter Phyllis. I heard later that there was seasickness on some of the boats due to the pitching and rolling.*

The remainder of the afternoon was consumed in games and races of all kinds, including a mountain marathon run, egg tossing, water balloon tossing, hands behind the back blueberry pie eating, eyes-closed pudding eating, hula hooping, sack races, tugs of war, and buoy bouncing. The latter event seems to be a local invention. Contestants seat themselves on large fluorescent orange crab pot buoys over two feet in diameter and bounce their way forward while grasping the buoy handles with their thumbs. I videotaped nearly everything except the hula hoop contest, although I didn't attempt to record all the iterations for each event if it was broken down into men's, women's, girls, and boys classes. The surprising thing about the tug of war was that the girls held the boys to a standoff, to the point where adults started jumping in to help each side. Eventually some men on the sidelines even joined the girls team, although at the end it seemed as though the boys got a slight edge.

There were also assorted arcade games (a ring toss, baseball toss at wooden milk bottles, another baseball toss into tilted cut-off cans, and a roulette wheel), a raffle drawing, and a queen contest, but the most spirited event of the day was the boxing. Spectators formed a large square and held onto the same rope used in the tugs of war to define the ring. Then for over an hour and a half the crowd cheered as one pair of boxers after another donned the gloves and went at it, from little tots to teenage girls and young men. They were all allowed to box until they had finished two rounds or until someone got hurt or drew blood. Emil Christiansen refereed all the matches and held up the gloves of both contestants if they went the distance. If one person got hurt, he stopped the fight and escorted that person to the sidelines but would never raise the glove of the victor.

The noisy enthusiasm of the crowd for this boxing made me re-evaluate the gentle and easygoing manners of Old Harbor people. I realize now that there is a fierce competitive spirit among the children and young adults which directly carries over into the salmon, herring, and crab fisheries.

I heard that there was to be a dance this evening but didn't see or hear this materialize. Nevertheless, many people attended a big bingo game held in the upstairs part of the city building. Surprisingly, there was no big fireworks display, although little firecrackers were in evidence everywhere.

Participants in this big Fourth of July party seemed to be limited primarily to purse-seine captains, their crew members, and their families, though it was difficult to tell whether or not all the children in the village were present. About 125 to 150 people attended the races and games, yet the total village population is about 284, so there were many who stayed home.

In Ouzinkie the Fourth of July is celebrated with a little parade, a carnival, some races, and fireworks. Although I am unable to provide any details, this Ouzinkie holiday is described as "a fun time thing."

The Pilgrimage to Monk's Lagoon

On the ninth of August each year there is a one-day spiritual pilgrimage to Monk's Lagoon on the southern end of Spruce Island to pray and pay tribute to the memory of Father Herman, who was canonized on that date in 1970. The people who go on this pilgrimage generally gather in Kodiak City and in Ouzinkie and ride over on fishing boats with Orthodox priests and lay readers. Villagers from all over Kodiak Island as well as people from the lower forty-eight states and Russia participate in this pilgrimage, and it is open to anyone who wants to go along (see Moss 1998b). In addition to this organized pilgrimage, many people visit Monk's Lagoon at other times of the year on their own personal pilgrimages.

At Monk's Lagoon there is a foot trail which leads to two marked graves, those of Father Gerasim Schmaltz and Father Peter Kreta. Father Gerasim died in the late 1960s and Father Kreta died in the mid-1990s. The trail continues on to Father Gerasim's two-room hut and chapel, and to a chapel that was built on top of Father Herman's former grave. Shortly after his canonization, the OCA removed Father Herman's remains to the church in Kodiak City. The trail to the chapel winds through a towering old-growth spruce forest, a place of tremendous natural beauty. On a sunny day the warm light filters down through the forest canopy onto the mossy branches of the giant spruce.

When the Orthodox faithful go to these sacred places, they gather a handful of soil from crawl space beneath the church where Father Herman was buried and carry it home in a ziploc bag. They also fill up pop bottles and plastic milk jugs of water from a spring near Father Gerasim's chapel. The soil and the water from this spring, regarded as holy water, is believed to have medicinal and curative powers. One Larsen Bay woman uses the water for her eyes and gives a bottle to her brother to help his arthritis.

People making the Monk's Lagoon pilgrimage, weather permitting, will usually have an outdoor picnic after visiting the holy sites. Since salmon berries abound along the trail, those on the pilgrimage gather handfuls of the ripe, juicy fruit and eat them on the spot.

I had a chance to visit this place in the company of Herman Squartsoff on July 31, 1996, just a few days before the annual pilgrimage. When Father Gerasim was still alive, it used to be an Ouzinkie tradition to visit Monk's Lagoon on the Fourth of July and have a picnic with the priest (Oswalt 1997).

Veterans Day

Veterans Day, observed in late October or early November, is one of the few days of the year when there is an Ouzinkie community dinner. On this day Ouzinkie veterans are honored, and they stand up and tell stories about their experiences in the military. Many Ouzinkie men served during the Korean and Vietnam Wars, while many others have served in the nonwartime military. Roy Chichenoff, the only casualty, was killed in action in Korea. Nick Pestrikoff Sr. has heard through the American Legion that Ouzinkie has the highest percentage of veterans of any community in Alaska. The importance of this to the community is evidenced by a half-page newspaper potluck dinner invitation printed in the *Kodiak Mirror* on November 11, 1998. The invitation was addressed to thirty-four current and former residents who have served in the armed forces.

Thanksgiving

Thanksgiving is a November holiday feast celebrated only by individual families, not at the community level. Turkey dinners with all the trimmings are popular. The Ouzinkie Native Corporation annual meeting provides another community feast in late fall.

MUSIC AND DANCE

There are two categories of Alutiiq dancing: the aboriginal style that virtually disappeared by the mid-twentieth century, and the western style introduced by Russian and Scandinavian immigrants.

Aboriginal-Style Music and Dance

Alutiiq aboriginal-style dancing did not resurface in Old Harbor until the early 1990s, several years after it was revived in Kodiak City by the Kodiak Alutiiq Dancers led by Connie Chya and Margaret Roberts and inspired by Old Harbor elders Larry Matfay and Mary Haakanson. By the time this dance group was formed in 1989, just a few months after the *Exxon Valdez* oil spill, nearly all of the traditional songs and dances were forgotten. The dance leaders collected a few songs and dances from elders, made their own traditional dresses (called "falling snow parkas"),

Fig. 5.4. *Larry Matfay, 1996. Photo by Craig Mishler.*

woven hats, and circular dance drums similar to those used by Yup'ik and Inupiat Eskimo dancers.

But traditional material was so hard to come by they had to borrow some songs and dances from Tlingits and Yup'ik dance groups in order to fill out their repertoire, and they decided to write some of their own material. By the late 1990s this group began to do outreach to the villages. In April 1998, Connie Chya and her son visited Old Harbor for a week to teach these dances to schoolchildren during Alutiiq Heritage Week, but Chya says she left the Kodiak City group due to its heavy performance schedule.

At the Elders-Youth Conference held in Cordova in August 1998, the Kodiak Soonaq dancers appeared under the tutelage of Caroline Kelly, originally from Old Harbor, who now performs with two of her children and another woman from Old Harbor. The reconstituted group now seems to reflect the desire of urban people to hold on to their village roots.

Popular Music and Dance

We have already noted in several places how popular social dancing and the playing of live music was in Ouzinkie, especially during Russian Christmas. Inventories at the Alaska Commercial Company store in Ouzinkie show that accordions were popular items as early as the 1890s. In 1894 a new accordion was valued at $3.50 (Alaska Commercial Company, 1894; 1898).

Martha Anderson (1997) says that during her youth: "dancing was a big thing. My brother Nick [Katelnikoff] Jr. was an accordion player, and we also had violins, mandolins, and guitars. Dances were generally held on Friday nights. Saturday nights were reserved for Russian Orthodox observances."

Dances were held all winter long and were very popular. Fred and Esther Chernikoff (1998) recalled five different dance halls: 1) Marzan's dance hall and liquor store, which flourished in the 1930s, 2) Arthur Levine's dance hall, which was the old schoolhouse, actively used in the 1940s, 3) Frank Hammerly's dance hall, also active in the 1940s at the same time as Arthur Levine's, 4) Ed Opheim's Pool Hall, which was used as a dance hall for two years during the late 1940s but relied on recorded jukebox music, and 5) Tim Panamarioff Sr.'s dance hall, later sold to Tommy Renshaw, which was active in the 1950s. According to Reed Oswalt (1997), "Tim built this dance hall, and it was built on a swamp in the middle of the town, and our house where we stayed was about 150 yards from the dance hall, but when he'd have a dance, between the noise and everything, it would make the whole area bounce [laughs], so it had quite a bit of resilience to it. It served a pretty good purpose."

Fig. 5.5. *Arthur Matfay, Old Harbor, 1998. Photo by Craig Mishler*

Some of the favorite Ouzinkie dances were square dances, and Julian Muller was the caller. The most famous musicians were all accordion players: Nick Katelnikoff Sr., Fred Katelnikoff, Peter Katelnikoff, Albert Torsen, and Moses Malutin. Zack Katelnikoff, Teddy Panamarioff, and Nicky Panamarioff played guitar in the bands. Nick was also good on the accordion and steel pedal guitar, while Waska Boskofsky played the ukulele and the mandolin. Virtually all of this music was instrumental; vocals were quite rare. After the postwar period, live music and dance halls began to diminish and disappear, and none survived the earthquake of 1964. This fading out of live entertainment may have been a result of the introduction of television.

It is somewhat surprising then that today virtually all of the dances held in Ouzinkie are for teenagers, and all of the music for the dances is prerecorded on tapes and CDs. The rambunctious dance hall days of Vasilli Pestrikoff and his friends (see Chapter 1) are long gone, along with a music and dance tradition carried on for almost one hundred years.

There are no more old-time musicians left in Ouzinkie, and I only found one musician, the late Arthur Matfay, still active in Old Harbor. Arthur played both guitar and accordion and acquired a piano in the early 1990s. Arthur's forte was the accordion, and he mostly played popular instrumental tunes from the 1930s, 1940s, and 1950s, tunes he heard during the time when he was growing up. He was self-taught, learning much of what he knew off of records and tapes, but he was also influenced by his late uncle, Alfred Azuyak, an accordion player. Arthur jammed with fishermen passing through Old Harbor and occasionally played for community social events. In February 1998, for example, he performed for a local wedding reception.

In April 1998, just a year before his death, I recorded Arthur on videotape outdoors and in his house. At that time he played a wide selection of tunes. One group came from the country music of the early to mid-1950s: "Cold, Cold Heart" and "I Can't Help It (If I'm Still in Love with You)" both recorded by Hank Williams Sr., "My Shoes Keep Walking Back to You" (Ray Price), "I'll Sail My Ship Alone" (Moon Mullican), "It Wasn't God Who Made Honky Tonk Angels" (Kitty Wells), and "Seven Lonely Days." Still older tunes include "Peg of My Heart," "My Happiness," "Has Anybody Seen My Gal?," and an untitled schottische. Taken from Alutiiq folk song tradition was a little number Arthur called "Unuguu" ("Tonight"). Although played by Arthur as an instrumental, "Unuguu" came from a traditional courting song that was very popular in the village as long as anyone can remember. Many people learned it from Arthur's father, Larry Matfay, and it is part of the repertoire of the Kodiak Alutiiq Dancers, who sing it in Alutiiq and English to the accompaniment of a skin drum. The lyrics, as translated from Alutiiq by Paul Kahutak and Carolyn Kelly are:

Tonight, tonight,
I'm coming,
I'll bring some tea for a snack.
If you hear the dogs barking at me,
Do not think I'm a Bigfoot (*Ahulaq*).

Old Harbor, like Ouzinkie, had a number of active musicians who formed themselves into dance bands. Alec Inga was well known for his ability to play almost any instrument—accordion, banjo, violin, harmonica, and guitar. Wilfred Alexanderoff played accordion and guitar, and Willie Shugak and Charlie Pestrikoff were active guitar players. As mentioned above, Paul Kahutak was counted on as a guitar, accordion, and piano player, while Walt Erickson was very good on the guitar but declined to play for dances. Local singers included Ed Pestrikoff Sr. and Moses Larionoff. During World War II soldiers stationed at remote camps on Sitkalidak Island would come into Old Harbor to get supplies, and this was yet another occasion for dancing. In the 1950s Larry Matfay operated a community dance hall that is still standing today next to Walt Erickson's store.

STORIES

The telling of traditional folktales and legends in Old Harbor and Ouzinkie seems to have faded away with the music and dancing. Even oral history, or at least that part of oral history reaching beyond an individual's personal life history, seems to be extremely rare in these communities. This raises the question of whether there is an indigenous Alutiiq view of history. Perhaps the indigenous view is that history is only important when framed within a person's own life experience. For the most part Alutiiqs are very present-minded.

In Old Harbor, as a result of the community's participation in archaeological excavations done at Three Saints Bay and at the Lighthouse site during the 1990s, young people have a much better sense of history than their parents. Naomi Klouda says: "The children growing up [here] have a firm understanding of pre-Russian history, Russian times, post-American, post-earthquake, pre–oil spill, post–oil spill, and so on."

So it may be that the elders know their cultural history very well but are simply reluctant to tell about it. As Nick Pestrikoff Sr. says, "We don't talk much about the past because we believe that it's something that's done with, something to be left alone, something we shouldn't bother or disturb." And Theodore Squartsoff, reacting to my chart of Ouzinkie families (Figure 2.3 above) and questions about the names of his ancestors, said: "Why are you digging up all of this? That's all behind us. We live for today and for the future. Our freezers are full. We're happy. So why worry about all these people who are dead and gone?" Later on, however, Theodore admitted that he does visit the graveyard to pray and pay his respects.

Some isolated fragments of folklore and oral history have been documented, but it would be very hard to make a case for an active living narrative tradition. In 1981, the late Philip Katelnikoff told a story of "The Crow and the Goose," which was published in the Ouzinkie High School book, *Ukulahā I* (1981), but this is the only traditional animal story to be recorded. In 1986, Laurie Mulcahy (1987) recorded some magical legends from the late Jenny Chernikoff in Ouzinkie. Jenny was joined in the interview by her son Fred Chernikoff and her daughter-in-law, Esther Chernikoff, who were already familiar with the stories.

> EC: Now, how about that pig or dog or. . . .
>
> JC: Oh yeah. And they used to see some kind of pig here on this island. About that big dog too, there was. Well, that pig! Well before, you know, Father. After Father Herman got here, all that evil stuff used to scatter all over. I don't know; that's what they say, anyway. Anyway, they used to make that, this big dog. He walked on his hind legs. Quite a few people saw it.
>
> LM: What was the name of this animal or creature?
>
> JC: I really don't know. But it was a huge dog. They say it walked on its hind legs.
>
> FC: Sabalahuk.
>
> JC: Sabalahuk, that's what they used to call it, see. And later, all that stuff went away when they have this holy prayer. Father Gerasim and Father Petellin. . . .
>
> EC: And now, how about that pig? Was it here the same time as the dog, or at separate times?
>
> JC: No, the pig was before the dog. That Yosakaguk, whatever it is, the mermaid, was before that pig. And that pig, well it was a pig, they say, but it had transparent legs.
>
> EC: Did it attack anybody?
>
> JC: No, but whoever would meet up with it, you know, would fall down and pass out, just faint.
>
> FC: Well, didn't whoever would see it would die or something? Or you know, worse yet?
>
> JC: No. They wouldn't die, but they would have kind of fits.

Jenny Chernikoff was also versed in stories about dwarves, called *yinchuns*, who could only be controlled by putting holy bread and holy water in their mouths. These dwarves would meet up with people and offer them tobacco or liquor or snuff. "And if a person takes it," Jenny said, "then you go nuts. And if you don't, they knock you down."

Jenny also believed in house mascots, called *susekas*, which appeared to the owner of a house in the form of a tiny little man. She believed that every house has a *suseka* and that to see the *suseka* in your house would bring you good luck (Mulcahy 1987).

Nick Pestrikoff Sr. says that some people in Ouzinkie still have visions of short hairy men with long beards, called *olaqs*. *Olaqs* are primarily associated with Afognak Island, but Nick's late mother-in-law used to see them inside her house in Ouzinkie. Magical and mystical, *olaqs* have the ability to enter through closed doors and windows. Nick's mother-in-law would get very scared and call him up whenever she saw them, and Nick would go over to her house to reassure her: "We know you see them, but they won't harm you. They *can't* harm you," he said.

As suggested by the "Unuguu" song, Old Harbor has an ongoing legend about *ahulaq*, another Bigfoot or Sasquatch-like creature with hairy arms and legs, exuding a powerful odor. Actually *ahulaq* may simply be a variation on *olaq*, but of a much larger variety. Sightings of this creature, which some people insist is a man, used to take place rather frequently, but are increasingly rare today, and no one has talked about seeing one in the ten years I have been visiting the villages. Paul Kahutak has never seen one himself but knows of several other people who did. One of them was the late distinguished elder Larry Matfay. It is believed that *ahulaqs* are very fond of snuff or *ikmik*, so Matfay once left a can of it lying on the beach as bait. After dark an *ahulaq* appeared, grabbed the can, and took off, all right in front of Larry's eyes (Klouda 1996a).

Marie Bailey, the schoolteacher in Old Harbor in the late 1940s, heard of several sightings of *ahulaq* and described him as "about seven feet tall with long black hair and very large hands and feet. He always carries a club" (Bailey 1949:38). People who see *ahulaq* generally get very scared. Unlike *olaqs*, *ahulaqs* stay outdoors and do not come into houses.

Although Ouzinkie and Old Harbor people are fond of telling personal experience stories, the only legend-like material I was able to record were some Ouzinkie anecdotes about a wild man named Toshwak, and the summary of an attack by some Russians at Fox Lagoon, near Old Harbor.

Toshwak

John Toshwak was a Native man who had a house at Sourdough Flats only a half mile or so from Ouzinkie. The 1940 BIA Village Census (National Archives, Anchorage) shows that Toshwak was born on January 7, 1886, that his wife Ana was born September 22, 1915, and that they had four children named Nick, Sergay, Pauline, and Daniel. Today there are no surviving members from this family, but the legend continues.

Nick Pestrikoff Sr. portrays Toshwak as a wild man who killed three or four people, including his own eldest son. Nick says that Toshwak killed his oldest son with a shotgun while he was sleeping because his son's snoring bothered him. Then he supposedly dragged his son's body down to the waterfront, put it inside a skiff, and anchored the skiff offshore. After a short while the skiff broke loose and washed up on shore, and someone called in the U.S. marshal from Kodiak. The marshal came out and arrested Toshwak but eventually released him, and Toshwak then went to Afognak.

When Nick was a kid, he and his boyhood pals used to hide in the woods near Toshwak's house and holler out at him just to get him riled up. When Toshwak heard these kids taunting him, he would come out and shoot at them with his .22 rifle.

Five years later, in 1947, Toshwak was apparently beaten to death by two men in a drunken brawl the morning after a dance was held in his house. According to Nick, one of the two men who beat him to death was his youngest son. Lola Harvey (1991:373–374), in covering these events, says that Toshwak had by that time acquired the nickname, "the Terror of Afognak."

There are plenty of variants on the stories. Theodore and Toni Squartsoff say that Toshwak shot and killed his son through the front door while his son was peeping at him through the keyhole. And Christine Kvasnikoff heard that Toshwak killed his son by rolling him up in a seine net and stabbing him to death with a fish pike.

The Battle in Fox Lagoon

Abalik (Paul Kahutak 1997a) tells a story about the Russians attacking an Alutiiq village in Fox Lagoon, Sitkalidak Island. This lagoon, which is about five miles from Old Harbor, is shown on topographic maps as McDonald Lagoon. Paul's story appears to be rather distinct from the story of the Russians attacking Alutiiqs at Refuge Rock, discussed above in Chapter 1 and reported in Holmberg (1985:59), even though Fox Lagoon was used by Russian ships to gain access to Refuge Rock.

CM: Did you ever hear any stories about the Russians, or the wars they had with the Russians?

PK: Oh yeah. Like they said in Fox Lagoon one time, you know. There was a village there. There was Russians there before. My aunt used to tell me. So this boat came in. So these Aleut [Alutiiq] people were there, and they had barabaras. So when they seen the ship, you know, they used those muskets. They got them from the Russians, you know.

CM: Muskets. Old guns?

PK: So when the boat come in, you know, they start shooting [at] it, them guys. Well, they didn't even know, but that ship got cannons. So the Russians they used the cannons, you know, and they killed them off. Just that one woman escaped. That Fox Lagoon is kind of far. I don't know. She [swam across the channel and] walked on the beach all the way to Old Harbor and made it. She was the only survivor.

The Haunted House

Another one of Abalik's stories concerns a haunted house and other strange happenings at Port Hobron, the old commercial whaling station on Sitkalidak Island that ceased operating in the 1940s. What brought on the paranormal events was the keeping of a whale fetus, in violation of an ancient taboo. Paul's body language is an integral part of this story, as captured on videotape (Kahutak 1997b):

PK: That whale station, you know? [at Port Hobron]

CM: Yeah.

PK: Me and Ralph we used to go duck hunting [over there]. These guys left, you know. At night time you couldn't go sleep! The [bed] covers making noise, you know [fingers of both hands trembling]. You figure, haunted house or whatever, like that. Boy, noise! [shrugs shoulders] Me and Ralph, you know [drops hand in slicing motion]. I used to tell him. Laying down in the bed, he said: "Did you hear that?" [turns head side to side] I said, "Yeah, holy smokes! Spooky!"

You know what the trouble was? They had that little whale baby, about so big [spreads thumb and index finger about five inches]. They had it in alcohol [cups hands to indicate a jar or bottle]. I told you about it, remember?

CM: No! I don't remember.

PK: When they had whaling station they got it in the stomach [uterus of a dead female whale], and they had it preserved in alcohol.

CM: Oooh.

PK: They kept it for years. So this guy, over there they're living, their son. He went cuckoo [spreads fingers of right hand and raises them up to his head] later on. And the old timer says, you know, they were kind of old-timers, they said: "Well, they shouldn't have took that baby whale. It's driving him nuts [circles right index finger next to head]. Yeah! [laughs] That's what them guys used to say here [in Old Harbor]. You should never take that, you know, whale [spreads thumb and index finger].

CM: Baby.

PK: Baby whale. So this guy went [circles left index finger next to head] off his head [shrugs shoulders]. Lot of people know [about it], here. And I asked them, "How come?" And they said, "Well, he shouldn't have kept that whale" [shakes head back and forth and cups left hand slightly to suggest the jar].

BASKETRY

Although Aleut grass basketry is well known and widely collected, very little has been written about Alutiiq basketry, and very few museums have any in their collections. It is a greatly underappreciated women's art form. One of the foremost practitioners of Alutiiq basketry was the late Fedosia

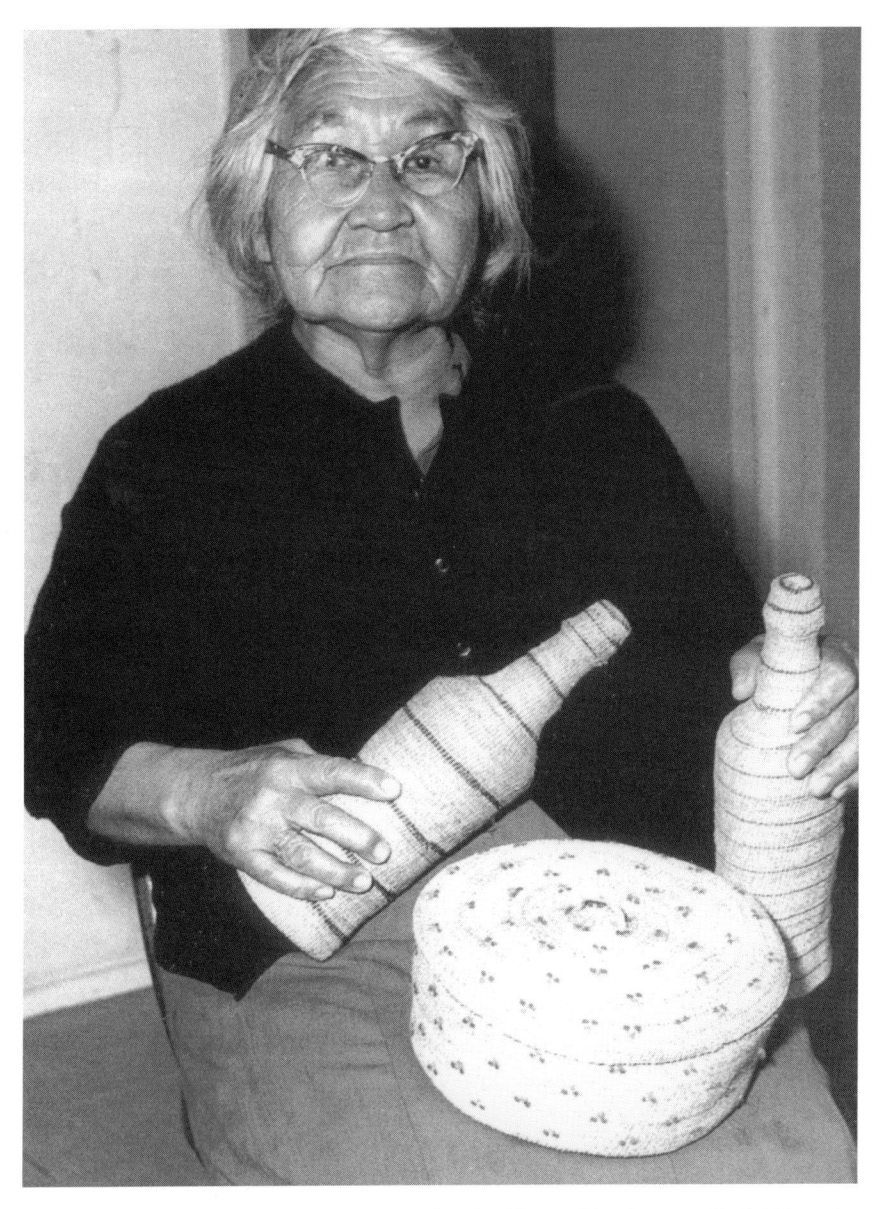

Fig 5.6. *Fedosia Inga, June 1970. Yule Chaffin Collection, Kodiak Historical Society Museum.*

Inga of Old Harbor, mother of George Inga Sr., Sophie Ignatin, and Polly Tunohun. Fedosia's grass baskets were round in shape and some were exquisitely woven over bottles of various sizes and shapes. They were much larger than the miniature baskets made today in Atka and other Aleutian Island communities, with "larger weave, larger objects, and more heavily decorated" (Murray and Corey 1997:1). Three of her baskets are now preserved in the Baranof Museum in Kodiak. The lid of one is decorated with Russian trade beads. During the 1940s Fedosia taught basketmaking to Old Harbor schoolchildren, both boys and girls, and also used to make broad-brimmed grass hats (Bailey 1949:39).

According to Martha Matfay (in Mulcahy 1987:84–85), who studied Fedosia's basketry with an eye to learning how to do it herself, Fedosia used to weave colored yarn and beads into her baskets and usually lined them with cloth. The grass was picked in the fall time after it had faded to a straw color, and the shorter grasses, beach rye and sedge, were preferred because they were finer.

Today only a few elderly women from Old Harbor still know how to weave grass baskets. These women are Martha Matfay, Christine Ignatin, and Marra Andrewvitch. While this group is now largely inactive, some younger women like Wanda Price are trying to learn. As a result, Alutiiq basketry has only a few remaining practitioners, and examples of it are very scarce. June Simeonoff, now living in Haines, was also a student of Fedosia Inga, and examples of her baskets are housed in the Alutiiq Museum in Kodiak and in the Sheldon Jackson Museum in Sitka.

GAMES

Traditional Games

Alutiiq games in Old Harbor and Ouzinkie are only spottily documented. Writing in the first decade of the nineteenth century, the Russian Davydov, for example, observed several Alutiiq games without saying where he saw them. Davydov (1977:182–183) identifies a men's gambling game called *kaganak* as "the principal game" played by the Koniag. This game was also documented by Holmberg during his visit to Kodiak in 1851 (1985:53–54).

Kaganak was played between two sides (either one or two players to a side), using "a bone dish about the size of a small coin marked around the rim with four black dots." This bone dish or plate is placed on two seal skins (which Davydov mistakenly identifies as "deer skins") separated by a distance of 3.5 to 4 arshins (8 to 9 feet). Players take turns tossing five convex round wooden disks (which Davydov calls "rings") as they try to cover the bone dish target or to knock an opponent's disk off of the target. The disks are marked to distinguish between the two sides. Points are awarded according to how close the disks come to covering the bone dish and the black dots, and score is kept using either 21or 26 counting sticks. The Alutiiq Museum houses over 200 kaganak disks from excavations in Karluk, identified by Larry Matfay.

To my knowledge this game is no longer played by the Alutiiq in any of the Kodiak area villages, although it has been preserved. The late Larry Matfay taught it to Joe Kelly, a non-Native employed by the Kodiak Area Native Association. Kelly now teaches the game in an effort to revive traditional Alutiiq culture. He made several *kaganak* game sets which he uses for teaching in village schools. Instead of a bone dish or plate, Kelly makes his targets out of flat wooden disks painted with four black dots.

When I was in Old Harbor in April 1998, for Alutiiq Heritage Week, Kelly flew down from Kodiak and spent two days teaching this game to

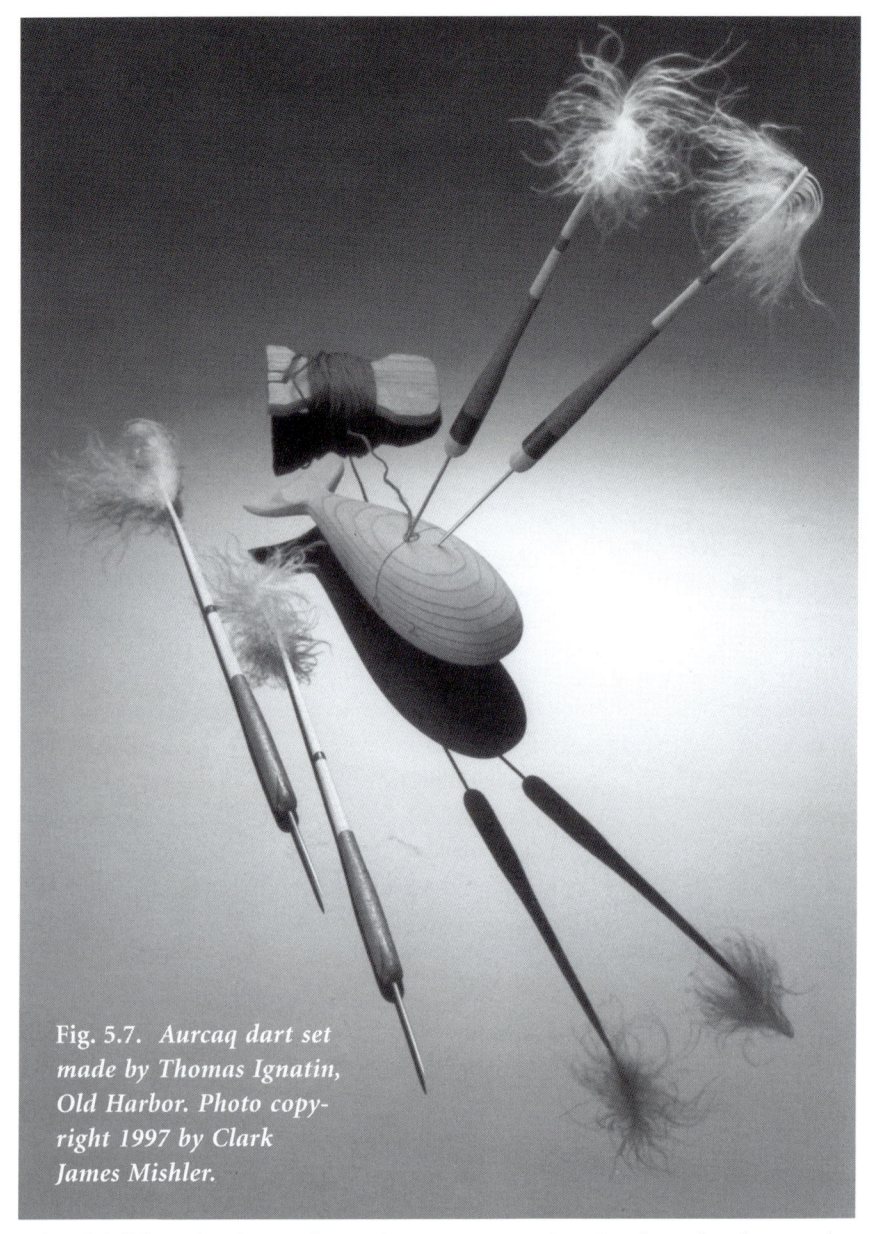

Fig. 5.7. *Aurcaq dart set made by Thomas Ignatin, Old Harbor. Photo copyright 1997 by Clark James Mishler.*

schoolchildren in the various elementary grades. In the school gym, he organized the students into small groups and started up several sets of the game simultaneously. By teaching this game at the public school, however, it became totally divorced from the traditional context of men's gambling, and for this reason it seems very doubtful that the game will ever be internalized and perpetuated by children on their own play time. Without its betting and gambling context, almost certain not to be approved by the school district, the game is reduced to a fairly lifeless formal exercise. It has form without function.

Another gambling game, which is still played occasionally (but only during Orthodox Lent) in Old Harbor and Akhiok, and which I have observed in a traditional context, is called *aurcaq*. Similar to *kaganaq*, *aurcaq* is a game that involves either two or four players. But instead of tossing wooden disks at a bone dish, players of *aurcaq* take turns tossing steel-pointed darts at a carved wooden whale or dolphin. This whale or dolphin (called a *manaq*) is suspended by a string from the ceiling of the room so that it hangs less than four inches off the floor. Points are awarded depending on where as well as whether the darts (sometimes called "spears") stick in the *manaq*.

In a recently published article, I described the rules of this game and the detailed social context in which I saw it and played it in Old Harbor on the evening of March 14, 1992. I analyzed the game from a folkloristic perspective, drawing attention to multiple social and cultural frames, each of which are "hot-linked" and contribute additional layers of meaning to the performance. In summarizing (Mishler 1997:200), I wrote:

> *Aurcaq can ultimately be framed in many ways: by the Lenten restrictions of the Russian Orthodox Church, by the norms of subsistence marine mammal hunting both past and present, by the lost technology and customs that historically and prehistorically defined dolphin and whale hunting, by the diffusion of Scandinavian folk beliefs, by gender roles, by kinship obligations, and by the immediate social setting in which the game is performed.*

Aurcaq was another game taught to Old Harbor schoolchildren by Joe Kelly in April 1998, during the Alutiiq Heritage Week held right after Orthodox Easter. In other words, the game was played outside of the customary Lenten period, and it was also stripped of its traditional gambling performance context. Although children are allowed to be present when *aurcaq* is played, they are not invited to participate. It is an adult game, and for the most part, a man's game.

In Old Harbor they had a bow-and-arrow game called *Koowaq*. This game consisted mostly of target shooting, and the target was made from a mound of mud and grass. On the side of the mound was placed the bulbous head of a big bull kelp. The players were separated into two teams of seven, and anyone hitting the bull kelp was given two points. If no one could hit the bull kelp, the person shooting the nearest arrow to it would be given one point. Bows were handmade out of yellow cedar or alder.

One other traditional game deserving of description is *Loptuq*, also known as "Aleut baseball." I have never seen this game played, but it is one which Old Harbor elders fondly remember, and purportedly it is still played today in Ouzinkie. It is governed by a set of rules and procedures very different from American baseball. In *Loptuq*, participants divide themselves into two groups of four or five players on a side. Boys and girls can both play, and the game is played with a wooden bat and a soft solid rubber ball.

No gloves are used. The traditional playing field is a packed gravel beach at low tide, but it could be played almost anywhere.

In *Loptuq* there is only one base and a home plate, and a runner must reach the opposite base or tag that base and return to home plate to be safe. Just one out retires the entire side, and an out is reached by striking out, by one of the fielders catching a fly ball, or by one of the fielders throwing and hitting a runner as he advances.

The pitcher stands ninety degrees to the side of the batter and does not try to strike out the batter but simply tosses the ball up so it can be easily hit. The pitcher may field a weakly hit ball or bunt and throw out the runner, or he may pick it up and throw it to a fielder so the fielder can throw out the runner.

No score is kept, but the object of the game is to keep batting as long as possible. *Loptuq* gets pretty exciting with a lot of hollering and cheering, especially when there are runners going in both directions, or when two or three runners are all on base at the same time. One strategy is to put the best batters at the bottom of the batting order so that they can drive home those who get on base. The best batters deliberately hit the ball to fielders who are clumsy and error-prone.

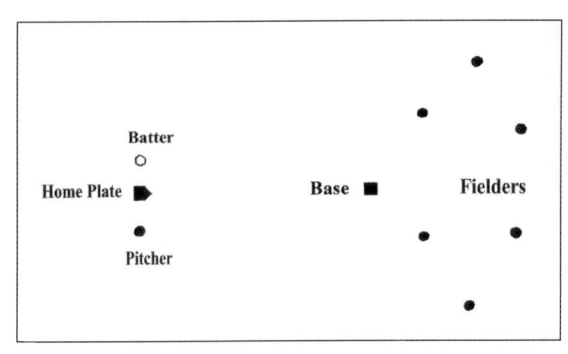

Fig. 5.8. *Loptuq* playing field.

Contemporary Games

Bingo – Bingo is a gambling game that holds an endless fascination for the Alutiiqs living in Ouzinkie and Old Harbor. Gambling has become engrained in Alutiiq culture through such historic games as *kaganaq* and *aurcaq*, and now that these games are on the decline, bingo has become a satisfying continuation of that same impulse. One major difference between bingo and these older games, however, is that women are active participants. Bingo was apparently introduced to Kodiak villages right after World War II, or perhaps in the early 1950s. Martha Anderson (1997) remembers that she ran the first bingo games in Ouzinkie, and that bingo would generally follow the showing of community movies. In Old Harbor, Larry Matfay's dance hall and movie house also served as a bingo hall shortly after he moved from Akhiok in the early 1950s. In Old Harbor today, bingo often follows school basketball games, wrestling matches, Tribal Council meetings, or other early evening events.

Bingo is run by the tribal governments an average of three nights a week in the Community Halls, and it provides part-time employment to three people: a cashier, a caller, and a checker. The cashier is the person who collects fees from participants for each game, pays the winners, and makes change. The caller is the person who announces each number as it is pulled out on a plastic ball from the mechanical sorting bin. The checker is the person who verifies that the first person or persons to shout "Bingo!" have all of the numbers called.

There are two ways of playing bingo these days. One is with cards that have little sliders over the numbers, and the other is with printed forms that are marked with colored ink balls. Players seat themselves on folding chairs around long banquet tables, and most play four or five cards at a time, both to make it mentally challenging and to increase their chances of winning.

On September 9, 1996, I made this entry in my field notes:

In the evening I shot some video footage of the bingo games being played upstairs in the community hall across from the lodge. I was surprised to see a "no smoking" policy had been instituted in the hall since I last attended several years ago. Tony Azuyak was the cashier and Wilfred Alexanderoff was the number caller. Another person verified the winning cards. I cut it short when Tony came over and laughed and said, "You're chasing away my customers."

Bingo, while not a traditional Native game, *is* a Native game. It provides an opportunity for Native people to gamble and socialize in a way that they would not be able to do otherwise, and it has only a very limited appeal to non-Natives living in the communities. In Anchorage, the sprawling Tudor Road bingo hall is a microcosm of the villages in south-central, southeastern, western, and northern Alaska. The twelve Native regions and many of the communities have signs hanging from the ceiling where people can sit and socialize with their friends back home. Every night hundreds gather to play this game.

Some households in Old Harbor and Ouzinkie seldom miss a night. George and Sophie Inga, for example, even have a door mat which says, "If we're not home, were probably playing bingo." George says that sometimes you can win at bingo in five calls, but usually it takes twelve or thirteen calls to get a winner. Village pots range from about $25 up to about $400. There is a large "early bird" pot held early in the evening to reward those who come to play early. Bingo games generally start about 7:00 p.m. and last until 10:30 or 11:00 p.m.

Card Games – In Old Harbor during the fall and winter, especially when there are rainy easterlies which keep everyone housebound, men often gather during the evening in the garage of one of the senior boat captains. They come to play cards, and their favorite games are Pan (short for Panguingue) and Pinochle.

Inside the captain's garage is a large green felt-covered table, a pool table, and a wood stove. There are cases of soda pop in various flavors piled high at one end of the garage, and the visitors simply help themselves when they are thirsty. A radio plays in the background. The programming could be rock and roll, opera, or a talk show. It makes little difference because the players are busy making small talk at the table, and the music simply fills the silence between words.

Pinochle is a widely known and well-understood card game, but Pan, although very popular in Alaska and California, is a little more obscure and deserves some description. Complete sets of rules for both games may be found in *The New Complete Hoyle* (Morehead et al. 1964: 111–115) or on the Internet, but Old Harbor men have their own variations.

In Old Harbor, Pan is a low-stakes gambling game, and the winner of each game gets $5 from each of the other players. At the beginning of a game each player antes up one $5 chip to make a pot. Pan requires at least five players but no more than eight, so the largest a pot can be is $40 and the smallest just $25. The host captain acts as banker.

There are eight decks of cards with all of the nines, tens, and jokers removed. Each player is dealt ten cards, and the object is to be the first to lay down all of the cards held plus one more drawn card. Each player, in counterclockwise rotation around the table, draws a card from the top of the deck or from the top of the adjacent discard pile. The draw card is shown face up on the table before it is played in a meld or discarded. Players may meld three or more of a kind (same rank but either the same or different suits) or three or more cards of one suit.

After selecting a card and playing down whatever he can in the way of a meld, each player places one card on the top of the discard pile. This continues until one player goes out. The winner of the hand becomes the new dealer and shuffles for the next hand. There are a few local slang words used in the game. *Paqoq*, an Alutiiq word, refers to throw-off cards. Kings are called "cowboys."

Whether Pan or Pinochle is the game of choice, participants arrive and depart with little ceremony and occasionally step outside for a smoke. If a seat is vacated there is usually someone else waiting around to get in. The game is relaxed and unhurried. The host captain's banya, located right next door, may also be going, so the men may leave the card game to take a little steam and then come back to play more cards.

All of this is reminiscent of what we might expect to find in a late eighteenth or early nineteenth century Alutiiq *qásxiq* or *kazhim*, the men's ceremonial house. Activities inside these dwellings were described by early Russian visitors to Kodiak Island (see Black 1977:93,104 and Clark 1984b:193), but such houses seem to have disappeared by the time Alaska became a territory of the United States.

FOLK SPEECH

There are a couple of regional speech patterns which give flavor to Kodiak Alutiiq communities, and these patterns shape a distinctive dialect of English commonly heard in both Ouzinkie and Old Harbor, as well as other Koniag communities. These patterns or traits are most evident in the English of elders whose first language is Alutiiq, but sometimes they also spill over into the speech of those who grew up speaking English as their first language. The patterns identified here are preliminary and incomplete, but they suggest some of the ways standard American English has been modified to suit the Alutiiq.

One distinctive pattern is syntactical. The months of the year are always referred to as "June month" or "October month" rather than "the month of June" or "the month of October" as found in standard American English. Alutiiqs also use a verb form not found in standard English. When people cut salmon fillets down to the tail, remove the skeletons, and hang them up for drying or smoking, they are said "to split fish."

One phonological feature of nonstandard English, apparently introduced by Scandinavian immigrants, has been adopted into the dialect spoken by many residents of Old Harbor and Ouzinkie. Their English lacks the *th* consonant, which is replaced by either a *t* or a *d*. For example, "Dat guy is crazy," or "Dis weader [weather] is rotten." Or if someone comes in empty-handed from a day spent out on the water and is asked what he got, the embarrassed person may exclaim, "No*t*'ing!" In this case the substitution is a glottalized *t*.

Father Michael Oleksa, a Russian Orthodox priest, thinks that this feature has crept into Alutiiq English due to the absence of the *th* phoneme in Alutiiq (Hunter 1979), but it could also be a holdover from the nonstandard English of Scandinavian immigrants. Oleksa, who once lived in Old Harbor, has apparently isolated twenty-four characteristics of Alutiiq syntax and phonology which carry over into English.

A similar feature appears when the first syllable of two-syllable words end with the phoneme *p*. The *p* is then glottalized, so that when a salmon throws itself out of the water, people will point and say, "Look! There's a jum*p*'er" or "There's a lot of hum*p*'ies in the creek."

Everyday speech as spoken in Ouzinkie and Old Harbor is also full of double and triple negatives, as in this utterance: "In them days they didn't have no doctors or nothing." Additional examples from the same speaker are: "They didn't have no lights or nothing," and "They never waste nothing."

BANYAS

Banyas or sweat baths are an essential and defining part of life in Old Harbor, Ouzinkie, and all of the other Native communities on Kodiak Island. While they may be regarded as cleansing and recreational, they also have much to do with the maintenance of mental and spiritual health, as well as socialization and ethnic identity. It is more than a coincidence that both the Kodiak Soonaq Dancers and the Tatitlek Village Dancers in Prince William Sound have a "banya dance" which includes back scrubbing and other washing motions. The banya is the perfect place to exchange local news and gossip, and for commercial fishermen, it provides an important end-of-the-day forum for sharing knowledge about fish locations, gear types, and strategies.

Banya is actually a Russian word, and it is used as both a noun and a verb, but there is strong evidence that the sweat bath was an ancient practice used for ritual purification and that the Koniags had sweat baths long before the Russians arrived in the late eighteenth century (see Clark 1984a:147; 1984b:191). The Alutiiq word for "sweat bath," *maqiwik*, attests to this. Heinrich Holmberg (1985:44), who visited during the Russian-American period, described the floor plans of sod barabaras after a visit to Kodiak in 1851:

> One of these earth rooms [in the barabara], whose number naturally depends on the number of inhabitants of the hut, serves as a steam bath, the use of which was already known to the Koniags prior to the appearance of the Russians. The steam and heat are obtained from glowing stones upon which water is tossed, and in place of scrubbing with a mop (cloth), they use a hard type of algae (rock lichen) [with] which no European of tender skin would allow themselves to be touched. After a Koniag has ended his steam bath he goes to wash himself in a river or the sea, whether it be summer or winter.

Banya Construction

The banya as found in Old Harbor is a frame outbuilding with a flat or pitched roof located close to the house, built out of plywood and covered with sheet metal (Figure 5.9). It usually has two rooms, a dress-

Fig. 5.9. *Anakenti Zeedar's banya, Old Harbor, 1997. Photo by Craig Mishler.*

ing room and a steam room, with wooden benches in each, and a connecting door or half-door. The average banya ranges from about eight to twelve feet wide and about fourteen to sixteen feet long. In Old Harbor it is a recent trend to attach smokehouses to banyas, giving the buildings more mass and wind resistance. Too often smokehouses get blown over.

The dressing room has hooks or pegs upon which to hang clothes and towels, and often a window for ventilation. The dressing room is not only used for dressing and undressing, but as a cooling off area. Bathers regularly go back and forth to the steam room and the dressing room. Some even step outside to cool down. Most banyas have a single light bulb in the steam room and another in the dressing room.

The centerpiece of the steam room is the wood stove, which is usually a fifty-five-gallon barrel that has been cut open on one end and fitted with a hinged door. The stove is placed inside an earth or gravel-filled wooden box that has been cut into one corner of the floor. On one end of the elongated barrel a fitting has been created for a six- or eight-inch diameter stovepipe that goes up through the roof. The earth or gravel base insulates the stove on the bottom and reduces the danger of fire. Piled directly on top of and on the sides of the stove is a mass of small to medium-sized rocks. Over the center of the top of the stove is a galvanized steel washtub filled with water.

On the wooden benches in the steam room are several plastic dishpans, which are used for washing. Soap and shampoo are also usually in evidence. There are also usually some thirty-gallon plastic garbage cans full of cold water and some five-gallon white plastic buckets, from which bathers may drink or splash themselves to cool off. A bucket dipper is also a prerequisite, and some households have manufactured their own using a coffee can nailed to a wooden handle.

A small woodpile sits either in the steam room or in the dressing room under a bench. Every thirty or forty minutes, the stove needs to be checked and replenished. A hot pad, heavy glove, or rag is available for this. Draft controls help to regulate the temperature of the fire, but chimney dampers are seldom found.

The Koniag-style banya used in Old Harbor and Ouzinkie is rather distinct from the style used until just recently in Tatitlek, another Alutiiq community in Prince William Sound. In Tatitlek, the wood stove was placed inside the dressing room, and when the rocks were hot, they were shoveled into the steam room, where water was poured upon them. This old Tatitlek style is probably closer to the style Alutiiqs used in antiquity. Presumably, when banyas were included as a room in the barabara, the rocks were heated outdoors in a roaring fire and then carried inside in some kind of heat-resistant container or tossed with a wooden shovel through an open window into the steam room. Just in the last few years wood stoves in Tatitlek have all been placed inside the steam room and rocks have been done away with altogether.

The Banya Experience

The ideal time for "making banya" is in late afternoon or early evening. Fishermen love to banya after a long day on the water. Most bathers wait to eat their evening meal until after they banya because eating a meal just before the banya causes bloating and discomfort. It takes about an hour to fully warm the banya, and if the weather is cold, sometimes longer.

Men and women usually banya separately, although husbands and wives often look forward to sharing the banya. In the early nineteenth century Father Gideon observed that prior to the introduction of Christianity the sweat bath was an important part of the Koniag nuptial ceremony and preceded a couple's first sexual intercourse by five days (Black 1977:95). Today washing and scrubbing each other's backs continues to be a treasured form of intimacy between spouses. In this regard, Old Harbor and Ouzinkie are again different from Tatitlek. In Tatitlek when husbands banya with their wives they get teased a lot from other men for doing so. There is social pressure in that community to maintain a separation of genders.

The algae or rock lichens that Holmberg wrote about in 1851 are called *tariqs* in Alutiiq (the plural is coined with an English-*s* ending), and they are still very much prized today for their ability to scratch and stimulate the flesh. In September 1996, Paul Kahutak took me and my daughter Susanna to a favorite place to gather *tariqs*. We combed the beach and almost gave up, but then suddenly I found a great big one tangled up in some rope at the high tide line. The heavy roots from this beach grass need to be plucked carefully to free the pieces of dry kelp and seaweed embedded in them. Then the whole thing needs to be soaked to get the sand out. *Tariqs* are the color of dry grass, and they curl up into a piece that fits easily into the palm of the hand.

The water dipper is used to mix hot water from the stove with cold water. The hot and the cold are mixed in a dishpan until the water is comfortably lukewarm. Each person has his or her own dishpan, and most banyas contain four or five. Most people like to wash with soap and washcloth, rinse off, and then stay around to get a good steam.

Every so often water from the washtub is dipped up and tossed onto the hot rocks to make the room hotter. When this happens, a heat wave travels across the room. Temperatures range from about 180 to 210 degrees Fahrenheit. If it gets too hot, bathers will sit or lie on the floor, where the temperatures are a little cooler. The average banya probably lasts forty-five minutes to an hour, but some people stay in for hours on end. Banyas are no longer followed by a plunge into a river or the sea, but some families use water hoses from their house to cool themselves off.

Here are my field notes from April 10, 1992:

After volleyball I was invited up to Sven and Mary Haakanson's place for a banya, and when I got there all the boat captains were in the dressing room having a lively conversation. Those I recognized included Carl,

Jack, and Rocky Christiansen, Rick Berns, and Rick Pewtress (the resident carpenter).

I undressed and went inside—the largest banya I have ever seen. It could seat 15 people. After I had been in for five or ten minutes Jack Christiansen came in and turned on the water hose and sprayed down the entire stove until the heat was just incredible. I realized that this was a test to see what I could take, and I lasted about another ten minutes before escaping to the dressing room. This was difficult because Jack was trying to engage me in conversation, and I was getting very woozy.

By the time I got out to the dressing room to join the other men, some had gone but others lingered and we talked about subsistence bear hunting and sea lion hunting. Carl told me that I stood up under the heat pretty well, but actually I had to move to a lower bench to breathe.

Banya Testimonies

Banyas are much more popular in Old Harbor than they are in Ouzinkie, but I asked people in both communities to tell me why they liked them. Some people are not fond of banyas, but they are in a distinct minority. Martha Anderson of Ouzinkie, for example, told me: "I never did like banyas. There's too much heat, and you'd always come out smelling like smoke." Here is what others have said:

Freddy Christiansen (1996):
  Banyas is right in the same category as seals. You got to have them.

Ron Bernsten (1997):
  CM: How often do you banya?
  RB: Three or four times a week. I get the wood every day.
  CM: Driftwood?
  RB: Yeah. Scrap wood or whatever I can get.
  CM: And does your wife like to go in too?
  RB: Oh yes. All of my kids. My kids were banya-ing before they could walk. That's no kidding, [at the age of] four or five months we took them in. And that's about the only major thing they miss [now that they are away in school] is their banyas.
  CM: So you like to banya better than a shower?
  RB: Much better. You get a lot cleaner. You feel a lot better.
  CM: How hot do you like it?
  RB: The hotter the better [laughs]. As you get a little older though, you kind of cool down. Not as hot as I used to take them.
  CM: You use those tariqs? Wunnaqis?
  RB: Oh yes.
  CM: Wunnaqis, alders are they?
  RB: Yeah. We call them oohisaqs. *In summer time when they're green and you've got a sore muscle or something, go get them and slap yourself with them. Boy. I don't know if it's the chlorophyll or whatever that's in the*

leaves, but boy it just draws that, fixes those aching muscles right up. If you've got any aches that calls for heat to fix them, you go into a banya with one of them and boy, I guarantee you'll be cured.

CM: You think they're good for colds too?

RB: Cure all. Lumbago. Banya will even fix a broken romance.

Walt Erickson (1997):

WE: Oh yeah. That's a way of life, banyas. [When I was young] we had no showers. We had to carry water and wood all the time. No running water, no.

CM: What do you like about banyas?

WE: I just like it. It's relaxing, and to me it's cleaner. Oh yeah. Showering, you just spread the dirt around, and it's still there when you get done. But a banya takes everything but the skin, believe me. And I think it's healthy. You don't have any skin problems when you have a banya twice, three times a week.

CM: I remember one time you came in from the banya. You'd just shaved. Do you shave in the banya?

WE: Oh yeah. I never cut myself in the banya. But I can do it in the sink at home, and I cut myself all the time. I shave three times a week, and it's always in the banya.

CM: And I guess the women like it just as much as the men, huh?

WE: Seem to be more so. Yeah, they stay in there longer. Well they get there and shoot the breeze. You know what I mean. They tell stories and make plans. This is where it all happens, in the banya.

CM: Do the women usually go in first and then the men later, or how does it usually work?

WE: Well, I don't know. I've always went banya with my wife. We've always done it. We're the only ones. It's mostly all men, and women. But my wife don't like to go in with crowds, and she likes to, you know, be with me, and she knows that I need help now that I'm old, you know [laughs]. She scrubs my back.

CM: And you scrub hers too.

WE: Oh yeah.

Nick Pestrikoff Sr. (1997):

CM: Do you really like banyas? Do you have a banya?

NP: Oh, I'm just about done building a brand new banya. There is no better way to bathe, you know. I mean, that's it, far as I'm concerned, anyway.

CM: Why do you like that better than a shower?

NP: Well, for the simple fact it's real wet heat, you know, damp heat, and it's going to make you pour with sweat like crazy. I mean, you just, it comes pouring out. You know boxers and those types, how profusely they sweat? They don't sweat, compared to us in a banya [laughs]. I mean it just *comes off in rivulets, you know. And that in itself is a real cleansing action for the body, you know.*

I mean, going in a shower and soaping down and rinsing up and going out—you're clean on the surface. But the banya-type situation cleans you inside out, you know. 'Cause your body is going to get rid of those wastes in your sweat, you know. . . . But in a banya situation, if you're a healthy person, everything that comes out of your body, your body would like to get rid of anyway.

CM: Well, generally do the women go in separate from the men, or do you like to banya with your wife?

NP: No, no. My wife and I banya together all the time, and once in a great while we'll take our grandchildren in with us.

Paul Kahutak (1997) had a terrifying experience in a banya, but it had nothing to do with the heat. He was enjoying a steam with his wife Martha when the 1964 Good Friday tidal wave hit Old Harbor:

I know Ashouwaks, they used to live right down a little ways from me. They used to make banya all the time. That's when she came up, you know, after that earthquake. So what you come, Lawrence came up. We were babysitting one of his boys. He said, "Could we take banya?" We said, "Go ahead. We'll babysit the boy, youngest boy." After while he said, "It's all over now, no more earthquake. You could take a bath." We did. Me and Martha. I walked in there, and after while Martha went out, and she looked out the window, and she said, "Holy smokes! The people are running up the hill." And I told her, "Yeah, there must be water coming up. Let's get out of here!" So, what you come, we run out, just grabbed the towel, put my coat on. Everybody hollering. I see the water coming right up to the road. It got so far and it quit. So we went up the hill, and all the people were all up there.

A Reflective Note

With banyas in mind I would be remiss if I did not admit that Kodiak Alutiiq culture has changed my own way of life. After enjoying the sensual stimulation and conversation of banyas in Larsen Bay, Port Lions, and Old Harbor over the years, I decided to take some measurements and build one beside my own home in Anchorage. My daughter Susanna assisted me, and we completed it in the summer of 1996.

Since then I have invited my Alutiiq friends who fly to Anchorage for extended stays to come and banya at our house because I know they miss their banyas back home. My wife Barbara and I entertain couples and serve them light refreshments afterwards. Although I did not have all of this in mind when I built the banya, hosting sweat baths has enhanced my friendships with Alutiiqs and has increased my opportunities to socialize and interview them about their traditions.

GRAVE ICONOGRAPHY

Throughout rural Alaska there are many different traditional ways of marking and identifying graves, and each ethnic group and each region has a defined style. Very little research on these ethnic and regional styles has been undertaken, even though they provide great examples of folk art. Alutiiq graves are always marked with wooden Russian Orthodox crosses and are often beautifully and richly decorated with real and artificial flowers. Many graves also have rectangular wooden "boxes" around them. They are sacred objects which seek to preserve the memory of the deceased, and they are artfully constructed and patterned.

In Old Harbor, grave crosses are painted three different colors: white, blue, and yellow, although one respondent said there was no particular

Fig. 5.10. *Old Harbor child's grave with toy boat. Photo by Craig Mishler.*

148   Black Ducks and Salmon Bellies

significance to the colors. White is the preferred color of the crosses on all of the Ouzinkie graves. The three-barred Orthodox cross that marks virtually all graves has a traditional symbolism:

The lower angled bar is believed to represent the agony of Christ's death, showing that he experienced true suffering. Another tradition holds that the upward thrust of the bar recalls "the good thief" who confessed Christ as Savior while they both were being crucified and was assured that he would be with Him in Heaven (Smith et al. 1994:109).

Within each regional style, there are family traditions, which could be called variants. Several of the graves I visited in Old Harbor, for example, have small toy wooden fishing boats, purse seiners, laid next to the cross at the head of the grave (Figure 5.10). I am told these boats are used to mark the graves of young boys. It used to be that every boy had a toy purse seiner, and they would pretend to be fishermen by catching minnows in a gunnysack and filling the holds of the toy boats with the minnows. The toy boats were made by the boys' fathers or grandfathers.

Fig. 5.11. *Old Harbor elder's grave, 1997. Note cap of deceased on top of the cross. Photo by Craig Mishler.*

One recent grave has the man's favorite cap draped over the top of the cross (Figure 5.11). Another has a rubber fisherman's boot (Figure 5.12). Still another grave has a beer can next to it. I debated about whether the beer can was negligently left there by someone who was disrespectful, or whether it was put there as a reminder of the dead man's jolly lifestyle. Knowing the man while he was alive, I finally decided to

Expressive Culture 149

support the latter interpretation, figuring that if his family didn't like the beer can there, they would have removed it.

In Ouzinkie the newer graves have a high white box structure over them that is filled with soil and allows the planting and arranging of flowers. One grave also has a red, white, and blue ribbon tied around the cross (Figure 5.17), a feature not visible in Old Harbor. The most elaborate grave marker displays a variation on the Orthodox cross, with thin angled slats covering the ends of the top two bars (Figure 5.14). This grave also features a miniature glass-sided "house" that could also be interpreted as a replica

Fig. 5.12. *Old Harbor grave with blue cross and old rubber boot. Photo by Craig Mishler.*

Fig. 5.13. *Old Harbor fisherman's grave overlooking Sitkalidak Strait. Photo by Craig Mishler.*

Fig. 5.14. *Ouzinkie grave with miniature chapel containing icon and Easter eggs. Photo by Craig Mishler*

of the Orthodox Church since it has a blue onion dome on it (Figure 5.15). Inside this "house" is an Orthodox icon, a candle, and three colored Easter eggs, suggesting the resurrection of Christ.

It is noteworthy that the names of the deceased are generally not included on the grave markers, although there are some exceptions. In Old Harbor, there are a few graves with the names of the persons laid to rest painted on the cross, but to identify a particular grave, you usually need assistance from someone in the community.

Clockwise from top left: **Fig. 5.15. *Closeup of Ouzinkie miniature grave chapel with Orthodox onion dome;* Fig. 5.16. *Ouzinkie grave with raised box;* Fig. 5.17. *Ouzinkie grave with red, white, and blue ribbon on the cross. Photos by Craig Mishler.***

CONCLUSION

It is through expressive culture in its various renewable and evolving forms—music and dance, folk art, games, folk speech, banyas, and holiday celebrations—that people find and maintain their social and ethnic identity. These symbolic forms, along with kinship ties and association with place, bond people to each other and make communities. While banyas continue to be popular and perhaps always will be, traditional games, masking, basketry, and traditional stories in the Alutiiq language are all rapidly fading beneath the twentieth-century horizon. Meanwhile, Alutiiq singing and dancing are enjoying something of a revival, and other forms such as buoy bouncing, bingo, Pan, folk speech, and graveyard art are just now coming into their own.

Chapter Six

Subsistence and "Food for the Day"

In Kodiak area communities, subsistence is a moving target. It is like a pair of black ducks flying low and fast over the water or a young bull sea lion diving off a rock, or the bright flash of a school of silver salmon moving in the bottom of a clear creek. To see those ducks and sea lions and salmon, it is necessary to visit the villages in every season, to see subsistence as an annual cycle of many activities focused on many kinds of wild foods found in many places.

Long before commercially processed foods became available, Alutiiqs in Old Harbor and Ouzinkie lived almost entirely off of the sea. And the Alutiiqs know that if American capitalism and the wage and cash economy ever collapse, they can always go back to living the ways of their ancestors. This is true, however, only if the traditional knowledge of subsistence practices and of wild resources is passed down by the elders to each new generation. Because their subsistence grew out of an autonomous and sustainable economic system, it seems likely that they will not starve to death. As Freddy Christiansen (1997) once said to me: "I think that's what holds rural Alaska together, is subsistence. You know, the economy of the world can fail, and by golly, we'll still live; we'll still eat, and you know that's very important to us."

One time when I was visiting the late Mike and Jenny Chernikoff at their house in Ouzinkie, they said: "We don't eat anything from the land. We eat from the sea." As elders, their diet was shaped along very traditional lines, lines established before the availability of big game such as deer and elk, which were introduced to Kodiak and Afognak in the late 1920s. The Chernikoffs were so conservative they didn't even eat hares, another introduced species, believing them to be related to cats. Still, they admitted to buying beef and chicken at the grocery store.

Figure 6.0 illustrates the seasonal round of resource use in Old Harbor and Ouzinkie. This table contrasts rather sharply with the one constructed by Aron Crowell (1994:228) for the Koniag of 1800. A major difference is that people today no longer hunt whales, porpoises, or fur seals, while the people of 1800 never hunted deer or elk. The only major difference between Old Harbor and Ouzinkie harvest patterns is that Ouzinkie makes no use of brown bear.

FALL AND WINTER

The subsistence way of life slows down just a bit in the winter months, for this is the time of year when weather conditions are at their worst, and regard for personal safety keeps people off the hills and off the water for days or weeks at a time. But there are breaks between the storms, and people do get out.

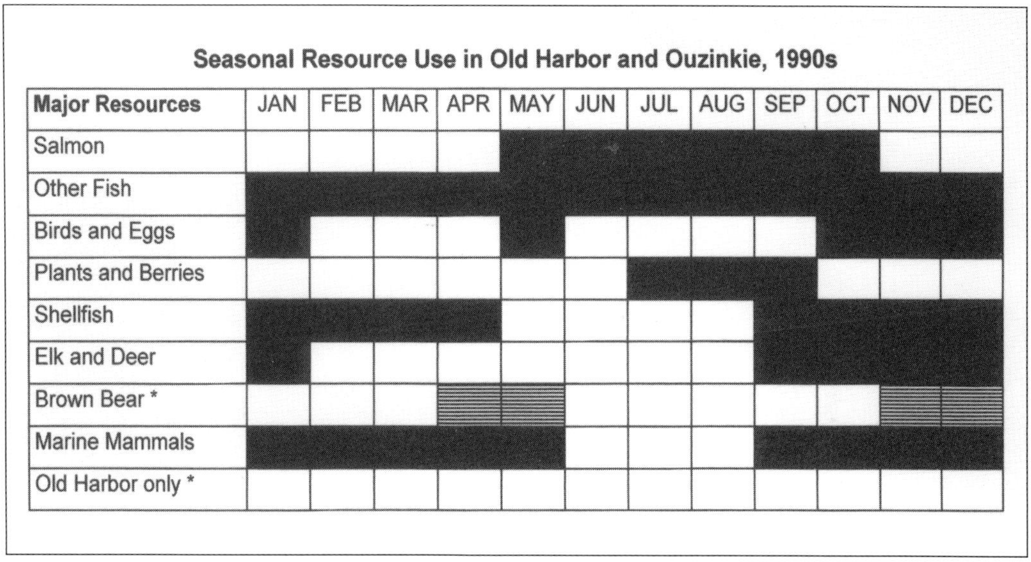

Seasonal Resource Use in Old Harbor and Ouzinkie, 1990s

Major Resources	JAN	FEB	MAR	APR	MAY	JUN	JUL	AUG	SEP	OCT	NOV	DEC
Salmon					■	■	■	■	■	■		
Other Fish	■	■	■	■	■	■	■	■	■	■	■	■
Birds and Eggs	■				■	■			■	■	■	■
Plants and Berries							■	■	■			
Shellfish	■	■	■	■					■	■	■	■
Elk and Deer	■	■									■	■
Brown Bear *				▤	▤					▤	▤	
Marine Mammals	■	■	■	■	■				■	■	■	■
Old Harbor only *												

Fig. 6.0.

One of the activities that people enjoy in the early winter is deer and elk hunting. Deer were introduced to Long Island in 1924 and to Kodiak Island in 1934, and for many years they remained on the north end of the island. Elk were first introduced in 1929. Two elders, John Nelson Sr. of Port Lions (1994), and Ed Opheim Sr. of Pleasant Harbor (1997), told me independently that they were present when the elk were released, and the biologist in charge told them that the elk were being put there for the benefit of the Natives, for their subsistence.

Since the 1950s deer have multiplied to the point where their numbers exceed one hundred thousand, and although deer did not migrate to Old Harbor until the late 1960s or early 1970s, by the 1990s the south end of the Kodiak Island had more deer than the north end. Elk numbers, on the other hand, have remained fairly low, ranging from about twelve hundred to fifteen hundred in recent years, partly because they are largely confined to Afognak Island and Raspberry Island. The animals seem to prefer timbered areas for cover. Occasional hard winters with heavy snows and low temperatures kill off many deer fawns and older bucks, as well as elk calves, but in successive mild winters deer and elk numbers quickly rebound.

Although deer hunting season on the Kodiak Island archipelago opens on August 1 and continues until December 31, except on the Kodiak road system, hunters in Ouzinkie and Old Harbor generally wait until late October or November to begin hunting. By this time the first snows of the year drive the deer down from higher elevations, and it is much less strenuous not to have to climb up into the mountains to find them and pack them out.

Federal subsistence hunting regulations off the Kodiak road system allow a bag limit of five deer per family each hunting season, while state general hunting regulations off the road system allow a bag limit of four deer. Both federal and state regulations also allow for "designated hunter" permits, although the federal system is more lenient. Recognizing that only a small percentage of each community actively hunts, these regulations allow Kodiak Island residents to take additional deer to be shared with families that are unable to hunt. In this way elders, persons with handicaps, and single women with children are provided for. These designated hunter permits were implemented to recognize a pattern of harvesting and sharing that was already in place.

By late November or December deer are sighted along the beaches, so hunters can often spot them when out in their skiffs. It is an easy thing then, to land the skiff and stalk and shoot the animals from the beach or from the dead grasses just above the beach. After beaching their skiff, hunters secure it by tying the bowline to a piece of driftwood and digging a trench in the gravel to secure the driftwood. An eye needs to be kept on the skiff on the incoming tide, however, to keep it from being washed away.

Since sport hunting and subsistence hunting for deer both occur in the same areas at the same time of year, there is an increasing amount of competition between sport hunters and subsistence hunters for the same animals. An Old Harbor subsistence hunter, for example, told me that in the winter of 1997–1998 he spotted a nice-looking buck while out riding in his skiff, so he landed on the beach, took out his rifle, and shot it. To his amazement a sport-hunting guide and his client came over the hill and claimed the deer, saying it belonged to them because they were stalking it before he shot it.

Elk have become a traditional Native food source since the 1940s, and until 1997 they have always been managed under Alaska sport hunting regulations. In 1997 the Federal Regional Subsistence Advisory Council for Kodiak and Aleutians and the Federal Subsistence Board approved a proposal that established the customary and traditional use of elk on federal lands, limited to the northwest part of Afognak Island. In 1998 both the Federal Advisory Council and the Federal Subsistence Board approved implementing regulations for the taking of elk. Elk may also be taken under state regulations all over Afognak Island and Raspberry Island, but only through general hunting regulations and not under subsistence regulations.

The prime area for elk hunting is on southwest Afognak Island, an area open only by state drawing permit. Although they participate, Ouzinkie and Old Harbor residents are not always successful in getting a drawing permit through the random draw. To get drawn for an elk-hunting permit in the fall, hunters must submit an application the May before they hunt and watch the newspapers for publication of the names of those lucky enough to get a permit.

When someone local from Ouzinkie, Port Lions, or Old Harbor is drawn, they generally organize a hunt through hunting partnerships. Hunting partnerships have gradually developed between several Ouzinkie, Old Harbor, and Port Lions Native families. Old Harbor men bring their purse seiners up to Ouzinkie or Port Lions, pick up their hunting partners, and then anchor offshore from Afognak Island while they go ashore and do day hunts on foot. At night they return to the boats to eat, shower, and socialize. If the hunt is successful, the meat is loaded on board and transported home. Elk is considered a delicacy and is cut into steaks for frying, butchered for oven roasts, made into stew, or ground up along with deer meat to make meatloaves.

Elk hunters are always worried about bears getting to their meat before they can pack it down to the boat. Theodore Squartsoff of Ouzinkie once advised me: "If you get a deer and can't get it back to camp, hang it up in a tree and tie your t-shirt or sweatshirt around it. Your body oil will keep the bears away. We did that once over in Afognak, and everyone around us lost their elk meat to bears except us."

Although I have never gone on an elk hunt, here is one elk hunting strategy used by Ouzinkie and Old Harbor men during the 1990s, drawn from my field notes for April 17, 1991:

A couple of the younger men climb up high on the mountains and spook the elk down to the lower altitudes, while the older men wait down below to shoot the animals as they come down the mountain. Last year a party of twelve men went over together. They have access to a truck from the Danger Bay logging camp to haul their meat out, and they also use float planes and motorized boats on Afognak Lake. With VHF radios they call a boat in whenever they have made a kill and have meat to move, but they can't use these radios to talk to each other while in the act of hunting. Despite all of this technology they claim that elk hunting is still extremely hard work. It takes at least five men to pack an elk out from a remote area.

At the same time that men go out to hunt deer and elk, they usually take along a shotgun and hunt ducks. On a day when deer don't show themselves, hunters will turn their attention to sea ducks, which winter over in the protected waters of the Kodiak archipelago. One favorite place to stalk and shoot ducks is on the flats. Flats are level areas dotted with small freshwater ponds, and the tall reeds make good cover for the hunters if they crouch down.

Surprisingly, stormy weather is prime time for duck hunting. This is because ducks take shelter during a storm and hole up in small lagoons or along creeks where they can be out of the wind. Hunters know these lagoons very well and are willing to brave the elements to get to them. Some areas can be reached more easily on a four-wheeler than in a skiff.

In the fall time Theodore Squartsoff and his son, J. R., always go up to their old family place at Barabara Cove, in upper Kizhuyak Bay, about fifteen water miles from Ouzinkie. They are often joined by Theodore's brothers, Martin and Peter, who also have their own cabins. For many generations this has been their family's traditional deer and duck hunting camp, and I was fortunate to spend a few days there in October 1996. From my field notes:

The steps in processing ducks is described as plucking, singeing, scrubbing and rinsing, gutting, rinsing again and soaking overnight, and wrapping and labeling. Theodore folds each duck in plastic wrap, slips the wrapped duck in a ziplock bag, sucks the air out of the bag with his mouth, and then seals it all tightly with masking tape. He labels each duck by species and by age: Y for young and O for old. I noticed he marked one duck O+. He says this is important when it comes time to cook them because it only takes about an hour to roast young ducks but two hours to roast mature

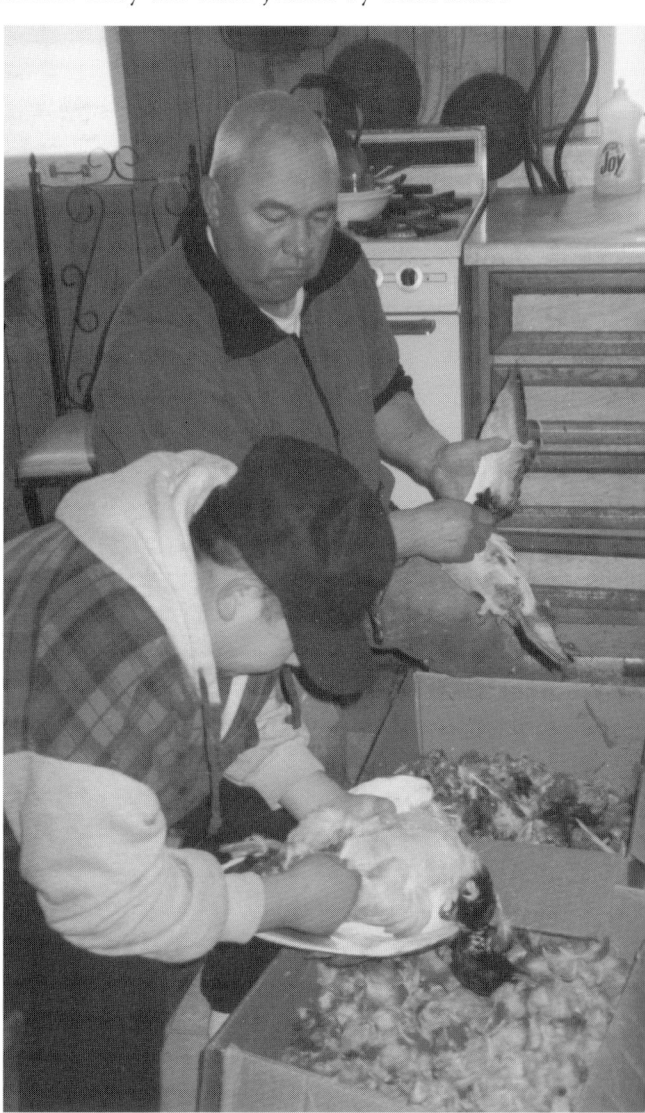

Fig. 6.1. *Theodore Squartsoff Sr. and Theodore Jr. plucking ducks at Barabara Cove, October 1996. Photo by Craig Mishler.*

158   Black Ducks and Salmon Bellies

ducks, and for obvious reasons you don't want to mix the two together. When he gets home he vacuum seals each duck individually and puts them in the freezer.

While visiting Ouzinkie in late January 1997, I was surprised again to find Theodore still going out to hunt ducks at the very end of the hunting season. But what he said was that it was his last chance to get fresh ducks for another eight months, and fresh ducks taste much better than frozen ones.

Here are some additional things I learned about migratory birds in Old Harbor, following interviews with Gary Price, Jeff Peterson, Buddy Pestrikoff, Glenn Clough, George Inga Sr., and Anakenti Zeedar (1994). The notes are taken from my trip report for December 15, 1994:

Fig.6.2. Theodore Squartsoff Sr. singeing a duck at his camp in Barabara Cove, October 1996. Photo by Craig Mishler.

1) Emperor geese are seen on the outside of Sitkalidak Island during the winter. They also come into Shearwater Bay during the early evening to drink fresh water. Apparently they feed offshore during the day. They are seen only singly as stragglers, or in pairs—no flocks. There are also a few found at the head of McDonald's Lagoon (aka Fox Lagoon), in Rolling Bay, at Sheep Island, and on the beach at Bush Point when it's blowing northeast.

2) Black brant come through in the spring but are too skinny to hunt. They are occasionally seen in McDonald's Lagoon, a resting and feeding area for many other species of birds.

3) Steller's eiders used to be heavily hunted in the Sitkalidak Straits during the 1930s and 1940s when they were very plentiful. Apparently they are still abundant locally. There are now an estimated 100 of them in McDonald's Lagoon, another 60 or so in the Sitkalidak narrows, some in Three Saints Bay, some at Port Otto, some in Kaiuganak Bay, and some in Natalia Bay. They are easy to confuse with rock ducks (harlequins) from a distance. One younger hunter said that no one hunts them today because of their taste, but this contradicts the statements by elders about traditional use.

4) *Eiders:* There are no common eiders or spectacled eiders around Old Harbor. However, one hunter reported seeing a few spectacled eiders north of Ugak Bay on the way to Kodiak, and another said there used to be some in McDonald's Lagoon before the 1964 earthquake and tidal wave. King eiders are seen in the Sitkalidak narrows, McDonald's Lagoon, and Newman's Bay, but the perception is that they are decreasing—fewer birds and smaller flocks. This decrease began well before the oil spill. Eiders mix in with black scoters. Most of the king eiders seen now are juveniles with only one or two mature drakes. They arrive in December or early January. King eiders are prized by sport hunters but not sought after by subsistence hunters. One respondent said that they have an iodine-like taste. Another is convinced that the king eiders are a local stock and has imposed his own bag limit of one adult pair for each hunter, even though ADF&G regulations allow up to 15 a day.

5) *Canadian Geese* (nuklluk): There is a flock of Canadian geese that were transplanted by ADF&G and which circulate between Seal Bay, Tanganak, and McDonald's Lagoon [aka Fox Lagoon]. Regarded by some Old Harbor residents as Fish and Game's "pets," they are seen virtually all year round. One hunter claims he takes them occasionally, even though they are protected by regulation from any hunting. He finds them very tasty and usually gets one for Thanksgiving and one for Christmas. Old-timers used to hunt them before they were protected.

6) The favorite ducks for Old Harbor subsistence hunters are black scoters (kugumiaq or whistlers), white-winged scoters (terpans), and mallards (niskayduk)—in that order, and they are hunted with shotguns while on the wing. Mallards are avoided in the early fall because they acquire a strong, bitter taste as a result of eating too many fish eggs. Harlequin ducks (kainyuq or rock ducks), buffleheads, and pintails were formerly hunted but are not sought after much today. Some species of ducks, such as canvasbacks, are not eaten at all. A good duck soup is made by putting the ducks in a roasting pan with water, rice, and potatoes, and "boiling the hell out of them." When they're done, you make a thick gravy out of a flour and water mixture stirred into the broth.

7) People in Old Harbor hunt ducks from early October through February. The season on freshwater ducks is fine as it stands, but some people

feel that the sea duck season should be adjusted to start later, on November 1, and run until late February or early March to provide more opportunity. This is partly because the sea ducks don't start arriving until November and December.

8) Lots of subsistence duck hunting is done in late afternoon or early evening. Surprising to nonresidents is the fact that bad weather is one of the best times to hunt ducks. A hard northwest winter wind will freeze over the lakes and creeks and force all the freshwater ducks down to inshore areas wherever fresh water meets salt water.

9) Old Harbor elders have noticed drastic declines in recent years of many kinds of sea birds, including parakeet auklets, oystercatchers, cormorants, arctic terns, and harlequin ducks. The decline in harlequins was most pronounced after the oil spill. All of these species were used for subsistence except the arctic terns. Two Alutiiq words used to describe declining populations of birds and animal species are iiyudut *and* iillut. *When populations are on the increase, they say* amaliut *(Zeedar and Inga 1994).*

*10) Tufted puffins (*tununak *or sea parrots) are also rapidly disappearing. There used to be thousands of them on the small islands, and when they took off the sky was black. Puffins and puffin eggs were traditionally gathered by hand from their nests burrowed along the cliff tops during the spring, but it was a risky proposition because the puffins would often bite and scratch [see also Davydov 1977:230]. Puffins would sometimes kill themselves trying to escape from their nests because they would be unable to get airborne quickly and would crash against the rocks below. Puffin skins were saved and sewn into winter parkas, and the brightly colored puffin beaks (*chuquwit*) were used to decorate the parkas.*

On December 9, 1994, I interviewed Pete and Melvin Squartsoff of Port Lions, and recorded the following information, supplemented later on by their brother Theodore:

1) Emperor geese sometimes land right in Settlers Cove during the spring, but they are not hunted. This is in contrast to Akhiok, where they are more abundant and are hunted.

2) Black brant come through in the spring when the weather is bad, but are not hunted because they are so skinny. They come into the lagoons and eat leaf kelp, and that's exactly what they taste like. If they came through in the fall when they were fat, they might be good to eat, but they are never seen in the fall.

3) In Port Lions and Ouzinkie the universe of ducks is divided into "saltwater ducks" (sometimes called "sea ducks") and "freshwater ducks" (some-

times called "puddle ducks"). This distinction may come as much from biologists as from Natives, but à la Levi-Strauss, there is also an emic structural opposition between "soup ducks" and "roasting ducks." This dichotomy directly corresponds to the opposition between "saltwater ducks" and "freshwater ducks." Where you get them determines how you cook them.

To make a good duck soup you have to have fresh sea ducks, because what makes the soup so good is the duck's fresh blood. Duck soup with lots of blood in it tastes a lot like a broth made from harbor seal meat. Freshwater ducks can be used for soup, but they do not have much blood in them. Saltwater ducks include all of the scoters, harlequins, oldsquaws, and mergansers. Freshwater ducks include mallards, buffleheads, goldeneyes (both Barrow's and common), widgeons, gadwalls, green-winged teals, and scaups (aka bluebills).

4) The favorite ducks for subsistence hunters in Port Lions and Ouzinkie are black scoters and white-winged scoters for soup, and goldeneyes and mallards for roasting. All birds are plucked and singed, never skinned. Skinning ducks is frowned upon as a lazy sport hunting practice. Oldsquaws also rank highly for soup and are heavily targeted. They are found by the hundreds in Whale Pass and stay around all winter. Black scoters are also very abundant.

5) Eiders: The only common eiders that have been seen anywhere in the area are just off a rocky island at the end of the Kodiak airport runway. Spectacled eiders have never been sighted anywhere in the area. King eiders are found in Whale Pass but are rapidly declining. There used to be thousands of them, but now there are only a couple hundred left. It is believed that many of them die by hitting the lights of crab boats. King eiders are sometimes hunted for subsistence.

6) Steller's eiders are very abundant and populations are increasing. There are big flocks of them in front of the old Afognak village and some come right into the Port Lions boat harbor. But Stellers are never hunted for subsistence. The old people called them "kelp ducks" and said they weren't any good to eat—that they would give you the runs.

7) Rock ducks (harlequins) are easy to get but not hunted very often because they get lice on them and their guts will turn blue. You have to clean them right away after you shoot them. Buffleheads and mallards also have lice. Buffleheads are occasionally hunted but are not preferred because of their small size. Common and red-breasted mergansers are seen but seldom hunted because so often they taste fishy. Occasionally oystercatchers and parakeet auklets ("sea quail" or "kanushkis") are taken. Parakeet auklets were traditionally hunted on the water on moonlit nights or at daybreak and were featured at Christmas dinner.

8) As for hunting seasons, mallards and goldeneyes are never hunted after January because they get so skinny. But black scoters ("whistlers"), old-

squaws, and scaups stay fat and are hunted until early March, at which time they leave. It was customary to hunt ducks in late winter (March and April) because the traditional Easter dinner always consisted of duck soup, pirok *(i.e. fish pie)*, and kolich *(a special bread)*. The scoters just come in a few at a time in December and slowly build up in numbers through the rest of the winter. Local hunters agree it would really be good to have the sea duck season extended until early March—especially for scoters and oldsquaws.

In addition to ducks, Alutiiqs also enjoy eating other birds, some of which have medicinal as well as nutritional value. When I asked Walt Erickson Sr. (1997) what his favorite Native food is, he responded:

I like ptarmigan because I guess it's almost impossible to get, but that's my favorite, is ptarmigan. Because that's what I was raised on, and my belief is that ptarmigan is a good medicine. We had no doctors. My Mom was the doctor. Dr. Mom, they called her. But that's what we use if you had a fever or anything, we'd always have ptarmigan, boil it and just drink the water, and this ptarmigan has all the herbs, and all the good stuff that comes out of meat, in the ptarmigan. Every time you have ptarmigan juice like that, boil the daylights out of it, and drink that and you'll get well, believe me. I believe in that. . . . Well, we take what we can get, you know. I even ate seagulls back when we couldn't get anything else. And the reason why we had that, we had no money to buy shells, so we'd take salt salmon and put it on a hook, and the seagull would eat the salt salmon, and we'd get our meat that way, from the seagull.

Fig. 6.3. *Theodore Squartsoff's scrubbed mallard duck. Photo by Craig Mishler, October 1996.*

The winter months have always been favorite months for digging clams and gathering other shellfish. Clams are a favorite Alutiiq food, and many of the old villages around Kodiak Island, such as Larsen Bay and Akhiok, are virtually built on top of shell middens. In ancient times when fish and game were scarce, clams undoubtedly provided a staple winter food supply.

Old Harbor and Ouzinkie people generally go after butter clams, littleneck clams, small bidarkis (chitons), and a few geoducks. Crab (dungeness, tanner, and king) is enjoyed but has not become a regular part of the diet. Crab came into prominence during the 1960s primarily as a commercially harvested species.

Around Old Harbor there used to be two favorite clamming areas, at Sheep Island, and at the Culvert. The Culvert, an area accessible from the road just outside of the lagoon, has not been actively used during the 1990s after we collected samples and ran a series of hydrocarbon laboratory tests on them. Although initially we suspected contamination from the *Exxon Valdez* oil spill, we discovered that the clams were actually contaminated from bilge oil coming out of the small boat harbor. Sheep Island remains the favorite area, especially when there are big minus tides. One time when I went there, four or five purse seiners had pulled up on the beach, and at least a dozen people were out digging and gathering *aridaqs* (bidarkis). One of the purse seiners had a tape deck or radio playing loud popular music, so there was a very modern air about this traditional activity. The *aridaqs*, which cling to the underside of rocks, are frequently eaten raw, or taken home and covered with boiling water. Their orange-colored fleshy "feet" are very chewy and palatable and are often tossed into a chowder. Butter clams and littlenecks (the latter also called "steamers") are eaten several different ways. In the words of Freddy Christiansen of Old Harbor (1997):

FC: We've got clam fettucine, we've got half-shelled clams, we've got clam chowder, we've got, I mean steamers. We've got a tremendous amount of ways of cooking clams, and that's a very important subsistence food also. You know my brother that passed away [Jack Christiansen]. He was a clam digger from heaven. He could dig clams like nobody else can dig clams, and one day there was two dungeness crab boats digging clams on Sheep Island for bait, and he went out and said: "That's not bait. That's a very important subsistence food in Old Harbor, and that's not showing much respect towards the community, taking that out and using it as bait."

CM: So did they stop?

FC: Yes they did. Yes they did stop.

CM: Well, it's good that people are standing up for their values.

FC: We really fight for what we believe in. Not just what's good for Old Harbor or good for, you know, there's a miscommunication as far as, we're very protective of our area, and that's not because we want everything, and we want to hoard everything in this area. It's because it's one of our ways of being.

CM: It's part of who you are, right?

FC: Yeah. It's part of who we are, and it's a way of being aware of conservation.

Around Ouzinkie there are several traditional places to dig clams. One of the favorites is Sourdough Beach, which is accessible on foot or by trail on a four-wheeler. Other areas, which can only be reached by skiff, are Cat Island (where the butter clams have black shells), on the Kodiak Island side of the Narrows, and Camel's Rock, where there is an offshore reef that goes dry during minus tides. At Camel's, the clams are not buried in sand as they generally are elsewhere, but lie under a layer of kelp and fucus. Instead of digging, clammers going to Camel's use their shovels to peel back the kelp and fucus. One shovelful can produce seven or eight clams, a mix of steamers and butters.

Before the 1964 earthquake Camel's Rock reef used to be home to abundant cockles, which were a favorite in Ouzinkie, but today only a few cockles remain. Old Harbor has also seen cockles disappear since the tidal wave. One traditional way they used to get them was to walk along the beach on a minus tide and push slender sticks down into the holes made by cockles as they dove into the sand. The cockles would then open up and grab onto the stick with their shells. At this point they could be pulled up and dropped into a bucket.

It used to be very common for Ouzinkie villagers to go clamming together at night during December on big minus tides. They would just pile into skiffs and take along Coleman lanterns to dig by. It was a major social activity. After the *Exxon Valdez* oil spill and numerous paralytic shellfish poisoning cases, including two fatalities, however, that tradition has disappeared.

Here is another entry from my field notes for Wednesday, March 14, 1990, when I was collecting oil spill samples near Ouzinkie with Theodore and Martin Squartsoff:

The wind came up this a.m., so Theodore decided not to take us out in the skiff. The harbor looked O.K., but there was a lot of chop and white water out in the Narrows. Instead, Theodore and Martin took us over to Sourdough beach to get samples, and we rode with them on four-wheelers over an icy, twisting trail. We arrived on the south side of Sourdough beach at 8:45 a.m. and found an abundance of butter and steamer clams, mussels, bidarkis, and a few urchins. One large rock at the far outer end of the beach is used as a tide marker—"We don't dig clams unless that rock is dry." This morning's tide was only a -1 but it was enough. According to Martin, the rock itself is a "hot spot" for clams, but all of the ones we got near it were very small. We tried digging some big geoducks, but they were deep into the sandy end of beach, and we were unsuccessful in finding any. You have to dig deep and dig fast to get geoducks. Theodore doesn't think it's worth the energy you have to expend for them. After collecting samples on the south side of Sourdough we sped across the peninsula to the windy north side where we collected more bidarkis from beneath high cliffs. At this spot the bidarkis are large and plentiful.

On May 19, 1992, when Theodore and I went across the Narrows to Soldier's Bay to collect shellfish samples, I became impressed with the importance of traditional knowledge. Although we had a -2.3 tide, to Theodore it seemed like a much greater minus because of the westerly winds. "Generally, when the winds blow easterly," he says, "you can hardly find any clams, even on a strong minus tide, because a big low pressure system out in the Gulf of Alaska brings in a large surge or undertow. But when there are westerlies (fair weather), the winds will turn a small minus tide into a big one, and you can find clams, bidarkis, and urchins everywhere." Most butter clams have very bright light-colored shells, but Theodore prefers to get the darker-shelled butter clams which can only be reached at extreme minus tides a couple of times a year. He believes these deeper clams are cleaner and safer to eat.

Clamming traditionally is done in Ouzinkie and Old Harbor only during the "R months," from September through April, due to the belief that this is the period when paralytic shellfish poisoning (PSP) is not a danger to human health. During the "non-R months," from May through August, clams are generally not harvested. Clam biologists say that the traditional Alutiiq belief that clams are safe during the "R" months (September through March) is a "myth," that you can actually get sick and die from PSP almost any time of the year (Toomey 1997). Shellfish poisoning was recognized as a major health risk on Kodiak Island even during the first few years of the nineteenth century, when eighty Native hunters died suddenly as a result of eating tainted shellfish (Davydov 1977).

However, elders such as Walt Erickson Sr. in Old Harbor have never stopped eating clams and claim to know how to sort out the bad ones. According to Erickson, the indicators to watch out for are: 1) clams with black inner shells, 2) clams whose meat is dark brown in color, and 3) clams whose shells are not completely closed and pull apart easily—suggesting that their muscles are not strong enough to close up properly.

In spite of this traditional knowledge, news of the deaths of an Old Harbor woman from eating mussels with toxic levels of PSP in 1995, and of a Karluk man from eating contaminated butter clams in 1997, has greatly reduced participation in the harvest of clams in Ouzinkie, Old Harbor, and other Kodiak Native communities. Villagers who still crave clams often resort to buying them from the store in cans, but there are a few, like Walt Erickson, who say they have never stopped digging the fresh ones.

In Kodiak villages, octopus or "devil fish" are often sought after under large rocks at low tide. The most traditional method for hunting octopus is as follows. Using a rubber hose and a bottle of Chlorox bleach, the octopus hunter sticks one end of the hose under the rock, pours down a cup of bleach in the other end, and blows on the end of the hose to disperse the bleach. Not liking the bleach, the octopus tries to escape from beneath the rock. The octopus hunter then grabs one of the tentacles and hoists the octopus out of the water and into a bucket. Sometimes octopus are also caught incidentally while people are bottom fishing with halibut skates.

One Ouzinkie man gets a fair number of octopus and has pointed out that you can use the same rocks over and over for additional octopus if you don't disturb the rocks. He uses the Clorox and rubber hose method but recalls that the old-timers used a stick with a sharp bent tip on the end to pull the octopus out with. He showed me a bowl which contained fresh octopus. He likes to eat the head (after gutting it out) especially. Before cooking it, however, he strips the suction cups and skin off of the tentacles.

Another winter food harvested and consumed for subsistence is marine mammals, particularly harbor seals and Steller sea lions. Formerly, Old Harbor and Ouzinkie men hunted humpback whales for subsistence, using nothing more than several kayaks and throwing harpoons. Today humpbacks continue to migrate along the east side of Kodiak Island on their way north and south from the Bering Sea to Mexico and Hawaii. One of the last of the traditional whale hunters was Ivan Karakin of Old Harbor (Figure 6.5), born in 1887.

Fig. 6.4. Theodore Squartsoff Sr. with live octopus near Ouzinkie in May 1990. Photo by Craig Mishler.

In 1996, out of all the coastal communities in Alaska, Old Harbor became the highest harvesting community in the state for Steller sea lions, a community that also takes a significant number of harbor seals (Wolfe and Mishler 1997). There are many communities in Alaska where hunters take only sea lions or only harbor seals, but there are very few that depend a lot upon both species of pinnipeds.

Fig. 6.5. *Ivan Karakin and his wife Keratina, better known as Mashataq. Photo courtesy of the Old Harbor Seniors Center.*

Sea lions are hunted primarily in the fall and winter months beginning in October, and hunting generally continues through April. This is partly because Steller sea lions leave the areas around Old Harbor and Ouzinkie in late May and early June and migrate to the big rookery on Marmot Island, where they have their pups. At the same time, attention in the villages turns to commercial and subsistence herring and salmon fishing. There is no contemporary or historical evidence that Alutiiqs hunted sea lions on the rookery.

The favorite sea lion hunting places around Old Harbor are at Cape Barnabas, where there is a big sea lion haulout, and Two-Headed Island, where there is another large haulout. Sea lions can also be seen swimming through the Narrows near Old Harbor. Although sea lions went through a big decline in the early 1990s and are now listed as an endangered species under the federal Endangered Species Act, Alaska Natives are still allowed unrestricted take of the animals for subsistence as long is there is no wanton waste of the meat. They are recognized to have exclusive rights to hunt sea lions and other marine mammals under the reauthorized Marine Mammal Protection Act.

On October 3, 1990, I went on a sea lion and harbor seal hunt out of Old Harbor to learn more about the means and methods used to hunt these animals. Excerpts from this hunt are shown in the video, *Alaskan Subsistence: the Kodiak Connection* (1991). Here is a selection from my field notes:

Rolfie Christiansen had to go to Kodiak at the last minute, so Sergie Alexanderoff picked me up at the Sitkalidak Lodge about 7:45 a.m., and we walked down to the small boat harbor to launch Rolfie's tiny skiff, a 14-foot Boston Whaler. The trailer without the tire on one wheel promptly got stuck in the soft gravel, and we had to wiggle the skiff off of it to get it in the water. As we were going out, Rick Berns's purse seiner, the Melissa Rae, *came steaming into the harbor with a small Chevy truck on the back deck— an unusual sight, to my mind.*

As we approached Cape Barnabas, on the northern end of Sitkalidak Island, the sun came up very pretty, and the water was calm, so we stopped the boat while I dug out the camcorder and took a scenic shot. We got to the Cape about 8:15 a.m., quite a long ride. As we rounded a big rock outcropping we saw about a half-dozen sea lions perched up high sunning themselves. Then on the beach there were 70–80 of them in a good-sized herd.

As we approached, Sergie expressed concern for the swells, saying he was reluctant to go in too close for fear of being swamped by the swells. So he hooted like a bull sea lion, took aim on an animal and showed me which one he was aiming at so that I could focus my video camera on it. He fired one shot with his rifle, a .243 Winchester bolt action with scope, but missed. The noise caused the whole herd to stampede into the sea, and we had them charging right towards us. The bulls came very close to the skiff with their heads out of the water, and Sergie was quite nervous about them attacking us, but mainly they just circled around.

Sergie, who only has one good eye, got off a second shot at a young one, but missed that one also. Every time he stood up to take a shot, they would dive under. He wanted me to shoot, but I had no confidence in my ability to handle the gun, and reminded him that only Natives could shoot marine mammals. We moved farther around the Cape to locate another haulout but couldn't find any more animals. So we returned to the first location, but none of the animals had hauled out again, so Sergie suggested picking off one of those sitting up on the rocks. Yet to get a good steady shot, he felt we needed to get out of the skiff and stand on one of the rocks. We located one and motored slowly up to it, and I jumped out with the camcorder and the rifle, while he tied up the skiff.

I climbed up high and positioned the camera, while Sergie lay in a small crevice in the prone position to get his shot off. He picked a young one which was just below a giant bull perched on top of the rock and squeezed off a shot, which hit. But at that very instant a big swell came up over the crevice and swamped him, causing him to let go of the rifle and grab onto the rock for dear life. The swell was not a wave but a massive surge of quiet water from the ocean floor. I stopped filming and put down the camera, but by that time the worst was over, and I saw that Sergie was simply drenched. It was a moment when he could have been swept out to sea, however, and scared both of us.

We got back into the skiff, and I noticed my gloves were missing. Sergie pulled the boat back up, and I climbed out looking for the gloves but couldn't find them. I did find one of Sergie's unused cartridges and grabbed that. We backed off the rock a second time and then saw the two gloves just floating on the water, so we recovered them quickly.

Sergie thought he had missed the sea lion, but I assured him I saw it fall as I looked through the camera viewfinder, and we pulled up close to the rock to see if we could find it in the water, but couldn't. I was ready to give up, but Sergie finally spotted it sitting on a little ledge, where it was neatly camouflaged. Its skin was almost the identical color of the rocks around it. It was only distinguishable by its rounded features.

Sergie said he didn't want to leave the skiff to go after it and suggested I climb up and roll it down to him. I said "O.K." but recommended we land on the back side of the rock where it was more level and easier to get out. So I jumped out on the backside and climbed around to the front side of the rock to find the dead sea lion, but on the way I ran into two more big sea lions which I had to avoid. After jumping across tide pools and steep crevices I found the animal but had great difficulty trying to move it. I finally found that moving the head worked best, and since I had gravity on my side, I told Sergie to pull the boat up into a certain spot, so I could slide it down to him. It took virtually all of my strength, but I finally did get it to flop right on the front deck of the whaler.

I then made my way back over to the backside of the rock, which took about five minutes, and Sergie came back in to pick me up. Success! We motored over to Table Island to gut out the animal, but Sergie was more interested in picking up a seal. He spotted several on the backside of the beach in the water but couldn't get a good shot off. He also took up a position where he could watch both sides of the beach at once. He says this beach used to be covered with seals, but there were none there today. We ate sandwiches and drank coffee that Sergie had thoughtfully brought along, and then Sergie gutted out the sea lion—a young female. Sergie did not like the looks of the liver—one of the prized parts of the animal—and was about to leave it behind. I asked what looked funny about it, and he said that instead of being smooth it had lots of little cuts and breaks in it. I decided to collect it and have it looked at by the NMFS lab, and put it in a plastic bag. I asked Sergie to open the stomach up, and we saw it contained only one thing—partially digested crab.

We loaded the sea lion back on the skiff and headed for Midway Bay and Big Creek, which flows into it, to look for the beach seiners. We got about a mile upriver and then started running into shallow water which eventually became impassable. So we got out and decided to see if we could hike the rest of the way up. However, we soon encountered lots of bear sign, *including the fresh prints of a sow with a cub. We were pretty worried that a bear might smell the sea lion and come after it.*

At the end of a big gravel bar we climbed up on the bank, and all of a sudden got a whiff of strong bear odor, and that spooked us. Sergie said he is very scared of bears, and agreed we should go back to the skiff. By the time we returned to the skiff the tide had come up three or four more inches, and we had to wade in water over our boot tops to get to it. We left the area and went back to Old Harbor, stopping at Three Sisters beach to gas up.

Returning to the small boat harbor in Old Harbor, we pulled the skiff up and unloaded the sea lion. I asked Sergie if he was going to eat the sea lion or give it away to somebody, and he said he probably would give it to his father-in-law, Kalumpi Larionoff. I'm beginning to think there's a special kinship relation between sons-in-law and fathers-in-law.

But when we saw Anakenti Zeedar on the dock, we hollered, and he came over to look at the sea lion and decided he would take some home as soon as he could get a three-wheeler to come down. He did not ask for meat, but just declared that he would take some. Perhaps our hailing him was enough of an invitation. Within about ten minutes he was back with son James and started cutting up pieces. I taped this, and Anakenti called out the Alutiiq words for various parts of the animal. He took a back flipper, a foreflipper, a slab of ribs, and some fat.

Anakenti also thought the liver looked funny, and I then decided to salvage the head for scientific purposes also, so he cut the head off for me. While Anakenti was butchering, Sergie told James Zeedar about his close call, ending with: "It scared the shit out of me." Sergie then decided that he would go up and offer some of the sea lion to his father, Wilfred Alexanderoff, whom he thought would like it.

A lot of local knowledge about sea lions and harbor seals in Old Harbor and Ouzinkie is already contained in the *Whiskers!* CD-ROM database published on diskette by the Alaska Department of Fish and Game, Division of Subsistence (1999), but recently I asked George Inga Sr. (1997), an Old Harbor elder, about how he cooks and prepares sea lion:

GI: I like sea lion better than seal. I'd rather eat sea lion than seal. Seal got too much blood.
CM: But the sea lions are harder to get, huh? Because they sink on you?
GI: I tell you, we ate a lot of sea lion too, in '40s, '50s, a lot of them.
CM: How do you cook that sea lion when you make a dinner?
GI: Well, my wife used to roast the chest part. The chest part, cut it up just like spare ribs. Same way. Put them in and put a gravy. Boy, that was good. And then boiled is good, soup is good.
CM: You guys eat the flipper too, huh?
GI: Oh yeah.
CM: How do you eat the flipper?
GI: I didn't eat it very much. I liked it cold. See boil it and then cool

it off and then boy, that's good. We'll eat it with fish, dry fish, good. Like Anakenti [Zeedar] said, you know, "just like pigs' feet" [laughs]. . . .

CM: Well, how often would you go after seal? Once a month?

GI: Whenever we wanted it. There were plenty then too, lots. Didn't have to go very far. This time of the year [September] was the easiest. They go up the creek, you know. All you do is go mouth of the creek and wait, and you could just see their eyes right by the bank. You shoot them. We didn't waste them either. We take fat and all. We use a lot of fat for grease, you know, with fish, humpies.

For many elders, seal fat and seal oil are even more desirable than seal meat. As Freddy Christiansen (1997) says:

You know the seal oil, which they call uguq, *you know, fermented seal oil, is very important. The elders cannot eat their wild fish without their seal oil. That's their butter [laughs].*

I talked with Sven and Mary Haakanson (1997) about sea lions. The introduction of powered purse seiners in the 1940s allowed local hunters to go out and get enough meat to feed the village:

CM: You mentioned to me one time that the way you hunted seal and sea lion, you would go out and get a whole bunch of them at once, instead of just one here and one there.

SH: Yeah. Once they got bigger boats. Mary's oldest brother Rolf used to do that. We'd go to Two-Headed Island, I remember, and he'd count, "Two more!" or so. One time we got 18 sea lions. The boat was just like loaded with fish, and we come back and radioed ahead, and we'd drop them off along the beach. Every family would pull them up, and next day you couldn't tell. There was nothing left.

MH: They salted them.

SH: They salted them and put them away, and everybody had food.

Although today hunters only take one or two animals at a time, marine mammals are still the most widely shared subsistence food in Kodiak villages. And even with the widespread use of chest freezers, some families still prefer salted sea lion.

SPRING AND SUMMER

With spring, everyone begins to think and talk about fish, but fish are not the only prized food. Late May or early June is the time of year when most birds lay their eggs, and the people of Ouzinkie frequently visit the rookeries to gather a few for their table. On May 28, 1991, I went out in a skiff with some Ouzinkie residents to catch early run red salmon, and we stopped on the way back to gather bird eggs. As much as these people wanted eggs, however, it became clear that care for the ecology of the birds was foremost in their minds. This is what I wrote:

We stopped by a couple of noisy bird rookeries on islets in Anton Larsen Bay to gather eggs. Locals distinguish between three kinds of eggs. The first birds to lay are the kittiwakes, then come the seagulls, and finally there are the herring gulls. Their laying comes about two weeks apart, so they harvest them in the aforesaid order. The seagull eggs are about twice the size of the eggs laid by the kittiwakes.

Eggs are not taken from nests with three or more eggs, because birds will not usually lay more than three in a season and thus would not raise any young until the next year. But if there is only one or two eggs in a nest, it's o.k. to take them because wild birds, like chickens, will continue to lay at least one more. Many of the eggs are taken just above sea level by pulling the skiff right up to the rocky cliff face. These eggs would all get washed away during storms and extremely high tides anyway. At one rookery, I was instructed to toss the fish heads from our twenty reds up on top of the rock. This was their way of paying back the birds for taking their eggs.

In May 1998, I again went out egging with this same group of people. Repeatedly, they would pull the skiff up to a bird rookery, and the kids would hop out, climb up on the rocks, and scour the islet for nests. If they returned with an egg or two, their faces lit up. We visited four rookeries over a period of an hour and gathered a half-dozen eggs. They say this has always been a fun thing for kids to do for as long as they remember.

Although traditionally some hunting was done in December, April and May is the time of year when villagers on the south and west side of Kodiak Island traditionally hunt brown bear, known in Alutiiq as *tarogaq*. Brown bear meat tastes the best just after the bears emerge from their dens and just before they den up again for the winter. Brown bears are not found on Spruce Island, and Ouzinkie residents have little or no interest in hunting them. In Old Harbor, however, brown bears were once an important part of the subsistence economy, and while today they have a greatly diminished role in the village diet, bears and bear hunting still have a high symbolic value.

At a U.S. Fish and Wildlife Service hearing held in Old Harbor on November 12, 1991, one key issue raised was the subsistence hunting of brown bear, which Emil Christiansen described as "something that has been taken away from us." A younger hunter, Jeff Peterson, made a strong case for the importance of passing down traditional knowledge, noting that his father's generation had never hunted bear for fear of being thrown in jail. Peterson said he wanted to learn from the elders who were still knowledgeable so that he could pass these skills down to his sons.

Since statehood in 1959, Kodiak brown bears have been declared illegal for subsistence hunting and have been allocated entirely to trophy hunters. Anyone wanting to hunt brown bears had to buy a hunting license and participate in a permit drawing. In 1996 the Federal Subsistence Board finally made a positive customary and traditional determination and implemented permit regulations so that members of Kodiak communities could freely hunt brown bears on federal lands. This determination was strongly opposed by brown bear hunting guides, who charge approximately $10,000 for a guided brown bear hunt and see every harvestable bear as a potential part of their income. The guides tried to appease the Natives by offering them bear meat from their guided hunts, but the Native village representatives on the Kodiak Aleutians Federal Advisory Council said they didn't want charity. It is a lesson in values to learn that Alutiiqs traditionally consumed the entire bear except for the head and hide, while sport hunters want to keep *only* the head and the hide and throw away the meat.

Alutiiqs see bear hunting, however, as something just as important as bear meat. Learning and understanding bear behavior, facing the danger of bear attacks, and going out on the land are considered just as important as killing bears and eating their meat. Knowledge about bear is an integral part of the culture that is passed on from older men to young boys, and some important rituals were attached to bear hunting. Paul Kahutak (1997) talks about the disposal of the bear's head: "So every time they kill a bear or something, you put the head there, you know, then they let it face northeast. I don't know why. 'Cause they won't leave it like that, you know. They let them face northeast."

There were also certain taboos that had to be observed, based on beliefs. Elder Old Harbor hunters say they had to throw away any clothes which were used to bury someone before going bear hunting or bad luck would follow. They also had to store their gun shells outside the house if there were menstruating women living there, or bad luck would follow.

Elder William Ignatin, moreover, says that after killing a bear on his first hunt, he put his arm down inside the bear's throat and grabbed a handful of the slime and mucous which he then rubbed on his bare chest. He was told that if he did this he would never be afraid of bears again after that, and it turned out to be true. Other bear hunters said they never had the courage to do this, even though it was a traditional initiation for a young bear hunter.

George Inga Sr. in recalling some bear hunting strategy, indicates that bears were not faced head-on. He says in the springtime you could hunt bears by climbing a small hill and scouting the countryside. After sight-ing one, you would wait for it to lie down in the brush somewhere and then go up and shoot it. But winter time was a lot more dangerous. Bears could be tracked in the snow, but sometimes they could be tricky and circle around and come back up to lie in wait behind you.

Old Harbor bear hunters used to walk for three hours up to Big Creek and then pack their bear meat in gunnysacks all the way back to the village. It would take five or six men to pack out the meat back for one bear. But the conservation ethic was strong. In Paul Kahutak's words, "They never leave nothing. You don't finish it, next day you go get it again. They never waste nothing."

Paul Kahutak's (1997) first bear hunt as a teenager, which served as a rite of passage into manhood, provides an exciting narrative from the mid-1940s:

PK: Like I said, you know, first time, William [Ignatin], you know, he took me to Kiliuda [Bay], North Arm. . . . He said, "Well, I'm going to let you get your first bear" or something, and he had a little boat, you know, William. So I think it was April month. William said, "We're going to go tomorrow if the weather's good," you know. And [it was] about April month, so he said, "Yeah. I'm going to let you take your first bear." I was kind of scared. I told him I had that lever-action .3030. That's what my dad used to use. So we went next day, that's where we went, and we stayed two days, you know. Second day, we see the tracks in the snow, but no bear first day. So I told him. William said, "I guess he took off for another bay or something."

So he had a little skiff, started rowing down the boat. [Before that] the boat was anchored. So I was rowing. Then after while he looked up, you know, William. He told me, "No, I could see it." You know, there was a little hill behind there. And he told me, "Yeah, you could see it! That black spot. It's slipping in the snow." And we turned around, and we got up on the beach. And he was happy, you know. There's a bear in there. So it was kind of steep. We take our time going up. There was quite a bit of snow yet. So we kept walking, and we got so far up, you could see it. He was sleeping. He wasn't up. So he was behind me. William says, "You got to get close, you know, get closer." Better range, you know, to kill it.

So I started walking in the snow. No noise. 'Cause he was laying down. I guess he heard me. By the time I got closer and closer, you know, I could see his ears, you know. That's when he got up, but he couldn't see. There was little trees there. There was a hill there. 'Cause before I took off, William was behind me, and he said, "Try and get a good shot at him, 'cause you'll lose him once he go over the hill." So, you know, I took my time, and I don't know how far, maybe a little further, yeah. He got up, you know, the bear got up. He looked around, but he couldn't see me. I figured, well, I better get a good shot at it. Otherwise, there's a hill there. We're going to lose it.

There was a tree there. I sat down, and my rifle was loaded. I took my time, you know. I figured well, I'll shoot it in the head, you know, best shot.

So I must have got it on the neck. That's how come, when I shot it, it fell on its, you know, when it was moving [laughs]. I could see that's when I was running towards it. I was just firing it. I had my shell. I know that thing was alive, so I wanted it dead. Like I said, this guy was hollering. William was hollering behind me. I didn't pay attention to him hollering. I kept going towards it. Finally I got so close, you know, keep shooting, didn't move. That's when he got up, you know. I asked him, you know. What he was hollering about. He told me to shoot it in the head, you know. He worried about the meat. I didn't want to worry about [the meat]. I want the bear dead. So I told him, "Now it's dead now. It's not moving." He was worried about the meat. He say it got blood clots in the meat all over. First time I shot a bear, you know, so. . . .

CM: Was the meat still good?

PK: Yeah, it was good, 'cause that's what I was aiming for, you know, when I was shooting it. 'Cause I don't remember how many times [I fired], you know. I know I was loading my .3030. I was running towards it, you know.

CM: And you were about seventeen at that time?

PK: Seventeen. I was only seventeen [in 1950]. I was surprised.

CM: There was just the two of you went out?

PK: Mmm hmm. In a boat. Yeah, when we got there he told me, "Yeah, you got a bear now." I feel kind of proud, you know, but it wasn't that big, though, but you know.

CM: Did they have any kind of party for you?

PK: No! Nothing. 'Cause see my dad was pretty proud of me when I told him, when I got home. You know he died in 1954 in Sitka; heart gave out, I guess. So I told him, "Yeah, dad. You know, I shot a bear, first one."

Except for brown bear, Alutiiq elders do not profess any traditional beliefs in animal spirits or souls, and they profess no knowledge of any ceremonies associated with killing animals. Unlike their Yup'ik neighbors farther north, for example, Alutiiqs do not have any rituals associated with the killing of seals, such as pouring fresh water in their mouths.

However, George Inga Sr. says that in Old Harbor they used to have a party for young boys whenever they caught their first bear, weasel, or fox. The boy had to give away whatever he got to elders. This tradition was still being carried on during George's lifetime (since 1925) but has now disappeared, along with the whole trapping economy.

The most exciting time of year for subsistence is from mid-May through mid-October, when the salmon are running. Salmon provide a staple in the Alutiiq diet, and around Kodiak Island five species are available: king salmon (chinooks), sockeye salmon (reds), silver salmon (cohos), chum salmon (dogs), and pink salmon (humpies). The residents of Old Harbor and Ouzinkie use all of these species. However, because red salmon do not spawn in the Old Harbor area, reds are not heavily depended upon there for subsistence. They must be received through sharing from other communities or taken out of the commercial catch of local purse seiners which travel around the island.

King salmon (*iliishaq* or *amasuq*): Because there are only a few king salmon spawning streams in the Kodiak archipelago, king salmon have not generally been targeted for subsistence around Old Harbor and Ouzinkie. They are too oily to be smoked or dried, so they are usually eaten fresh or frozen. In recent years king salmon have been targeted during the winter months and are caught by trolling in deep water using fancy downrigger gear, a newly introduced technology.

Red salmon (*nikllik*): The earliest reds have come in through the Ouzinkie Narrows is around the seventh of May, but the early run doesn't develop until much later in the month. One of the main places people look for them in May is at Litnik, on southwest Afognak Island. Red salmon do not spawn in the creeks around Old Harbor and are seldom caught there.

Pink salmon (*amakayaq*): Humpies show up around Ouzinkie in early July and peak around the last part of August. They are eaten fresh and dried. Theodore Squartsoff (field notes September 27, 1989) says: "Natives don't like humpies when their meat is still pink; they like it when it's white. So they should be caught in fresh water when they start turning color and start getting their humps. When they are a mottled color they have less oil in them and they dry better. White people are just the opposite. They want all their fish bright and shiny." Humpies taste best when they are boiled for just a few minutes, not long. In Old Harbor people like to eat their humpies with seal fat or seal oil.

Dog salmon (*aliimaq*): Dog salmon, also known as chum salmon, usually arrive around Old Harbor about the same time as the humpies. Dog salmon make excellent dry fish, as long as its not raining, but unlike silvers, dogs are seldom smoked. Some of the best places around Old Harbor to get dog salmon are at the Culvert, in Barling Bay, and in Dog Bay, which is part of Kiliuda Bay.

Silver salmon (*kakiiyaq*): Silver salmon are probably the favorite fish for subsistence in both Ouzinkie and Old Harbor because they are large and can be put up in quantity for winter. They are caught in beach seines and on rod and reel and are eaten fresh, smoked, salted, and pickled. In my field notes for September 14, 1989, I wrote: "I decided to look up Theodore Squartsoff, who was down at the waterfront cutting fish with wife Toni and uncle Fred Squartsoff. Some fish were already hanging—cold smoked with cottonwood. Theodore was very talkative as he quickly and expertly cut his day's catch of silvers into fillets. He complained about having to use rod and reel to get his subsistence fish from Katmai Creek."

Salmon Gear Types

An essential piece of gear for deploying salmon nets or fishing with hooks is the skiff, and the skiff is also widely employed in hunting deer and elk, ducks, and marine mammals. Residents of Old Harbor and Ouzinkie use a variety of skiff sizes and styles, but most have a V-bottom or semi-V bottom, are made of aluminum, and are powered by a large motor or "kicker." The skiff is a powerful tool that greatly enhances subsistence opportunity and efficiency. Included in the skiff illustrated in Figure 6.6 are: a 115-horsepower Yamaha motor, a five-gallon metal gas can, a second five-gallon plastic jug of gasoline, a twelve-volt electric winch (crab pot puller), a wooden paddle, an upright control console with a compass and a steering wheel for the skiff driver, a tote holding a fifty-fathom subsistence gill net and an anchor, a round basket holding a subsistence herring gill net, and two rear storage lockers (on each side of the motor). The right rear locker holds survival gear such as a first-aid kit, flares, life jackets, a spare VHS radio, and a GPS chart plotter. The left rear locker is the grub box, which contains food and soft drinks as well as emergency rations.

Red salmon, pink salmon, and silver salmon are generally caught today with nets. Two of the most traditional and efficient nets are gill nets and beach seines. Gill nets are more popular in Ouzinkie, while beach seines are more popular in Old Harbor, but it is hard to know why that is the case. Obviously both of these gear types were introduced first through commercial fisheries and were later adapted to subsistence.

However, I was curious to know how Alutiiqs caught salmon before they had gill nets and seines, and in September 1997, George Inga Sr. of Old Harbor drew a sketch for me of something they called a *malik*, a lance with a toggle hook. The *malik* was used to spear fish when they were swimming upstream in their spawning creeks. The spear, which resembles a gaff, was made by bending a sharp steel spike into a round semicircle. The base of the spike was set into the slotted end of a wooden pole and attached to the shaft with about twelve inches of braided twine. When the fish was speared, the spike came loose from the pole, but the wriggling fish was held fast by the braided twine. It could then be easily tossed up on the stream bank. Presumably the modern-day *malik* has a prehistoric correlate, shaped from some kind of bone, that predated the introduction of steel spikes.

Another old way of catching salmon was by trolling with lures. Trolling would seem to be a fairly modern sport fishing method, but apparently for the Alutiiqs it was used back in the 1940s and 1950s. George Inga Sr., for example, says they used to catch most of their subsistence salmon right out in front of the village rather than up in Big Creek. The silvers schooled up in such large numbers inside the strait that it was very easy to catch them. Because they did not have any money for spinners and lures, they made their own out of polished teaspoons and tablespoons and attached big halibut hooks to them.

Gill nets are frequently used for subsistence around Ouzinkie. Some men manufacture their own nets by purchasing the webbing and then hanging the nets with lead lines and cork lines. When a gill net is set, it

Fig. 6.6. *Theodore Squartsoff's aluminum skiff. Photo by Craig Mishler.*

is usually anchored on one end to the shore and on the other end to an anchored buoy, although it can also be deployed offshore with both ends anchored to buoys. The net is allowed to soak for several hours until the tide changes, but the person setting the net may pick the net several times before pulling it up. Since deploying the gill net takes a lot of time, fishermen use the net soaking time to eat their lunch, rest, or jig for halibut, always keeping one eye on the corks to see if there are any entangled fish. When a salmon is caught in the webbing, it usually causes one or two of the corks to bob up and down.

Another way of setting a gill net is to toss one end out without any anchor, just fastened to a buoy, and then use the skiff to form a circle around the fish. This "roundhauling" method is used when fish are jumping out of the water and schooling up. In this case the gill net functions like a seine, except that the fish still must swim into the webbing and get caught.

One trick used to pick fish while the net is still in the water is to bring the skiff up alongside the net, then pull up the lead line first and cradle the fish between the lead line and the cork line as it is being untangled. This way, if the fish gets loose from the mesh, or the fisherman loses his grip, the fish can't just flop down into the water and swim away. When the net is picked as it is being pulled, at the end of a set, the fish are untangled after they are pulled on board the skiff. Theodore Squartsoff always likes to bleed and gut his fish as soon as they are caught, believing that they taste better when the blood is out of them.

The other major subsistence gear type, the beach seine, is employed a lot in Old Harbor for catching silver salmon. The beach seine, unlike a gill net, is heavier and more finely woven. Approximately ten fathoms long, the beach seine is used in freshwater creeks to catch salmon which are migrating upstream but are temporarily resting in clear, deep pools. Although more people often participate, hauling fish with a beach seine can be done successfully with only two persons.

As I observed it near Old Harbor on September 12, 1992, the seine was first deployed from the side or back of the skiff, with one person in hip boots holding on to the end of the net on the bank of the creek, a second driving the skiff, and a third feeding the seine out from the back of the skiff. The skiff immediately crosses over to the opposite bank while feeding out the net and, with the motor set at trolling speed, slowly moves downstream. The person holding the shore end of the net walks downstream along the bank perhaps thirty or forty yards, until a decision is made to bring the entire net ashore. When this happens, the skiff comes back and lands on the same shore as the anchoring person. In the act of landing, the skiff pulls the net part way up on the beach. The fishermen count on the fact that the salmon will not turn tail and swim back downstream because they are averse to shallow places. Instead, they school up at the upstream end of the net. After beaching the skiff, the skiff driver and the shore-end person work together to pull the rest of the net up on the beach. By this time the salmon are splashing and flopping all over the place. The entire process takes only about twenty minutes.

Altogether, a good haul may bring in ninety to one hundred silvers. When the net is picked, people announce how many they need, and the fish are divided according to the person who owns the net and the skiff. When I videotaped a beach seine haul near Old Harbor (Mishler 1992), a second skiff appeared shortly after the fish were beached, and the passengers of the second skiff retrieved and received part of the catch. Sometimes the fish are just thrown in the bottom of the skiffs and sometimes people bring along a big clean plastic garbage can to put them in.

The salmon are generally hauled back to the village for cleaning. This is when the women join in. On September 17, 1991, I observed almost the entire Christiansen family cleaning fish on the beach. My notes from that day:

I wandered down to the beach near the lodge and found a whole bunch of people splitting fish—mostly Christiansens but others as well. They offered free fish to everybody who came by, including me, and talked about "feed-

ing the whole village." After watching for a few minutes I asked permission to go get my video camera and they said O.K.

The weather was sunny and calm, and it was a joyous activity to observe with dogs and four-wheelers running all over. The fish cutters paid hardly any attention to me or the camera and kept up a lively chatter that included several personal experience stories and discussions of various methods of preserving and putting up their fish.

Most people worked on their hands and knees in front of a huge pile of silver salmon which someone had brought back from Big Creek. Some Alutiiq was spoken by the elders. I used my tripod and captured thirty minutes of delicious footage. Oscar Christiansen, speaking of subsistence off camera, said, "It ain't nothing but a lot of hard work." Learned that Mary Haakanson and Wilma Berns are sisters to Harold Christiansen. Mary was putting fish heads into a white five-gallon bucket.

Anakenti and James Zeedar's skiff came in. Anakenti disappeared someplace, but James said they just came back from Big Creek and got nothing because the fish had all moved up the creek overnight. This foiled George's plans to take me up there this afternoon and illustrates the importance of timing.

Salmon Processing

There are at least five ways of "putting up" salmon: drying, smoking, salting, pickling, and freezing. Freezing, the newest method, was developed only after the villages were electrified in the 1960s, after the earthquake. While a significant amount of fish is frozen, the Alutiiqs recognize that smoking, salting, drying, and pickling salmon are all methods which make their foodways culturally distinctive. Besides this, some elders still eat parts of their salmon raw, especially humpies.

1) Dry fish (*tamuq*). Old-timers like to make dry fish out of silver salmon in late September or early October, after all the bugs are gone. By this time the fish in Big Creek are all mottled. To make dry fish, you have to hang the fish outdoors for many days. It is a difficult thing to do because of the region's wet rainy climate, and it's impossible to make dry fish while it's raining.

Also, flies like to lay their eggs (locally called "fly blows") on the flesh of fish so the fish have to be closely checked once or twice a day, or the fly eggs will hatch into maggots. If fly eggs are found, they are quickly cleaned off the fish with the flick of a fingernail. Some people, like Theodore Squartsoff, have modernized the process by building a large box out of screen wire and putting the fish inside the box. Then he sets up an electric fan right next to the box. With this method he has dry fish in just one or two days instead of two weeks, and flies are not a problem.

2) Smoked salmon (*baliq*).

Field Notes (March 13, 1990):
Theodore and Toni Squartsoff served us "cold smoked salmon" cut into thin strips, along with blueberry muffins and coffee. To "cold smoke" salmon, you hang it high up in the smokehouse for twenty-two days over a very slow fire. Anything quicker is considered "hot smoke" salmon.

Field Notes (October 2, 1990):
Sven Haakanson Sr. showed me his smokehouse, covered on the outside with corrugated aluminum. He hangs his fish on a multi-tiered wooden rack which sits on a set of wheels—a cart—so that he can pull the entire fish rack out of the smokehouse all at once. The wheeled rack sits up on platform reached by a short set of stairs, while access to the wood stove is through a crawl space underneath the platform. Sven salts his fish for a day or two, rinses them off in fresh water, and then smokes them with dry cottonwood for about three days.

Field Notes (September 17, 1991):
George Inga Sr. showed me his salmon smokehouse, located right next to his banya, and told me in some detail how he puts up his smoke fish and his salt fish. I took mental notes and wrote them up when I got back to the lodge. George smokes his fish for four days with dry cottonwood and then hangs them under a roof eave for about two weeks to dry them properly. Then he puts them back in the smokehouse for a few more days until they collect a little mildew. But the mildew wipes off very easily, and then he cuts the salmon up into strips and freezes it.

Field notes (Monday, September 9, 1996):
Susanna and I went up to Paul Kahutak's house and checked out his smokehouse. He built it out of 4 sheets of 4 x 8 foot plywood (very simple) and a slanted roof. The fire is contained inside a cut down 55-gallon barrel covered with two sheets of corrugated roofing. Paul smokes his fish for five days. Then he either freezes it for making sikiaq [half-smoked salmon] or air dries it. The smoking is all done with cottonwood. I took a couple pictures of Paul and his smokehouse.

3) Salt salmon (*salunaq*). Some Old Harbor people salt the whole fish, while others like to salt just the bellies (*aksuk*). These are called salmon bellies or salt bellies. It used to be that salmon were salted in wooden barrels. Now they are put into five-gallon plastic buckets with sealed lids. The top portion or back of the fish is then saved for smoking and drying.

Another method of preparing salmon for salting is to clean it, remove the backbone and tail, and open it up butterfly style. These double fillets are placed in the salt barrel or bucket "skin to skin" and "meat to meat" to prevent the meat from getting slimy by coming into contact with the

Fig. 6.7. Paul Kahutak (Abalik) at his smokehouse in Old Harbor, 1996. Photo by Craig Mishler.

skin. Paul Kahutak says they cut off the tail but leave the head on and just cut right through the head so that it also splits.

On September 11, 1997, while people in Old Harbor were actively putting up fish for the winter, I made some detailed notes about salt salmon:

This afternoon I came upon Walt and Jenny Erickson putting up their salt fish in a thirty-gallon plastic garbage can. They were using coarse grade

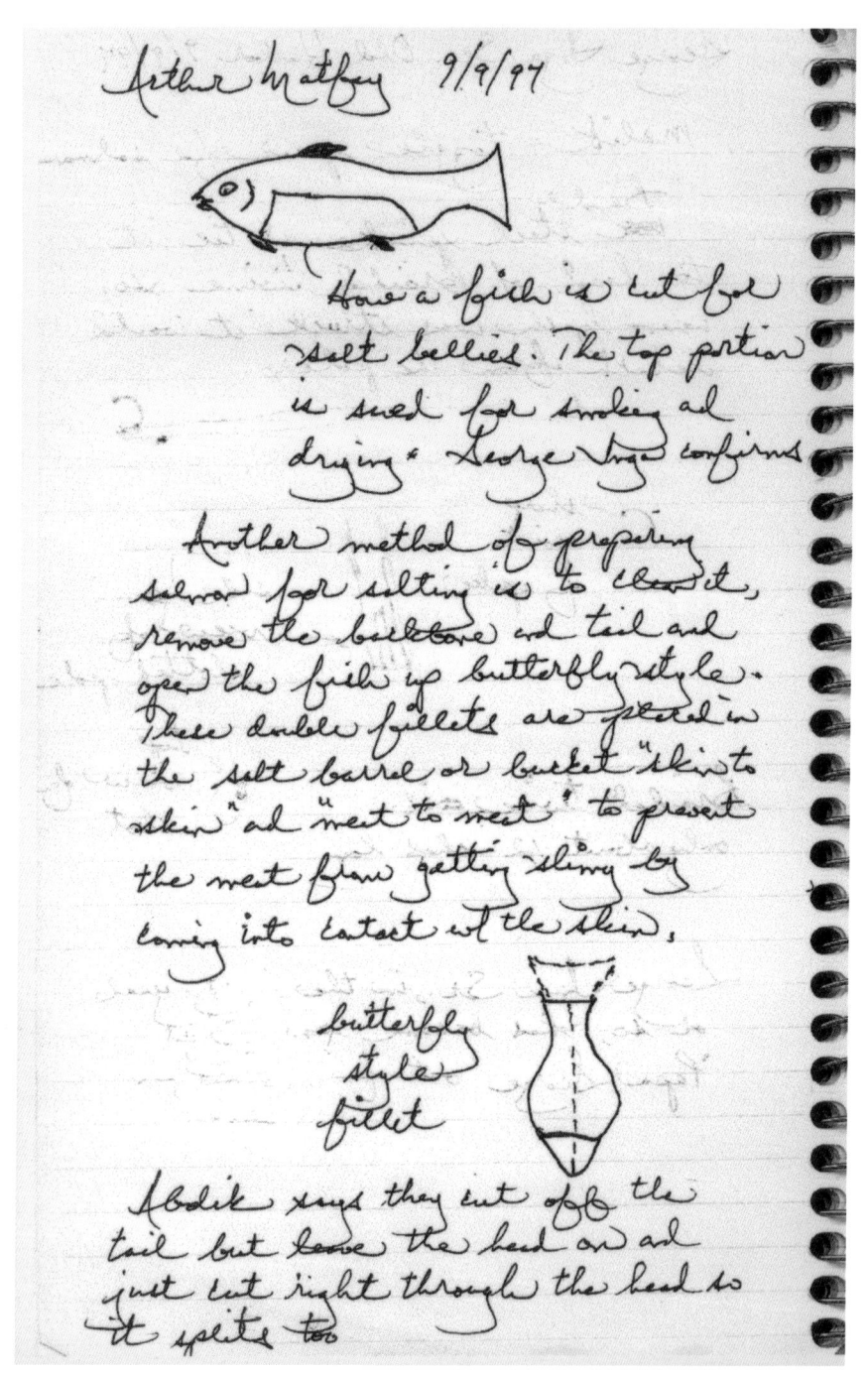

Fig. 6.8. *Page from the author's field notes on cutting a salmon for salt bellies.*

rock salt. But first they soak the fillets in another clean garbage pail to get all the blood out. Then they layer the fish and add salt, but not heavily, just a few grains. Walt says they are cured within seventy-two hours.

But with salt fish you have to soak the fish out in fresh water for about 12–18 hours before cooking and pickling. A separate bucket is used for the split heads and "collars." The collars are the bony parts of the fish right between the heads and the gills. I took a picture of Walt with the bucket tilted into the sun. In his words, "We hardly get into them until after the holidays, and then after Lent, well that's all we eat."

Abalik says he pours off the bloody water of the salted fish after two weeks and then makes a fresh clear brine to replace it, but the Ericksons soak the blood out before packing the fish in order to conserve salt. The fish will make their own water, and Ericksons put a board inside the barrel with a heavy weight on it to keep the fish fully immersed in the brine. This way, the fish stays moist until you're ready to use it, but no air can get to it. Abalik simply covers his buckets with a sheet of visquane (clear plastic). Carl Christiansen does it Walt's way and says be sure to seal the lid tight and not allow any water to get into it.

4) Pickled salmon. George Inga Sr.'s recipe for pickled salmon: Soak out your salt fish overnight in fresh water. Chop up one big onion, add one-half can of pickling spice, three cups of cider vinegar, and 3 cups of cold water. Cut up the fish into small pieces and soak in a glass jar with the onion for at least two days. Eat with saltines or pilot bread. It should be added that some people like to boil the vinegar, water, and pickling spice and let it cool before adding the cut-up fish. Others add half a cup to two cups of brown sugar to the mixture.

5) Frozen salmon. In freezing salmon, it is important not to allow it to get freezer burned. After sitting for too many months in a freezer, even small amounts of air next to the fish start to turn the flesh yellow, called "burned." To avoid this, some families double wrap their salmon in freezer paper, and some freeze their salmon in containers of water. Others, like Theodore Squartsoff, have invested in vacuum sealers and plastic bags. When vacuum sealed,

Fig. 6.9. Walt Erickson salting salmon in Old Harbor, 1997. Photo by Craig Mishler.

Subsistence and "Food for the Day" 185

fish are not exposed to the air at all, and they may be kept frozen for years without spoiling.

6) Raw salmon. In the early days, George Inga Sr. says they ate raw salmon bellies and the raw backs of male humpies, and today people such as George still eat salted salmon bellies and salted salmon heads without cooking them. Paul Kahutak says sometimes they even eat the heads of silver salmon without salting or cooking them. Raw fish, shellfish, or meat of any kind is called *qashaq*.

Other Fish

Although the five species of salmon constitute a primary part of the Alutiiq diet, the importance of all species of fish was brought forth at a public hearing in Ouzinkie on June 27, 1989, shortly after the *Exxon Valdez* oil spill washed up tar balls on village beaches. One man spoke up and said, "If there's no fish to eat, then there's no reason to live here."

Theodore Squartsoff and other Ouzinkie fishermen are very fond of black rockfish, which they call "black bass." These black bass and an occasional greenling are caught by jigging with lures in deep holes off the sides of rocky cliffs. Sculpins are caught offshore along with gray cod, halibut, and an occasional octopus. Some other species that are occasionally used are red snapper, Dolly Varden, steelhead, and herring. In Alutiiq, herring are called *allaklokpuk*; in Russian, *sildik*. Here are my field notes from Ouzinkie on April 18, 1991:

This evening we saw Theodore Squartsoff coming in with his skiff and unloading a couple of sacks full of fish. Shortly thereafter we got a call from his wife Toni to come on up and see the king salmon he brought in. When we went up we saw that it was not king salmon but halibut, cod, and sculpin—beautiful looking fish. All of the skin is trimmed off the fillets. Theodore considers his part of the work finished when he gets the fish filleted and cut up into pieces—the wrapping and storing are delegated to Toni. Toni put all of the fish out on the dining table to dry, daubed them with paper towels to absorb the moisture, and then put them in plastic bags. A bright orange label saying what kind of fish it is was put on each bag. Then all the bags were placed inside a big cardboard fish box, loaded onto the back of their four-wheeler, and taken to the community freezer for vacuum sealing.

During the oil spill, our Division of Subsistence staff went to traditional subsistence sites near oil spill communities to collect various species of fish that could be biosampled for hydrocarbon contamination. On August 6, 1990, my daughter Susanna and I accompanied Anakenti Zeedar on a fishing trip to Barling Bay, just outside of Old Harbor. Here is what I wrote:

At 3:15 p.m. we moved out to the mouth of Barling Bay (sampling site OHA2) and changed over to jigging gear (hand lines) to catch bottom fish. In less than an hour we caught more than seven gray cod (5 to 8 lbs. each) and saved four of them for sampling, giving the remainder to Anakenti, who calls them "codfish." These were caught at a depth of over twenty fathoms. Anakenti has devised his own homemade jigging gear, and I took photographs of him holding it after we returned to the village about 4:45 p.m.

Anakenti's gear (which may well be traditional) is in the form of a horizontal toggle stick suspended by a heavy hand line. One side of the toggle

Fig. 6.10. *Anakenti Zeedar holding cod and halibut jigging gear in Old Harbor, 1990. Photo by Craig Mishler.*

has at least a one-pound lead weight on it. This is counterbalanced on the other side of the toggle stick with a large halibut hook baited with a piece of salmon. However, the hook dangles about three inches shorter than the lead weight on the opposite side. The toggle is lowered via a heavy hand line wrapped around a piece of plywood notched widely on both ends. When the line is all the way to the bottom, the plywood holding the remainder of the line can be dropped in the bottom of the skiff, while the line already in the water is jigged up and down off the bottom.

Only a slight pressure is needed to pull the line up about four inches. When a cod hits, it is only felt as it first takes the bait. When this happens, you have to snap the line and set the hook. Pulling in a cod by hand is slow, and the fish doesn't struggle much, so it's difficult to know when you really have one hooked. The same gear and line are also used to catch halibut.

Anakenti's handline gear, shown on page 187 in Figure 6.10, is very similar to cod fishing gear reported to be in use around Kodiak in 1851 (see Holmberg 1985:47). In the 1850s, however, a heavy round stone took the place of the lead weight.

Being part Norwegian, Ed Opheim Sr. (1997) is very fond of cod but disdains halibut, an opinion that has also been adopted by many Alutiiqs:

EO: *The thing is, a cod fisherman was never a halibut eater. It's the truth. We never, very seldom we ever took home a halibut to eat. And if we did, we just took the head. Because what could we do with a halibut? We'd catch 'em on our codfish gear, and if they came up with a hook down in their stomach, they'd die, so all we could do was release 'em and let 'em go to the bottom. And I remember fishing codfish alongside of a big halibut schooner, and we were cod fishing, and they were halibut fishing, and here they were throwing the codfish overboard, and saving the halibut, and we were throwing the halibut over[board] and saving the codfish.*

CM: *You just didn't have a taste for halibut, is that the main reason?*

EO: *That's it. I don't know. Halibut has an odd smell to it. They have a smell that's, I don't know, none of us liked it. But a codfish, you know, is a fish like a schmoe, you know. You can make anything out of it, you know. I suppose you could even make cakes or something, bread, I don't know. You could cook a codfish in so many different ways, and it's a fish that you like to eat.*

CM: *Did you like the tongues? You eat the tongues?*

EO: *We used to have a bucket on board. Coming home from the fishing grounds, well we'd get busy as boys, and we'd start cutting codfish tongues, and man, we'd have buckets of codfish tongues, you know, and we had 'em fried, and we had 'em creamed, and we had 'em, and we had 'em cooked in every way you could think of. So we were living really better than a millionaire.*

Fig. 6.11. *Toni Squartsoff making pirok with a Russian Orthodox cross in the top crust, Ouzinkie, 1997. Photo by Craig Mishler.*

Theodore Squartsoff eats almost any kind of fresh fish, even sculpins and Irish lords, which he claims are some of the best tasting. He likes his cod or *amutaq*, however, from deep water: "As far as I'm concerned, shallow water fish [except salmon] are pretty much your trash fish. If you want really good clean fish you've got to go to deep water." He believes that shallow water cod are living off of human garbage.

Sven Haakanson Sr. of Old Harbor (1997) has a similar perspective:

And they used to use them pogies [greenlings] and sculpins, long as they caught them way off in the deep. But they'd never eat them, the ones around the dock, 'cause they used to call them "gurry suckers." All the toilets and everything going on. They'd never eat them. The ones that stick around under the dock. Filipinos ate them all the time; we wouldn't. 'Cause you know the sewers going down [into the ocean], and we'd cut them open, and they got stools in them and everything, so they called them "gurry suckers." No one would eat them.

Subsistence and "Food for the Day"

Here are some local fish recipes:

1) *Pirok*. Fresh or salt salmon *pirok* is a traditional Alutiiq food that may be thought of as a fish pie, but *pirok* can also made by substituting corned beef in place of salmon. Roll out a sheet of pie crust dough, insert it in a large baking pan, and add a layer of cooked white rice, a layer of stir-fried vegetables (which can include carrots, onions, green pepper, cabbage, and rutabagas), a layer of fresh sockeye salmon, another layer of vegetables, another layer of cooked white rice, and optionally a layer of something else, like hard-boiled eggs. Cover ingredients with a top crust of more pie dough and bake in a 350-degree Fahrenheit oven for about an hour and fifteen minutes. Some people like to garnish their *pirok* with ketchup after it is served. Toni Squartsoff cuts the outline of a three-barred Russian Orthodox cross into the top crust before baking. One of Toni's *piroks* made on May 14, 1997, fed fourteen people with lots leftover.

2) *Piroshkis* (Herman Squartsoff's favorite). Stuff large dinner rolls with cooked or canned salmon and rice or corned beef and rice. Fried vegetables are optional. Herman says the old way of making these, as learned from his father, was to use a heavy pie crust dough rather than yeast-leavened bread. *Piroshkis* are a lot like *pirok*.

3) Fish hash (George Inga Sr.'s favorite). Chop up any kind of fish and pan-fry it with cooked potatoes.

4) *Kinuwaq* (boiled fish; Carl Christiansen's favorite). Boil water with onions and bacon and lots of Johnny's Seafood Seasoning. Then add potatoes, and when the potatoes are almost done, toss in the salmon steaks. They will be done in just three or four minutes. The broth is really good too.

5) Boiled fish heads and roe (Abalik's favorite).

6) *Sikiaq* (half-smoked salmon). Put some fresh salmon fillets in a salt brine for an hour or two. After removing the salmon from the brine, cold smoke the fish for one to three days, using a mild wood, like cottonwood. Top the fish with sliced onions, margarine or butter, and bacon, cover, and bake slowly for about thirty to forty minutes in a low oven.

7) Halibut chowder (Rolfie Christiansen's favorite). Toss chunks of fresh halibut into a big pot of boiling water and thicken with carrots, macaroni, rice, potatoes, and onions. Season with Johnny's Seafood Seasoning.

8) Red salmon gravy dinner (Theodore Squartsoff's favorite). In a

large roasting or baking pan add two cans of stewed tomatoes and two cans of water. Add one chopped onion. Dice up one red salmon into one-inch cubes and add to base. On top of mixture place two whole red salmon fillets side by side. Season with salt and pepper. Cover fillets with one pound of sliced bacon. Bake at 375 degrees for one hour. This is good even without the bacon.

Plants and Berries

The Alutiiq diet would simply not be complete without plants and berries. Every year each person in Old Harbor and Ouzinkie on average consumes about eight pounds of berries. Starting the last week in July people in Old Harbor and Ouzinkie go out berry picking and get gallons of salmonberries, blueberries, blackberries, mossberries, and cranberries, which are made into jam or frozen for later use. This activity continues through the month of August. Theodore Squartsoff's favorite dessert is *chiidaq*—salmonberries with milk and sugar. George Inga freezes his salmonberries and then during the winter thaws them and eats them with boiled fish.

Unlike other subsistence foods, which are widely shared, Alutiiqs tend to hoard their berries and keep their favorite berry patches secret. In Old Harbor, while visiting Larry and Martha Matfay, I tasted *piinaq* for the first time—this has a very sour taste. *Piinaq* is made with fermented salmon eggs whipped together with sourberries, mashed potatoes, and sometimes a little sugar. It is sometimes referred to as "Aleut ice cream."

Two wild plants they used to eat are *laq* ("wild rice"), a plant with a maroon flower that grows about twelve inches high, and *aaduunaq* ("wild rhubarb"). People also like to chop up the stem and the leaves of plants called pushkis or petrushkis and boil them with fish. These plants give the fish a very special flavor. In Ouzinkie, some families use high bush cranberries for sore throats and cottonwood or *ciquq* for hangovers.

An inventory of the many plants used by Ouzinkie residents for food and medicine is contained in the richly illustrated book, *Plant Lore of an Alaskan Island* (Graham 1985). One of the highlights of the book is the transcription of an interview with elders Jenny Chernikoff and Sasha Smith, but it also contains numerous local recipes using wild foods.

CONCLUSION

In January 1997, when I was visiting Theodore Squartsoff in Ouzinkie, it was on the last two days of duck hunting season, and Theodore felt an urgency to go out and get a few more ducks. The urgency was so great that he pulled his son J. R. out of school to go with him. When I laughed and pointed out that he already had lots of ducks in his freezer, Theodore turned and said to me, "It's just not the same. They don't taste the same. And besides, the important thing is to get food for the day, not for the year." This side of subsistence is seldom appreciated or understood by residents of Alaskan cities who only go out to hunt and fish once or twice a year. For Theodore and many others, subsistence means having the freedom to go out and put fresh food on the table every day all year round. It is a traditional and sacred way of living, a way of thinking about the world, a way of seeing the world, and a way of being in the world.

Meditation Upon a Pirok

Layer upon layer
The earth's crust, rolled out dough.
Rice, cabbage, and rutabagas,
Fresh red salmon, salted and peppered,
More cabbage and rutabagas, more rice, hard-boiled eggs,
Orthodox cross cut into the top crust,
Baked for an hour in the oven.
Just add ketchup.
Yum.

Layer upon layer
Alutiiqs, Russians, Scandinavians, Americans,
More Americans, more Scandinavians, more Russians, more Alutiiqs.
This is how the villages were made:
Akhiok, Ouzinkie, Old Harbor, Karluk, Larsen Bay, Port Lions,
Chenega Bay, Tatitlek, Nanwalek, Port Graham,
Perryville, the Chigniks, Ivanof Bay.
Layer upon layer,
Baked two centuries until brown.
Just add ketchup.
Yum.

Chapter Seven

Social and Cultural Change Since the Oil Spill

Social and cultural change is something which has always been present in Kodiak communities, but it has a special place in this ethnography because during the past nine years since I initiated my field work, the rate of change appears to be greatly accelerated, and it is having a dramatic impact on the old way of life. In 1989, for example, most homes in Ouzinkie and Old Harbor only received one channel, the Rural Alaskan Television Network (RATNET). With cable TV and numerous personal satellite dishes, villagers are now tuned into dozens of channels across the nation twenty-four hours a day, even if the nation is not tuned in to them. And the surprises keep coming. When I visited the home of Sophie and George Inga Sr. in Old Harbor in the spring of 1998, I was stunned to find these elders playing computer solitaire. Since then they have added e-mail, and we now correspond.

One fairly obvious thing is that Ouzinkie and Old Harbor are no longer isolated by their distance from urban areas. Instead of two or three commercial flights a day, which was the norm in 1989, these villages are now serviced by six or more flights a day when the weather permits. Residents can fly to Kodiak in less than half an hour, arrive in Anchorage in two to three hours, and end up in Seattle in seven or eight. The use of telephones and VHF radios has greatly increased, and during the *Exxon Valdez* oil spill all of the village councils acquired fax machines.

THE CHANGING ECONOMY

While during the Russian and early American periods cash or credit became available to the Koniag through sea otter hunting and fur trapping, the cash or credit was used primarily for luxury items. People in the villages were able to make a living doing subsistence off the land and sea. The Russians also taught them cattle herding and gardening.

If they received money from fur trapping they used it to buy guns, skiffs, and gear so they could do more subsistence.

During the 1920s and 1930s villagers started working in the canneries and became involved in the commercial fisheries. The canneries not only supplied wages but also sold material goods and groceries. Every cannery on the island also had a store. Villagers purchased clothing items and staple foods such as tea, coffee, sugar, flour, salt, and rice.

When power dories became available in the 1930s, Alutiiqs found many opportunities to crew and to captain the vessels. Ownership was still a distant dream, since at that time all of the boats were owned by the canneries. In the words of Tom Shugak (1992:49) of Old Harbor, "The end-of-season payoff was not large by current standards; $300 bought a winter's supply of grub, .22-gauge shotgun shells were a quarter for fifty rounds." By the 1940s, through technical fishing skills acquired largely from Scandinavian immigrants, some men prospered and accumulated enough capital to acquire their own boats. They became independent businessmen. By the mid-1950s those who had purse seines began to acquire power blocks for pulling in their nets, which reduced the amount of back-breaking hand labor. Also in the 1950s they started to fish for king crab during the stormy winter months, and power blocks were the

Fig. 7.1. *Ouzinkie houses with rooftop satellite TV dishes, 1996. Photo by Craig Mishler.*

Fig. 7.2. *Old Harbor purse seiner, the* **Carla Rae C.** *Photo by Craig Mishler.*

key to hauling in heavy crab pots. In 1959 nine boats and seventeen men from Old Harbor were fishing king crab, yet all of their summer and winter fisheries combined only brought an income of "somewhat less than $2,000 per employee" (Befu 1970:33).

After the State of Alaska limited-entry permit program was instituted on January 1, 1973, many families in Old Harbor and Ouzinkie were in a good position to acquire permits to go with their boats. Limited entry was instituted as a conservation method to restrict the number of vessels catching salmon in Alaskan waters. For those individuals who could demonstrate prior involvement in the fisheries for the previous four years, purse seine, gill net, and beach seine permits were issued by the state free of charge. In the Kodiak district, 368 purse seine permits, 183 gill net permits, and 27 beach seine permits were issued, and those numbers have remained relatively constant ever since. Those who did not receive permits were much less fortunate and either had to buy a permit or work as crew members for those who received a permit.

Commercial fishing permits amounted to instant capital. They could be used as collateral to get boat loans. They were like money in the bank, subject to supply and demand in the marketplace. In the late-1980s purse seine permits were highly sought after and sold for $150,000 or more each. However, salmon prices began to collapse in the early 1990s (Figure 7.3), largely due to salmon farming in Norway and Chile. With

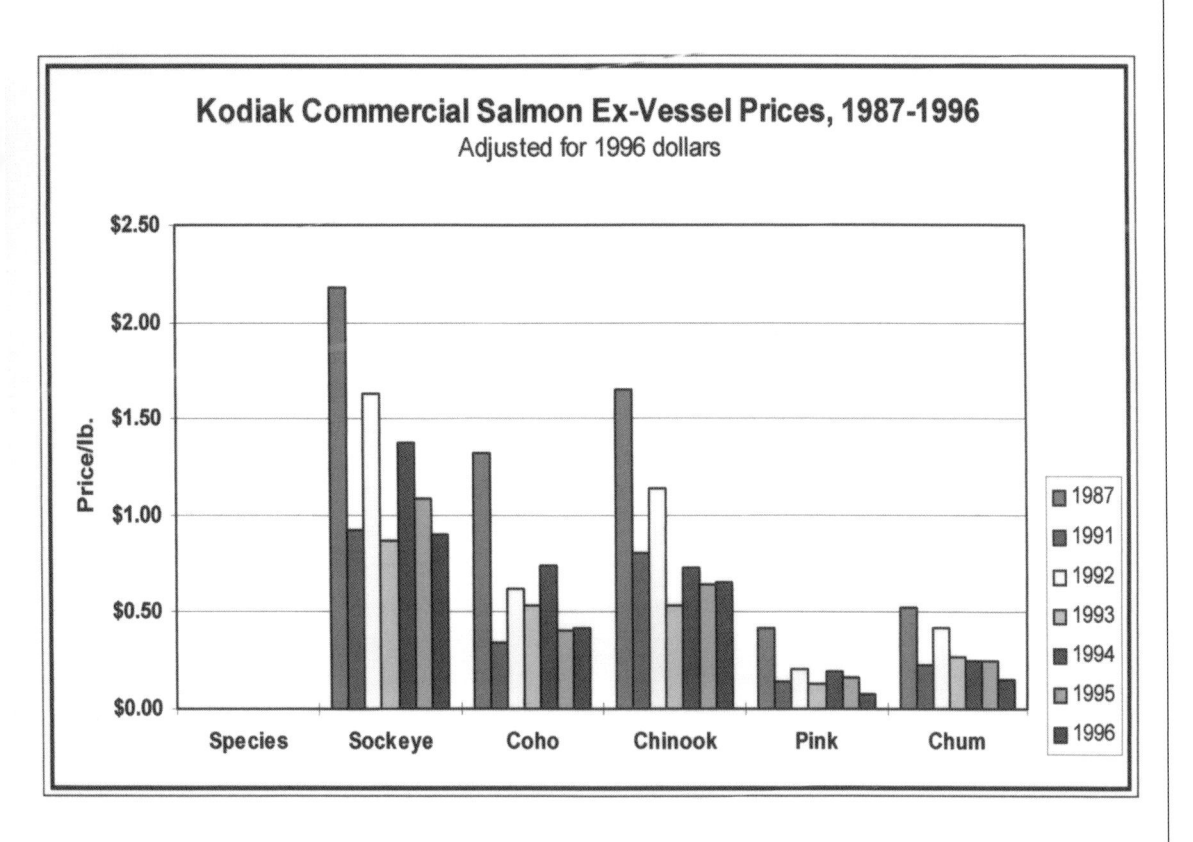

Kodiak Commercial Salmon Ex-Vessel Prices, 1987-1996
Adjusted for 1996 dollars

Fig. 7.3.

Kodiak Commercial Salmon Ex-Vessel Prices, 1987-1996
Adjusted for 1996 dollars

	1987	1991	1992	1993	1994	1995	1996
Species	$/Pound	$/Pound	$/Pound	$/Pound	$/Pound	$/Pound	$/Pound
Sockeye	2.18	0.92	1.63	0.86	1.38	1.08	0.90
Coho	1.32	0.35	0.62	0.54	0.74	0.41	0.42
Chinook	1.65	0.81	1.13	0.54	0.73	0.65	0.65
Pink	0.42	0.14	0.20	0.13	0.19	0.16	0.07
Chum	0.53	0.23	0.42	0.27	0.24	0.25	0.15

Compiled from Kodiak Management Area Commercial Salmon Annual Reports, ADF&G Div. Of Commercial Fisheries, 1987-1996

Fig. 7.3A.

Fig. 7.4.

Kodiak Commercial Salmon Ex-Vessel Values (In Millions), 1987-1996
Adjusted for 1996 dollars

	1987	1991	1992	1993	1994	1995	1996
Species	Income	Income	Income	Income	Income	Income	Income
Sockeye	24.6	26.8	38.6	20.8	19.7	24.9	25.3
Coho	2.1	0.8	1.4	1.0	1.9	1.0	0.7
Chinook	1.0	0.2	0.4	0.4	0.2	0.2	0.1
Pink	7.5	6.7	2.4	18.0	5.9	26.3	0.9
Chum	2.8	1.6	2.1	1.0	1.4	3.2	0.7
Total	$38.0	$36.1	$45.1	$41.1	$29.2	$55.6	$27.7

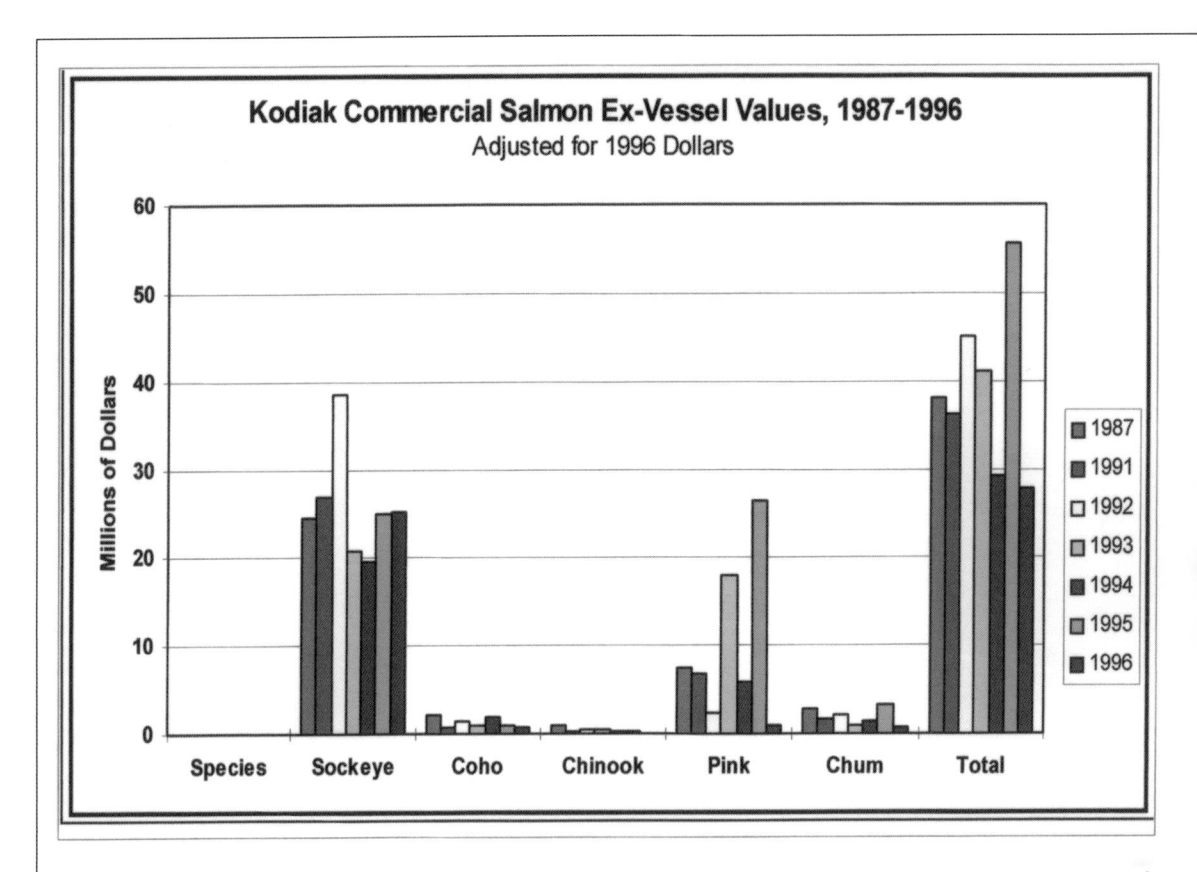

Sources: Kodiak Management Area Commercial Salmon Annual Reports, ADF&G Division of Commercial Fisheries, 1987-1996.

Fig. 7.4A.

lower fish prices, the value of limited entry purse seine permits around Kodiak fell to about $40,000 each in the mid-1990s (Berntsen 1997).

Compared to 1987, a pre-spill year, fish prices in 1993 collapsed to less than half of what they were. Both 1994 and 1996 were disastrous years, and even though 1995 was a bumper year for fish volume, with record runs of pinks and chums and strong runs of sockeyes, prices still remained depressed (see Figure 7.3). The downward stairstep effect is very evident over a ten-year period (Figure 7.3). In 1994 and again in 1996 the ex-vessel values, an estimate of the money paid to fishermen by the canneries, dropped to below 1987 levels (see Figure 7.4; Figure 7.4A). By 1996 pink salmon were only bringing in seven cents/lb. (Figure 7.3A). The trend towards higher volume catches has tended to benefit high-tech purse seiner crews at the expense of low-tech gear operators such as beach seiners and set gill netters, but even the purse seiners have been unable to keep up with inflationary rises in the cost of fuel, gear, and groceries. In the mid-1990s boat owners have found they often cannot earn enough to make their boat payments and pay their operating expenses. Some fishermen spend as much as $10,000 per year on nets. A new seine skiff motor costs as much as $8,000. Permit holders and captains are lucky just to break even, while crew members find themselves working for almost nothing.

In order to maintain a standard of living above 1987 levels, Kodiak fishermen in the 1990s have had to catch a great many more fish. In 1987, 7.7 million fish were caught; 1993 saw a record harvest of 39.3 million fish but this did not translate into record profits. Harvest volume in 1993 increased by 500 percent over 1987, but the total ex-vessel value of the salmon increased by only 17 percent, not even keeping pace with inflation (ADF&G 1993:61–62).

To make up for lower prices, many village fishermen realized they not only had to catch more fish but they also had to fish all-year-round to come out ahead. However, after king crab stocks were depleted in the early 1980s, the king crab fishery was closed and it has not reopened since then. Herring and salmon still provided the core income, but it was still a fairly meager existence from a cash economy point of view. Understandably, a lot of fishermen in Old Harbor and Ouzinkie began participating in twice-yearly twenty-four-hour halibut openings, and they also started fishing tanner crab from January through March. By 1995, however, tanner stocks in the Kodiak area were also depleted, and that fishery has remained closed.

In 1996 halibut fishing went to an individual fishing quota or IFQ system, based on previous participation levels and harvest tickets. This has amounted to another form of limited entry. In response to the closure of tanner crab, many fishermen have converted their crab pots into cod pots or have gone to fishing cod with long lines. Cod is now the only major fishery that does not require a limited entry permit. It is still open to everybody.

During the early and mid-1990s herring prices were the only prices which remained high. For a few years herring, a spring fishery that runs from mid-April until mid-May, was considered the new "money fish," and Kodiak fishermen counted on herring to subsidize the other fisheries they were involved in. In 1996, for example, they received $2,200/ton for herring, but in 1997 herring prices suddenly collapsed under a weakened Japanese economy, falling to $200/ton (Parker 1997). In 1998 prices only rose modestly to about $500/ton. In 1998 the price of halibut tumbled to $1.35/lb. compared to $2.25/lb. the year before (Buckley 1998).

In 1998 persons with Old Harbor addresses had twenty-nine salmon purse-seine permits, three salmon gill-net permits, one salmon beach-seine permit, and three herring purse-seine permits. This is three more than the thirty salmon permits counted by Davis in 1986 (1986a:200), but a closer look reveals that the extra three are actually nonresidents using Old Harbor as their address. In 1998 persons with Ouzinkie addresses held ten salmon purse-seine permits and two salmon gill-net permits (Alaska Limited Entry Commission 1998). This is identical to the twelve limited-entry salmon permits counted by Davis in 1986 (1986a:214). With the salmon fishery no longer very profitable, one might expect that villagers would sell their permits, but the going price for permits, which can be bought and sold on the marketplace, has dropped as precipitously as the prices paid for salmon.

The weakened commercial fishing economy, moreover, has resulted in a reduction in the number of boats and a loss of jobs, particularly to crew members. A significant number of salmon permits have remained idle in recent years. In the summers of 1997 and 1998, for example, there were only two purse-seiners and two gill-netters still fishing in Ouzinkie. Eight other permit holders declined to fish.

Throughout the 1990s, young men in Ouzinkie and Port Lions have made a fairly good alternate living longshoring in Danger Bay, where they load logs onto Japanese logging ships. However, in 1998 timber prices, like fish prices, plunged as the result of a weakened Asian economy, leaving many of these young men unemployed. In 1993, for example, there were fifteen jobs and households involved in stevedoring. The average reported earnings for these jobs was $10,650, or an estimated $185,939 to the community (Alaska Department of Fish and Game, Division of Subsistence, Household Surveys, 1994). The loss of these jobs was strongly felt in 1998, even though some men were able to pick up temporary jobs in housing construction and remodeling during the summer months.

In Old Harbor commercial fishing is a little bit better off than it is in Ouzinkie. While very competitive with boats outside their community, Old Harbor fishermen nevertheless cooperate through something called "the combine." The combine seems to be very effective when they are fishing herring. Leroy Gregory, who fished for many years as a crewman but

Fig. 7.5. *Japanese logging ship in Danger Bay, 1994. Photo courtesy of Ed Opheim Sr.*

later drove a taxi and delivery van in the village, explained to me how the combine works (field notes April 13, 1992):

Since each herring boat cannot afford to have its own spotter plane, the captains pool their money to hire one pilot for the whole fleet. Accordingly, they work together to catch the fish and share their profits equally. If one boat has engine trouble and breaks down, that captain and crew still get a share of the money made by the others. The Christiansen brothers have a smaller combine for salmon that does not include the other Old Harbor boats, but spotter planes are seldom used for salmon, so costs are lower. Leroy says, "Old Harbor fishermen are known to be very aggressive. We don't give way to nobody!"

The people with smaller older wooden boats that fish only salmon are gradually being forced out. In the words of Ron Bernsten (1997) of Old Harbor:

Everyone that lives here loves it here. But with the lack of jobs—once that's gone, you lose hope. And without hope you're nothing. You lose hope, you lose faith in your community, and you tend to get desperate, and then you start hitting the drugs and the bottle.

The main choices available to struggling fishermen are to fall into poverty and depend upon welfare, move away to another community where there are jobs, get college or technical training, or look for a new occupation. Bernsten (1997) sees government welfare as a form of humiliation:

The government right now is trying to stop welfare, in which a lot of our people I'm sorry to say, are on. But they have no choice. We're a proud people; we don't want food stamps. We want to work. We want to do what we've always done, and that's fish. We used to make a living as fishermen, salmon fishing. But that's been taken away. The farm fish has screwed that up. The price is so screwed up you can't make a living any more, and we used to. In the older days too, when we had a bad season, the canneries were more closely knit with the people than they are nowadays. They say, "O.K. You had a bad season. Good. We'll grubstake you for the winter. 'Cause, you know, there's better years comin." Which was the case. But it's not. Prices have gone to hell, and the canneries' attitude is saying, "You go to hell" because the canneries—I don't know who's controlling them—but we can't make a living.

Fig. 7.6. *Transportation Old Harbor style: the purse seiner* Glennette C. *Photo by Craig Mishler.*

202   Black Ducks and Salmon Bellies

Leroy Gregory, another former crew member, found an alternative to commercial fishing in his taxi service and delivery business. But the most attractive new occupation, which still involves the operation of boats and life in the outdoors, lies in sport fishing and ecotourism. As I became aware of this trend, I asked George Inga Sr. (1996) of Old Harbor and others about the future of commercial fishing. George was somewhat optimistic:

CM: What do you think is going to happen to commercial fishing now? Do you think it's going to have a chance to stick around, or do you think it's going down?

GI: I really don't know. If the price goes up. You know, right now they're having a hard time. 'Cause the price is so low. It's getting the fishermens down, you know. They can't make a living on that fishing any more. The fuel costs so much, you know. I think if the price goes back up, I think the fishing is not going to die out, no way. No way. One year it might be bad, the next year we'll hear [have] more. It just depends on what kind of a winter you've got, you know.

I raised the same question to Nick Pestrikoff Sr. in Ouzinkie, who points to younger men in the village for much of the decline in commercial fishing.

NP: Well, like I referenced earlier, you know, the fishing thing, the big income of the past, it's fading away. Our young people are not interested in it any more. The generation that's coming up, virtually none of them are participating in it. And the locals that still have boats better rely on outside help from somewhere else, just to crewmember their boats, you know? So that thing is pretty much gone, and the people that show any ambition at all are moving into these other areas. You know, the six-pack license [for U.S. Coast Guard approved charter boat captains] and—primarily that's it. And then there's other things. There's more and more talk about other things in the tourism area now, which I think is going to be the big and upcoming thing.

One of the first ones to take advantage of opportunities in sport fishing and ecotourism in Old Harbor was Freddy Christiansen, a seasoned commercial fisherman. Along with Jeff Peterson, who began taking out sports fishermen and duck hunters in 1988, Freddy Christiansen (1996) has been something of a visionary in this arena:

FC: Well, I would have to say that I think that the commercial fishing industry as everybody is aware of, is in a slump, and I do believe that there is some changes in the air, and not only Old Harbor, but as well as other places in rural Alaska, and I think it has a lot to do with welfare reform and trying to become more self-sufficient and being creative and trying to bring more jobs to the community.

The commercial fishing industry, specifically the salmon, salmon and herring, we have lost our prices, you know. Of course there's always been a trend of the prices fluctuating up and down, you know, and that's been in the history. But to see it as devastating as it was after the oil spill, there was never a period, a five-year period where the prices were ever that low for that period of time, that long period of time.

One of the things that I really feel that the community should be involved in [is] tourism—that it is coming. Some people want to be naive and not accept that, and are against it, and I respect that because I'm concerned about it as much as they are because you know, the main thing that got me involved was being the tribal council president for quite a few years.

Christiansen's first foray into ecotourism was building the Sitkalidak Lodge in partnership with another local purse-seine captain, Rick Berns. Berns's wife Wilma is Freddy's aunt, so this was a business created through affinal kinship. The Sitkalidak Lodge, a $100,000 facility with television sets in each room and a cafe, opened in 1989, right after the oil spill, although the timing of its opening seems to have been a coincidence. The Lodge was built right next to the old airstrip and close to the ocean, where guests have a spectacular view of the ocean and the mountains on Sitkalidak Island.

Eventually, Christiansen bought out Berns and formed a new partnership with Gary Price and Charlie Powers, two non-Natives, to form First Frontier Adventures. Price's wife Wanda, however, is Christiansen's cousin, so kinship again helped to bond the business relationship. This group invested $160,000 to buy a large fifty-three-foot charter boat, *The Sitkalidak Straits*, which they converted into a deluxe cabin cruiser. *The Sitkalidak Straits* slept six and allowed comfortable side trips all over the south end of the island, but recently this boat was sold and replaced with several smaller vessels. Their business has been catering to conservation groups such as the World Wildlife Fund, the Great Bear Foundation, the Izaak Walton League, and the Nature Conservancy. Most of the guests are middle-aged affluent men, who pay more than $400 per day each for guided fishing, meals, and lodging. One recent investment has been the remodeling of the old pool hall into a lounge area and freezer facility for lodge guests. This cottage industry provides a significant number of jobs for young people in the village, who are hired to clean boats, process and freeze fish, clean rooms, cook gourmet meals, and wash dishes. One night I was graciously invited to join the guests for dinner and was treated to grilled steak and fresh crab right off the boat, with baked potato and tossed salad, topped off with a large slice of "Better Than Sex Cake."

Other Old Harbor Natives involved in sport fishing and chartering include Jeff Peterson (see Klouda 1996b) and George Gatter Jr. Peterson specializes in deer and duck hunting, taking clients out in his twenty-six-

Fig. 7.7. *Left: Old Harbor sport fish and touring boat, the* Sitkalidak Straits, *1997. Photo by Craig Mishler.*

Fig. 7.8. *Below: The Sitkalidak Lodge in Old Harbor, 1997. Photo by Craig Mishler.*

foot cabin cruiser, while Gatter has found a specialty niche in guided fly fishing and runs a small tackle shop next to his house. It is important to recognize that Peterson identifies himself as an "Alutiiq Native Guide" and that the Sitkalidak Lodge promises customized trips on "Alutiiq Culture." Many of the visiting sport fishermen are not so interested in eating their fish as they are in being entertained by the outdoors. Although these sport fishermen almost always take home some frozen vacuum-sealed salmon and halibut for their family and friends, much of their fishing is catch-and-release. This is in direct contrast to the ethic of local subsistence fishermen like elder Paul Kahutak, who eats everything he catches and never throws anything back.

In addition to sport fishermen, Old Harbor outfitters also entertain deer hunters, who arrive in October, and duck hunters, who arrive in December and January. These hunters, most of whom are from the Midwest, are not interested in eating ducks as much as they are in collecting many species of ducks to mount and display in their trophy rooms. Likewise, they are not so interested in putting up deer meat as in taking home a big set of antlers.

Not everyone in Old Harbor has been receptive to tourism development. As sports fishing and sports hunting increase, there is more tension within the community, and subsistence users sometimes feel like they are the ones being squeezed. One of the most outspoken critics was Walt Erickson (1997), a retired commercial fisherman and grocery store owner who disliked the clientele. As an elder, Walt's opinions carried considerable weight:

> WE: The people are getting so enthused or brainwashed by what they call tourism, and there's people even in Washington, D.C. that are working

Fig. 7.9. *Magazine display ads for Old Harbor Guides and Outfitters.*

on us to help the people that want to go into this business get loans and everything. Truly, I'm against it. I'm against it because I think it ruins a village lifestyle.

It brings an influx of bad things to villages, like drugs and alcohol, and all the people who can afford to come to the village to do this sport fishing are all well-to-do people, and well-to-do people they know the weakness of the Native people, and they bring it with them. Drugs and alcohol. They bring it. I know it.

They bring it there, and give it to the people, thinking, "Oh he's a good man; he's a good guy. He brings us alcohol and drugs and everything. Boy, they must be nice people," you know. And people will eat that up. Same time they're raping the villages. They really are. The only people that are going to benefit is like the lodge or the people that are in to make big bucks off of this, and believe me, it's big money.

Starting in 1996 Old Harbor began hosting passengers from small cruise ships, which stop at the village en route from Prince Rupert, B.C., to Provideniya, in the Russian Far East. Larger cruise ships would certainly

Fig. 7.10. *Jeff Peterson dressing out halibut caught by his sports fishing clients, Old Harbor, September 1999. Photo by Craig Mishler.*

overwhelm the community, but the *Akademik Shokalskiy* only carries about forty passengers, which for now is quite manageable (Richardson 1997).

In Ouzinkie a similar trend towards tourism is underway, although on a somewhat smaller scale. Andy Christofferson, who runs a Bayliner cabin cruiser under the business name Marmot Bay Excursions, and Herman Squartsoff, who operates a large open skiff under the name Spruce Island Charters, are two emerging operators who have started up in the 1990s. Both have been Coast Guard certified and have "six pack" licenses to transport up to six passengers in their boats.

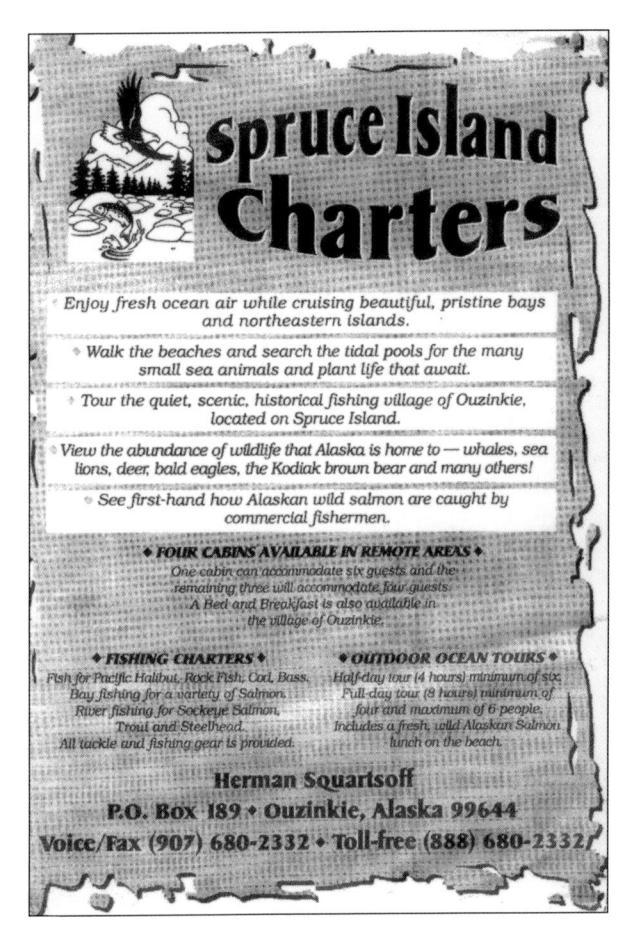

Fig. 7.11. *Herman Squartsoff's charter skiff display ad.*

While Ouzinkie still has no lodge for visitors, Herman's brother, Theodore Squartsoff, and his wife Toni have started running a low-profile bed-and-breakfast during the fall, winter, and spring months. They do not advertise, but they house Herman's clients as well as other visitors to the community such as nurses, doctors, and dentists. Here again, kinship between two siblings has enhanced a business venture. Not to be left behind, the Ouzinkie Native Corporation has invested in tourism by becoming the new majority owner of the Katmai Wilderness Lodge, located on Kukak Bay inside Katmai National Park (Dobbyn 2000).

Elsewhere around the island, Randy Christiansen in Larsen Bay and Mitch Simeonoff in Akhiok, two other commercial fishermen, are transitioning into charter and outfitting businesses. Although lots of brown bears are found in the area around Old Harbor and are frequently seen at the village dump, tourists who come to Old Harbor and specifically want to view brown bears are now sent to Mitch Simeonoff, who has ready access to some sites where bears can be seen feeding on salmon all summer long. In this way, the villages are cooperating with one another to enhance each other's businesses.

A newspaper feature article, "Defending Old Harbor," written by Naomi Klouda (1997), describes in considerable detail the changes brought to that community by the recent boom in tourism and estimates that in 1996 there were seventeen full- and part-time jobs created in Old Harbor to cater to the new visitors. Based on her interviews with Freddy Christiansen, Jeff Peterson, and others, Klouda brings out two fundamental beliefs guiding this development.

First, they are convinced that if Old Harbor people don't develop tourism, someone else from outside the community will, and they will be left behind. Second, by being involved, Old Harbor people have a fair amount of control over where visitors go, what they see, and what they do. Local guides protect sensitive subsistence salmon streams, for example, so that by common agreement outsiders do only catch-and-release fishing there, and only four clients per day may accompany each guide.

Because all of the lands adjacent to many salmon streams are owned by the Old Harbor Native Corporation, shareholders can effectively control public access and limit competition with local subsistence users.

In 1999, a number of new operators began operating sportfishing charters out of Old Harbor, including Buddy Pestrikoff, Alex Shugak, and Al Cratty. All of these men have spent many years working in commercial fisheries. Little more than a big skiff equipped with a fast outboard motor and some life jackets often suffice for start-up costs since some sports fishermen like to fly in on the morning plane, fish all day, and return to Kodiak City on the afternoon flight. Others come for several days at a time, hoping to catch both salmon and halibut. In response to this pattern, Al and Johnetta Cratty have started a bed-and-breakfast business, and Ray and Stella Krumrey have also opened one.

Naomi Klouda (1999) writes that "You can hardly name a family that has *not* benefited from tourism." She says that what really kicked off tourism as a new economy in Old Harbor was the National Geographic television special, "Island of the Giant Bears," now retitled and available on video (Bayer, 1994) and a related *National Geographic Magazine* feature article (Eliot 1993).

LAND BUYBACKS: THE LARGE-PARCEL PROGRAM

In Old Harbor, but not Ouzinkie, land buybacks are having a major impact on the community. These buybacks have largely been enabled by funds authorized through the *Exxon Valdez* Oil Spill Trustee Council, an organization devoted to restoring the wilderness habitat of birds and other animals damaged by the oil spill of 1989. The Trustees received their funds through the damage settlement reached between the Exxon Corporation, the State of Alaska, and the federal government as approved by the courts on October 9, 1991. Soon thereafter, the Trustees began to initiate both large- and small-parcel buybacks, and primarily what they have been buying back are Native lands in Prince William Sound, Lower Cook Inlet, and the Kodiak archipelago. Large parcels were defined as parcels greater than one thousand acres.

The Trustees first went to the Native Corporations, which owned the largest parcels. Following the Alaska Native Land Claims Settlement Act of 1971, the Old Harbor Native Corporation received thousands of acres of federal lands in the vicinity of the village to develop into profit-making ventures and to protect their subsistence areas from encroachment. To do this, they selected large chunks of the Kodiak National Wildlife Refuge, many of them at the mouth of major salmon-spawning rivers (Map 4). The managers of the Refuge, however, were worried that the development of these Refuge inholdings into sports hunting and fishing lodges and private homes would have a negative impact on the habitat of salmon, bears, deer, and other animals living on the Refuge. The villagers did not really want to see this development occur but felt that was the only way they could lift themselves out of poverty and dependency on government transfer payments.

In May 1995, the Trustees bought back 31,609 acres of Old Harbor Corporation lands and immediately gave them to the Kodiak National Wildlife Refuge, at a total price tag of $14.5 million (Anonymous 1995). Of this amount, the Trustees paid $11.25 million, and the federal government anted up the other $3.25 million from its share of the spill criminal settlement. Consequently, shareholders were paid for not developing their lands and for keeping outside interests from coming in. Most notably, the Council purchased a conservation easement for virtually all of Sitkalidak Island, setting it aside as a private wildlife refuge.

The urgency of this settlement was undoubtedly prompted by the downturn of commercial fish prices in the early 1990s. Old Harbor's economy is focused on commercial and subsistence fishing, and the Old Harbor Native Corporation's Board of Directors is controlled by active and retired commercial fishing captains. The settlement and the subsequent distribution of corporation dividends has cushioned the loss of fishing income and has allowed boat owners to continue making payments on their vessels. The Old Harbor Native Corporation has kept most of its large buyback monies in Seattle real estate investments, paying out modest dividends to its 350 shareholders (under $10,000/year).

This stands in sharp contrast to the Akhiok-Kaguyak Corporation, which has seen a great deal of internal feuding over the distribution of their buyback proceeds. Akhiok-Kaguyak, which negotiated side by side with Old Harbor, sold back over 118,674 acres and received $42 million, more than twice as much as Old Harbor. But Akhiok-Kaguyak shareholders fought against their corporation president and Board and went to court to win a dividend payout of $30,000 (Phillips 1997). The corporation's Board of Directors finally settled out of court.

At one point, however, it was brother against brother and brother against sister. On November 3, 1997, the Akhiok feuding made the front page of the *Anchorage Daily News* (Phillips 1997) and the *Kodiak Daily Mirror* (Associated Press 1997). There was resentment over the $1,500/month salaries paid to corporation Board members, and the dissidents wanted to dissolve the corporation and liquidate its assets, which included an apartment complex in New Mexico.

Once the dust settled, the 147 Akhiok-Kaguyak shareholders voted out their longtime corporation president by petition. But before he was recalled, the president invested a portion of the sale proceeds into a trust fund consisting of stocks and bonds. This trust fund paid shareholders about $500/month and the corporation also paid them about $500/month. Akhiok-Kaguyak shareholders improved their standard of living by investing in new satellite dishes, four-wheelers, boats, and outboard motors, but

Fig. 7.12. *Old Harbor Native Corporation office. Photo by Craig Mishler.*

they are still feuding. In the fall of 2002 Akhiok shareholders voted to liquidate three-quarters of their $40 million settlement trust, awarding their 147 shareholders a sum of $200,000 each in two equal payments of $100,000 (Anonymous 2002). Still, this big payout has had a noticeable ripple effect on the Old Harbor Corporation, which at this writing is facing a similar asset liquidation initiative by some of its shareholders.

Old Harbor and Ouzinkie corporation shareholders, who are also shareholders in Koniag, Inc., the regional profit-making corporation, also benefited directly from a $20 million payout in January 1999 by Koniag, Inc. In 1995 Koniag, Inc., sold back many of its lands along the Karluk and Sturgeon Rivers to the Kodiak National Wildlife Refuge. With most Koniag shareholders having about 100 shares and each share dividend worth about $60, the average payout was about $6,000 (Koniag, Inc., 1999). And the money keeps on flowing. As major partners in Afognak Joint Ventures, Koniag Inc. shareholders stand to receive another $32 million from the sale of AJV lands and timber on Afognak Island to the Trustee Council.

It is ironic that many shareholders of the corporations that have sold lands to the Trustee Council remain confident that they still retain subsistence hunting and fishing rights on those lands, even though the Trustee

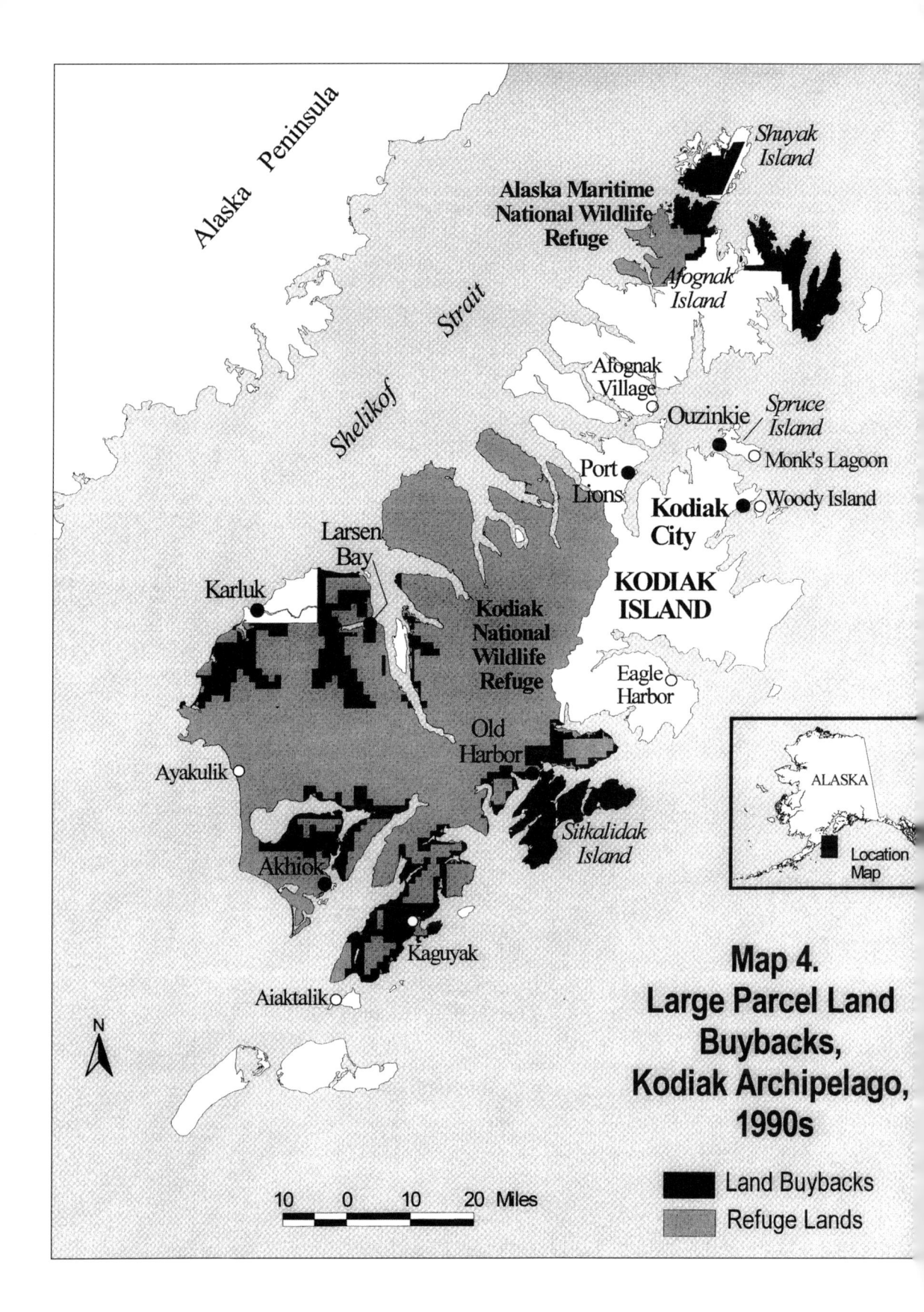

Map 4. Large Parcel Land Buybacks, Kodiak Archipelago, 1990s

Council and the federal agencies who now manage those lands actually have no authority to make such guarantees, since subsistence is regulated solely by the Alaska Board of Fish and Game and by the Federal Subsistence Board. By law, all the shareholders can actually receive from the buyers of their lands is guaranteed continuous access to those lands, and indeed in fine print this is the way the agreements seem to be worded (see for example, U.S. Department of the Interior 1995). Except for Seldovia and Nanwalek, which sold off *all* their rights to most of the lands they sold, shareholders in most of the village corporations have retained an easement for subsistence access. In other words, they cannot be cited for trespassing on lands they sold to the Trustees, but they can still be prosecuted for taking a deer out of season while they are on these lands.

At the very same time, since federal subsistence hunting regulations are generally more lenient and favorable to subsistence uses than state regulations, it appears that residents of most oil spill communities stand to benefit strategically from the sale of their lands to federal management agencies. Those lands they continue to hold onto privately will still be subject to stricter state regulations that do not favor rural residents.

THE SMALL-PARCEL PROGRAM

The Trustee Council's small-parcel buyback program has been targeted at individual Native allotments, many of which are also in the Refuge. Between March 1996 and 1998, the U.S. Fish and Wildlife Service purchased twenty-eight Native allotments, mostly from elders, and it has plans to buy several more. The funding for the small-parcel program has come from a variety of sources, including the *Exxon Valdez* oil spill civil restoration funds, and Congressional appropriations from the Land and Water Conservation Fund. The parcels are largely located along the coasts of Kiliuda Bay, Sitkalidak Strait, and Three Saints Bay.

The total acreage purchased so far for these 28 parcels is 2,923 acres, for an average size of 104.4 acres each, and the total amount paid to allotment-holders is $3.49 million, an average of $124,704 per parcel (Jerry 1998). According to an earlier estimate (Davis 1986a:193), this is still only a fraction of the 215 parcels and 13,316 acres originally filed for by Old Harbor residents. This means that the majority of those with allotment parcels are still holding on to them.

The impact of this much cash, all tax free, has been quite noticeable in the village. The small-parcel buybacks have immediately translated into luxury goods. Some people have purchased new cars (referred to as "allotment cars"), new trucks, new boats, and new houses with their allotment money, while others have invested in large satellite dishes that bring in hundreds of TV channels. All of these acquisitions are an indirect result of the oil spill.

In a community already heavily stratified into haves and have-nots (see Mishler and Mason 1996), Old Harbor now has another class of affluent people created through the buybacks. Unlike the situation in Akhiok, this affluence has not created much additional tension and conflict in the community because most of the sold allotments belonged to elders, people who were used to getting by all of their lives on very low incomes, and everyone is happy to see the elders treated well.

Some allotments were jointly held by the heirs of the original allotment-holders and accordingly subdivided the money within the family. And, very importantly, some of the allotment money has stayed in the community. Several villagers now have jobs installing and maintaining satellite dishes and cable TV.

CORPORATION DIVIDENDS

Members of the Ouzinkie Native Corporation have also recently benefited from affluence, though their affluence is of a different kind, completely unrelated to the spill. As a result of wanting to develop their lands on Afognak Island, in 1977 the Ouzinkie Native Corporation formed a joint venture with three other Native corporations to form Koncor Forest Products Company, a logging and timber export firm. The other corporations in the joint venture are the Natives of Kodiak, Inc., Yak-Tat-Kwan of Yakutat, and the Chenega Corporation of Chenega Bay. The Ouzinkie Native Corporation has derived two major benefits from this partnership: a share of Koncor's profits paid in dividends to corporation shareholders, and a local hire provision that gives longshoring jobs to over a dozen Ouzinkie men. In 1993 Koncor had over 2 billion board feet of timber inventories and revenues in excess of $64 million (Sturgeon 1994:12).

Under the leadership of the late Andy Anderson, corporation president, the ONC has become one of the most profitable Native corporations in the state, and the dividends paid out to Ouzinkie Native Corporation shareholders have been increasing since the mid-1980s. From 1973 to 1992 cumulative dividends per shareholder reached $34,000 (Berger 1993:26), and the dividends have been getting larger and larger. In 1991, for example, each shareholder received $8,000 in dividends. In 1997, each shareholder received $12,500 in dividends, paid out in quarterly installments. For a married couple, this amounted to $25,000/year, and several individuals made even more due to additional shares inherited from their deceased parents. This may all be coming to a close, however, since nearly all of the logging on Afognak was shut down in 1998 due to low demand in the Asian market. Although the corporation has investments on Wall Street outside of timber and logging, the big dividends have largely come through profit-sharing with Koncor.

Despite massive clearcutting efforts, Anderson insisted the Natives are among the biggest environmentalists and he went public with several letters to the editor of the *Kodiak Mirror* to say that they were reseeding Afognak, using seedlings from southeast Alaska, which seem to be hardier and grow faster than local stocks.

One of my questions has been whether this "easy money" from corporation dividends during the 1990s has been linked to the reduced effort in commercial fishing. After all, why should men go fishing, which is enormously difficult work, when the free money just rolls in anyway? But my hypothesis was not supported by Arthur Haakanson. While he believes his people are being spoiled by the cash dividends, Haakanson (1997) does not believe that the dividends have diminished their work ethic (see below, Appendix A).

If commercial fishing is on its last legs in Ouzinkie, this begs the question, of course, as to what is happening to subsistence harvests. For many decades subsistence fishing has been closely linked to commercial fishing because the same boats and gear are used for both harvests, and subsistence fish are frequently taken out of commercial catches for home use. With all of the new cash in both communities, are people buying more of their food and doing less subsistence? The answer to this question may only be resolved via another comprehensive subsistence harvest survey which compares harvest quantities and participation in the late 1990s with the years just before and after the oil spill.

THE NEW AFFLUENCE

The other major question raised by the new affluence in both Old Harbor and Ouzinkie is whether the communities are losing or enhancing their culture. By turning more and more towards logging and tourism for their income and by buying satellite TV dishes, are Alutiiqs being absorbed into world culture and losing what is distinctively theirs? The answer to this question seems to be yes. But are they using their newfound wealth to enhance and promote their culture? To the extent that all of the village and regional corporations financially support the Alutiiq Museum and Archaeological Repository in Kodiak City, a facility built with oil spill settlement funds, the answer to this question is also yes.

Anthropologists have been interested in these issues for some time. A 1981 symposium sponsored by the American Ethnological Society demonstrated that affluence can threaten cultural survival, turning indigenous peoples like the Alutiiq into consumers of mass marketing and making them dependent on national and global forces beyond their own control (see Salisbury 1984). Since the early 1970s such a dependency had already quietly taken place in Alaskan commercial fisheries and timber sales, two industries dominated by Japanese financial interests.

By turning to ecotourism during the 1990s, Alutiiqs are now shifting their dependency to non-Native sportsmen and conservationists who, as noted above, are themselves an affluent group. As Richard Salisbury

(1984:6) wrote in his introduction to the proceedings of the 1981 symposium, it is very much a two-edged sword: "A simple dichotomy between cases of cultural enhancement and those of cultural dependence is inappropriate. Neither is automatically the cultural consequence of affluence, but both are potential consequences."

ENCULTURATION OF YOUTH

One of the questions which confronts the analysis of social change is whether traditional knowledge and traditional values are being passed on to younger generations. In the Native world, nothing may be more important than providing young people with the love and strength and confidence to carry on the traditional way of life. As the western world swallows up small-scale societies and attempts to assimilate them through mass media, more attention has been turned toward youth who run the risk of losing their identity. According to Gordon Pullar, former director of the Kodiak Area Native Association, "It is believed by many that a loss of heritage and ethnic identity has made it difficult to feel a pride in who they are as Native people. This condition, it is said, produces a loss of self-esteem that manifests itself in self-destructive behavior such as alcohol abuse, family violence, and suicide" (Pullar 1992:182).

Three newly established and visible efforts to transmit traditional knowledge and values such as self-esteem to youngsters in the Alutiiq region are Native Heritage Weeks, Spirit Camps, and Youth-Elder Conferences.

Native Heritage Weeks are set aside each spring in Kodiak Island Borough communities to recognize the importance of preserving and reviving Alutiiq culture. In most Kodiak villages, the school rather than the church has now become the center of community social life. This is so not only because people want to see their children get a good education, but because the schools provide a central place for the community to gather and interact with one another. From September through May, Old Harbor and Ouzinkie schools provide a setting for recreational volleyball and basketball ("Little Dribblers"), intervillage basketball and wrestling matches, and high school graduations. Both children and adults attend these events, and Native Heritage Week has become a regular part of the community's social calendar.

In April 1998, I attended the Native Heritage Week celebration in Old Harbor. The activities I saw at the school were instruction in Native dancing, conducted outdoors by Connie Chya of Kodiak, instruction in Native games, conducted by Joe Kelly of Kodiak, instruction in bentwood hat making and spirit bag sewing conducted by the schoolteachers, Ray Krumrey, Phil Johnson, and Carla Lam. Although the children seemed genuinely engrossed in these hands-on activities, my impression is that the teachers' attempts, however sincere, are superficial, and that the school provides a highly artificial setting for the revival or continuation of Alutiiq traditions.

One of the best parts of the 1998 Heritage Week was the cooking of Alutiiq foods by elders Sven and Mary Haakanson. All week long they came in to the school kitchen to prepare and serve delicious traditional dishes such as boiled seal meat with rice and potatoes, ducks baked in brown gravy, sikiaq, salmon pirok, and alajiks (fry bread). Throughout the week some of the older girls worked as helpers in the kitchen and were interested in learning recipes and cooking methods.

It is also telling that the school did not schedule any time for the teaching of the Alutiiq language during the Heritage Week, even though an Alutiiq teacher was on the school staff. The Alutiiq language has been sadly overlooked during Heritage Week. In Alutiiq people talk about traditional place names, use kinship terms, play games, and tell stories and jokes that are lost on the younger generation, and the number of people speaking the language is rapidly declining.

I arrived at this rather pessimistic evaluation partly because all of the Heritage Week instructors were either non-Natives or nonresidents, and partly because the students only get exposed to these activities for one week each year. Still, it is clear that Alutiiq Heritage Week has some salutary effects. One student, Geri Pestrikoff (1997), writes about her experience:

My favorite Alutiiq week activity is skin sewing and beading. I'm making a headdress of white fur, blue felt, and black, white, and blue beads to wear when I am Alutiiq dancing. I like this headdress because it is beautiful and useful and makes me feel connected to my culture in a tangible way. Alutiiq week is a welcome break from regular school—books and paper. I miss this kind of learning throughout the school year. This is great fun and we're learning a lot.

In 1995 and 1996 Old Harbor students were involved in excavating the historic Lighthouse site on the edge of the village overlooking the Sitkalidak Narrows. Under the leadership of Ben Fitzhugh, a young graduate student, students in grades seven through twelve spent two seasons excavating two late Russian period house pits. During the time they were excavating, school was held outdoors, and students learned to do applied math and science in the process of excavating. At the end of the project the students gave reports to the adult members of the community about what they learned about their own heritage. The artifacts were placed on display. During the third year of the project, Fitzhugh and Rolf Christiansen along with a couple of the older students built a *ciqlluaq* or barabara near the site they had excavated the previous two years. One major difference is that traditional barabaras were covered with grass (see above Chapter 1, Figures 1.2 and 1.3), while the new one is covered with moss (Figure 7.13).

The Old Harbor School also gets involved with subsistence. Every fall teachers take the older students on a field trip to Big Creek, where they teach them how to catch and cut fish and how to share their fish with elders. Jeff Peterson has designed a teaching unit on duck hunting, duck cleaning and dressing, and gun safety, so in these ways the school curriculum is becoming more and more relevant to the lifestyle of the village. But if these techniques and values are not taught at home or by parents, how can they expect to be passed on through the school program? Subsistence, like language and culture, cannot be artificially propped up and institutionalized unless there is support for it in everyday life.

Another popular venue for teaching Alutiiq culture is the Spirit Camp. Spirit Camps and Culture Camps are a product of the 1980s and 1990s and have become part of a very broad social movement throughout rural Alaska. Like Native Heritage Weeks, Spirit Camps attempt to enculturate youth through teaching and role modeling. Most importantly, they provide a wilderness outdoors camp setting where youth, elders, and middle-aged people can mix.

The first Kodiak area Spirit Camp was started in 1996 under the sponsorship of the Karluk IRA Council and the Kodiak Area Native Associa-

Fig. 7.13. *New barabara in Old Harbor, built in 1997. Photo by Craig Mishler.*

tion. It was funded for $250,000 for two years by the Alaska Department of Community and Regional Affairs using oil spill criminal settlement funds appropriated by the Alaska state legislature. The camp consisted of two one-week sessions and involved a total of about fifty youth, ages twelve to eighteen. The primary objective, according to a final report, was "to transfer knowledge and awareness regarding subsistence restoration to youth on Kodiak Island" (KANA 1997).

The KANA Spirit Camp started out as an adjunct to the already established archaeology school, "Dig Afognak," held each year at Litnik on Afognak Island, but it quickly broadened to include other activities, including subsistence and Native arts and games. During the first two years participants helped build a barabara at the site and studied geology and archaeology with Patrick Saltonstall, Libby Ponti, and Amy Steffian of the Alutiiq Museum. Alutiiq dancing was taught by Denise Malutin, and drum-making was taught by Teacon Simeonoff of Akhiok. Teacon also taught several ways of splitting fish using an ulu and a knife. Vicki Vanek, of the Alaska Department of Fish and Game, Division of Subsistence, taught a workshop on harbor seal biosampling methods. A boat trip was taken to the old village of Afognak. Participants took turns hauling water and firewood to heat the banya. Ceremonies included the lighting of a stone seal oil lamp at the beginning of each week, and the performance of Alutiiq dances around a bonfire on the last night.

In 1998, its third year, the KANA Spirit Camp was moved to Sitkalidak Island, near Old Harbor, while the Dig Afognak program continued with its own agenda. On Sitkalidak Island a temporary camp was built with sleeping platforms, toilet pits, and eating facilities. Two banyas were also erected, one for the men and boys, and one for the women and girls. About fifty youth again attended the camp. Activities included advanced kayaking, Native dance and language, traditional arts and crafts, gill-netting, arrow-making and archery (taught by Joe Kelly), first aid, medicinal plant education, and archaeology. Sven Haakanson Jr. taught mask carving, the use of masks during ceremonies, and area history. Leroy Gregory spoke about the dangers of substance abuse and how he turned his own life around. Akhiok residents Mitch, Judy, Speridon, and Teacon Simeonoff taught kayaking, cooking, and archery.

In contrast to the Native Heritage Weeks, Spirit Camps are geared exclusively to older youth, and they tend to be run by the Natives themselves rather than non-Native schoolteachers. Because Natives are in charge, the Spirit Camps are more authentic in the direct transmission of traditional knowledge and values, and therefore should be more successful than the Heritage Weeks. The major drawback, again, is that Spirit Camp sessions only last one week a year.

Since I have not attended any of the camps or interviewed those youth who attended, I am unable to say whether they have had any profound or lasting impact on the youth who attended them, but most people think they are excellent. It is noteworthy that thirteen-year-old Ken

Michener of Kodiak City, who is a member of the Kodiak Alutiiq Dancers group, said he had a supernatural experience at the Sitkalidak Camp in 1998. He was awakened at 3:00 one morning to the sound of a beating drum and a voice: "It was raining that night and I remember the sound of rain turned into a drumbeat. After a few seconds the most beautiful voice chanted a short song. I think it was a welcoming song," he said (quoted in Moss 1998a). Others in the camp also claimed to hear the song that night.

A third venue for the enculturation of youth has been the Youth-Elder Conferences held for twenty-two days each October in Anchorage just before the annual convention of the Alaska Federation of Natives. For the past ten years, Old Harbor high school students have been accompanied on this trip by Phyllis Clough and various elders. Sponsored by the Old Harbor Native Corporation, this trip enables the youth to come to terms with important political issues such as subsistence and sovereignty and to talk to one another about health concerns such as drug and alcohol abuse, AIDS, and other sexually transmitted diseases (Klouda 1996a; Rostad 1997a).

Inter-regional Alutiiq Youth-Elder Conferences held in Kodiak City in 1997 and Cordova and Kodiak in 1998 have facilitated not only the learning of youth from elders but the acquaintance of elders with other elders and youth with other youth. But beyond the organized phenomena of Heritage Weeks, Spirit Camps, and Youth-Elder Conferences, it is useful to look at other aspects of youth culture in the villages. Teachers in Old Harbor disagree over whether drugs and alcohol are serious problems. Theft and vandalism, however, are chronic.

In September 1997, when Paul Kahutak and I parked his new boat at the harbor dock, we were advised by a local fisherman not to leave the engine battery or gas can in the boat overnight. "It will be gone in a heartbeat, if you do," he warned. This is the same sentiment expressed to Nancy Yaw Davis twelve years earlier: "[You] can't leave anything in your skiff" (1986a:202).

Arthur Matfay told me that some teenagers came by his house on a four-wheeler late one night in 1996 and maliciously shot his dog while it was resting on his front porch. In 1998 Walt Erickson's grocery store was broken into four times by teenagers who stole cartons of cigarettes and (just before the Fourth of July) fireworks. On one occasion they also managed to run off with some cash. These crimes have all been attributed to three bored high school dropouts.

There is a kind of desperation involved in seeking cheap thrills. On the sunny afternoon of October 2, 1998, as I was walking along the gravel road between Middle Town and Downtown, I saw three young people racing their four-wheelers side by side at about forty miles per hour. As I jumped off the road, I was engulfed in huge clouds of dust. None of the drivers had on protective helmets, and they had to stay dead even with each other to keep from eating each other's dust. One errant move would have spelled disaster for all.

And in 1992 when Tom Shugak was the principal at the Old Harbor School, I was invited to make a presentation on subsistence to the middle school and high school grades. At the end of my talk I asked the students what they would do if Penair and Markair stopped flying to the village tomorrow. That is, if the supply of groceries was suddenly cut off. I expected them to say they would fall back on subsistence and live off the land and the sea as their ancestors did. Instead, what they said was: "We'd leave for Kodiak tomorrow. We'd catch the next boat out of here. We can't live without our pizza and our Pepsi."

In Ouzinkie, while many teenagers stay busy listening to rock music on their portable Walkmans, riding around on their four-wheelers, or watching videos, Theodore Squartsoff Jr. (J. R.) goes out in the skiff with his father to hunt and fish and even skips school to be in Barabara Cove because his father believes that there are many important life skills that cannot be taught in school. Actually, the school excuses him up to so many days a year for this. In Old Harbor, Loren Peterson also skips school to go with his father Jeff on hunting and fishing trips. Certainly J. R. and Loren also like to watch videos, but in their love for the outdoors and in the quality time they spend with their fathers, they are the exceptions that prove the rule.

Fig. 7.14. *Ed Gregorieff, left, of Tatitlek and George Inga Sr., right, of Old Harbor in Cordova for the Youth-Elders Conference, August 1998. Photo by Craig Mishler.*

Social and Cultural Change Since the Oil Spill

THE MONK'S LAGOON CONTROVERSY

Since the settlement of their land claims in the 1970s under the Alaska Native Land Claims Settlement Act, the Ouzinkie Native Corporation has owned and managed the buildings and sacred sites at Monk's Lagoon where Father Herman lived and died in the early nineteenth century, and where Father Gerasim Schmaltz resided off and on from 1935 through the mid-1960s. Monk's Lagoon, most of the rest of Spruce Island, and large portions of Afognak Island were all included as part of the ninety-three thousand acres conveyed by the federal government to the corporation. Another twenty-one thousand acres or so still remains to be selected (Arthur Haakanson 1997). Monk's Lagoon has been described by one scholar as "the foremost Holy Place and spring of Holy Orthodoxy in America" (Golder 1968). On July 31, 1996, I was fortunate enough to visit Monk's Lagoon and these sacred places in the company of lay reader Herman Squartsoff and a visiting Russian Orthodox couple. When we landed with Herman's skiff, we were greeted by a young black-robed bearded monk, one of a dozen or so who were living just above the beach. In the early 1990s a group of these monks led by Father Iosaph arrived from their seminary in northern California. They called themselves the Brotherhood of St. Herman of Alaska, a group founded in 1963 and distinct from the Orthodox Church of America or OCA. The OCA, Alaska Diocese, has operated the seminary in Kodiak City and for decades has served all of the Kodiak villages with priests or lay readers. The Brotherhood's spiritual leader was named Abbot Herman, but in 1988 the OCA defrocked Abbot Herman and excommunicated him for establishing a monastery without the approval of church leaders.

Still wanting to be near Monk's Lagoon, the monks under Abbot Herman first acquired a parcel of land on Spruce Island at Pleasant Harbor. They purchased the land from Ed Opheim Sr. and built a monastery on it, which they called the New Valaam Monastery. Eventually they turned the monastery over to an order of nuns, the St. Herman's Sisterhood, and returned to California. But a couple of years later, in 1994, the monks returned. They asked and received oral permission from Andy Anderson, then president of the Ouzinkie Native Corporation, to build a chapel at Monk's Lagoon and to restore Father Gerasim's hut.

However, the monks were not satisfied with this and began to build some additional houses, huts, and other structures on the site, including some barabaras. Their numbers also began to grow, and they announced plans to build a large monastery and boys' school. However, after hearing that the monks had prevented some shareholders of the Ouzinkie Native Corporation access to the holy sites, Anderson gave written notice to the monks saying they would have to tear down the monastery and vacate the area by May 15, 1998. They were summarily evicted.

This eviction created a tremendous stir in Kodiak City and in the village of Ouzinkie, where families were divided over what should be done.

Many letters to the editor were written to the *Kodiak Daily Mirror* supporting the monks and their spiritual dedication. Nevertheless, the dean of St. Herman's Seminary, Father Michael Oleksa, in a letter to the St. Herman's Sisterhood (the nuns) declared all of the monks to be "imposters." Nevertheless, many others supported them, including Ed Opheim Sr. and the Pestrikoff family in Ouzinkie (Jeffrey 1998).

The Pestrikoffs sold the monks a town lot in the center of Ouzinkie so that they could build their monastery there, but this would have been highly contentious, since the lot was located right next door to the main office of the Ouzinkie Native Corporation. To defend its actions, the corporation published a paid ad in the *Kodiak Daily Mirror* defending its decision (ONC 1998). At last notice, a compromise position was reached as the monks still had to vacate Monk's Lagoon but were able to receive a $1/year annual lease to Nelson Island, a privately owned tract of land located near Pleasant Harbor and quite close to Monk's Lagoon. Nick Pestrikoff Sr. says some of the monks built new houses and other structures on Nelson Island.

For now, the controversy has cooled down, but it illustrates that there is considerable friction between some Ouzinkie families over how the monks should be treated and received. Although the monks were evicted from Monk's Lagoon, the Ouzinkie Native Corporation has not barred them from visiting the site, only from living and building there.

Unlike the students at the OCA seminary in Kodiak City, most of whom are Alaska Natives, all of the monks in St. Herman's Brotherhood are non-Natives from California. This new population, albeit conservative, threatens to bring religious and social change to Ouzinkie and its surroundings, change that has not been altogether welcome. For better or worse, depending on one's point of view, this is one of the first times in history when Ouzinkie people have exercised the power to make major decisions regarding the activities taking place on their own land and sacred sites. As Gordon Pullar (1992:189) has written: "Alutiiq peoples long have allowed others to define who they are and how they should act. This power that has been relinquished must be reclaimed for pride in heritage and ethnic identity to be instilled."

CONCLUSION

While most of the changes discussed above cannot be attributed to the oil spill per se, living conditions are noticeably different in the villages now. If there is a lower level of participation in subsistence today than there was ten years ago, it may not simply be because butter clams and steamer clams continue to contain high levels of paralytic shellfish toxins, a phenomenon not directly connected to the oil spill. It may be because people are spending more and more of their time watching satellite television and videos. It may also be because they are finding it easier and easier to have fast foods such as hamburgers, french fries, and hot fresh pizza delivered by airplane.

And if young people are only getting one or two weeks of heritage education a year, it is because most of their education continues to be derived from a non-Native–designed school curriculum. A sincere effort has been made to correct this problem through the Alaska Rural Systemic Initiative, a statewide multimillion-dollar program funded by the National Science Foundation and sponsored by the University of Alaska and the Alaska Federation of Natives (see Rostad 1997b). One of its goals has been to produce a cultural atlas CD-ROM for Kodiak Island. This CD was compiled through the efforts of a panel of elders, including Walt Erickson of Old Harbor and Nick Pestrikoff Sr. of Ouzinkie, among others.

Faced with rapid social and economic change and globalization, the Alutiiqs themselves are aware of some positive, beneficial changes. Tom Shugak, who was raised in Old Harbor and returned there to become the school principal for several years, noticed a change for the better in the way outsiders were treating the locals since he had left the village three years earlier: "The residents control how our community is to grow. Outside agencies approach the community in a different way, giving people credit for intelligence and knowledge on how to handle certain problems" (Shugak 1992:53). This newfound respect gives renewed hope that the good people of Old Harbor and Ouzinkie, whether fishing or guiding tourists, will at long last be able to guide their own destinies.

APPENDIX A

ARTHUR HAAKANSON'S ORAL HISTORY
OF COMMERCIAL FISHERIES IN THE KODIAK REGION

Interviewed by Craig Mishler in Ouzinkie, Alaska on May 15, 1997. Edited transcript.

I was born in Deadman's Bay in a fishing tent in 1931, August sixth. And I don't remember much of Deadman's Bay. I do remember some of Alitak where there was a large cannery there belonging to the PAFCO or the Pacific American Fishery Company in Alitak. And it was pretty large.

The boats were real small, and it wasn't until a few years later that another outfit in Moser Bay under a man called Serian, brought the three first modern fishing boats to Alaska: the *Carrie*, the *Sherry*, and the *Don't Worry*. They were thirty-two-footers. They had masts and booms and winches, and they revolutionized the fishing industry which was done mostly by siwash seines, which meant that they were pulled in by hand with no purse lines. But the advent of the winch brought along purse rings and purse lines and modernized fishing. There was still a lot of work to do. Seines were then pulled over the stern.

The main fishing areas at that time were around Olga Bay, Karluk, and then later up in Afognak Island. Another cannery, the Kadiak Fisheries Company, started there, and in Larsen Bay and in Olga Bay the Alaska Packers built canneries. Canneries were springing up around Kodiak Island. And way up on Shuyak Island, there was the Washington Fish and Oyster Company called WAFICO. And later in the early 1930s. O. L. Grimes in Ouzinkie started his Grimes Packing Company cannery.

There was a great influx of fish traps. The boats were small. Their cabins were small. The lengths were about twenty feet, and they had small houses in the bow, three men with a small seine box in the stern, and a little teeny engine with five or ten horsepower that was just enough to propel them here and there. Mostly when they went to fishing bays and areas, they were towed by the larger tenders.

During these times there was a great abundance of what we now call subsistence. There was many ducks, seals. There were bears, there was fish, and there were lots of berries of different kinds—blueberries, salmonberries. Some of these were made into jam. Some were put away by Natives in their own methods. Salmon were smoked and salted and put away. There wasn't much to do with electricity, so the freezers and stuff were still unheard of. Mail boats came. Sometimes around every three or four months, three times a year. Later on grew more modern. A Coast Guard cutter then was bringing mail call, the *Discover*, once a month around the island to the main villages of Akhiok, Kaguyak, Karluk, Larsen Bay, Ouzinkie, and starting from Kodiak.

Other small canneries were starting up too. There were three herring plants in Raspberry Straits: Port Vida, Port Iron Creek, and Port Wakefield. The herring industry was quite a thing then. Before the herring died out. They had large huge herring seiners that used to come into the Malina Bay area and around Afognak Island and fish herring.

The salmon industry was just starting. Before that the people, the villagers, and many other people had salteries where they fished for cod. Codfish was popular, and the salmon were so plentiful no one dreamed of utilizing them until finally the Syrians and the Italian groups that came to Alaska started their small canneries on the south end of Kodiak. And they brought about the salmon industry, and later on they brought in the fish traps, which outfished anything and caused a great depletion of the fishing industry.

And back to subsistence. In those days it was nothing for a man to go out with a single-shot shotgun, and the ducks were so plentiful, it is true they could catch around twenty ducks in one shot! Seals were plentiful. The salmon streams were full. It was an abundant life.

And the groceries that came usually came by steamer, which wasn't very plentiful. W. J. Erskine and Company in Kodiak started the first store. And they used to bring groceries around the island on a boat and peddle them to the villagers. Later on another store started by the name of O. Kraft & Son in Kodiak, and they started to disperse. And then much later came along the famed but never forgotten till now, I guess, the Sears Roebuck catalog. [laughs] And this was all in early Alaska days. I'm speaking of the early 1920s until the possible 1940s.

After Alaska become a state [in 1959], the canneries lost their huge political pull, which was depleting the salmon, and they had to pull out their famous fish traps. After the fish traps went, the fish started to come back again in somewhat larger runs.

But hindrance followed upon hindrance in the fishing industry. First, there was the tidal wave, which upset and lost some canneries, brought a low to the fishing prices. And then there was a botulism scare on fish, which brought the prices down, and this wasn't helped either by later on the Alaska oil spill, and fish prices kept depleting and declining until nowadays many people in the villages don't even feel that it's worth it to go out, with the high price of oil and groceries, and the low price of fishing. It's a disaster for the economic system here.

Do you think subsistence is important today?

I think subsistence is *very* important to the community. In itself I know we're having a downtrend now in our clam digging and everything. A lot of people claim it was the aftermath of the oil spill, and lot of people claim it was this red tide that causes a paralytic poisoning of a human being from the beaches. So there isn't much activity in the clams or the other seafood along the beaches.

And there is an abundant amount of salmon now, but just no fishing price for them, and many fishermen they have to go out and they have to catch fish that in the earlier days would have made them very wealthy people, had they retained the same prices. Now the fish is down to just pennies a pound, whereas before even humpies, humpback salmon, was at least 47¢/lb.and red salmon were over a dollar/lb., in some places as high as three dollars depending on who was buying them. Silvers averaged around 70¢/lb., dog salmon 40-45¢, and there were big money in fishing then. Many people bought new fishing boats. After the traps went out, as I said earlier, the fishing again became abundant around the island.

But the disasters like the botulism, the tidal wave, and the oil spill all helped to deplete the Kodiak fishing industry money-wise.

Were you fishing, yourself, in those days?

Yeah. I started fishing with my father [Arthur Haakanson Sr.]. I went gill netting with him when I was about ten years old, up to Paramanof [Bay]. Later on he got a small boat, and I was around twelve then. My brother Herman was fourteen; he was a man then. And I could pull web. My father would pull the lead line and Herman would stack corks. We'd fish all summer long. Sven was too small to come with us then. He did later on, though. So we fished as a family, and we made a living catching our fish. We had many different kinds of boats. Some of them my dad owned. Some were company boats. Until my dad retired. He retired from fishing because he had a serious rupture and had to wear a truss. There was no power blocks in them days, and the heavy gear was too much for him, so he become a cook on a tender until he retired.

Did he run a purse seiner too? Was that all hand work?

It was all pulled by hand. First we started with half-purses. That is, we'd have a hundred fathoms of seine without a purse line, and we'd pull that over the stern until we came to the purse line. Then we'd take the purse line to the small winches we had and winch the purse line in, making it purse seine, and thereby the fish would be in the bag, and then we'd pull the rest of the seine aboard until we either brailed the fish into the boat, or if they were a little enough bunch of them, we would roll them aboard the boat.

And during the early days there was hardly any fish. For about fifteen years it was *very* bad. Hardly anybody ever made a living. There was no such thing as welfare or help or anything like that around here then. And we had to make do with what we had to do. And many of us became very good hunters during that period. And this depletion of fishing I believe was because of these traps that were circulating in strategic places around the island actually capturing fish until statehood, when they were ordered to take them out. Then the fish runs returned again.

And how about herring? Was that a big fishery in those days?

Herring was a large, huge fishery around Kodiak, but it was, like everything else, overutilized.

Did people use herring for subsistence? I know the Danes love their pickled herring.

My dad would pickle them. He tried smoking some once. Sven and I caught a dory full down there by the dock one evening. But they were too fat. They wouldn't smoke good. Herring was too fat.

And crab. Did you fish crab too?

Yeah. We fished crab. It was in the beginning when we first used tangle gear. Then we had old rickety crab pots. And then later on our pots become round pots. Our boats got bigger. Then we had the Kodiak Island square six-by-six pots. And we first started, I started fishing with Nicky Katelnikoff around Kazhuyak and tangle gear, that was horrible. Those crabs would be all tangled up in web we laid along the bottom of the ocean and then pulled it in by hand over the stern, catching what crabs were tangled in it. And then later on we made small drags, about thirty-foot spread drags. We had little small boats, and we towed these drags and catch the king crab. Then we started to make pots. We used to take our crab and put 'em in what we called our own live boxes, made out of barbed wire, where we could hold up to five hundred crab, which is all our small boats could pack. But we were getting a dollar a crab in them days, and five hundred dollars was big money.

We would take about a week to get five hundred crab, and then we'd take them into Kodiak to Walt Muller or Pete Devoe, the first two crab canneries in Kodiak and deliver to them. Sometimes they were short of help, and some of us would stay and work all night helping butcher the catch we brought in too. [laughs] This was just the beginning of the king crab. Then Ouzinkie had a small king crab cannery too. That went out on the tidal wave too. There was another king crab cannery across the bay from Ouzinkie. That was burned down, run by a fellow called George Grant.

In addition to king crab you've got dungeness and tanner crab too, but they never did much with tanners up here, did they?

They became a major industry for a few years. I remember when I was crabbing down around Jap Bay mostly we'd get pots full of these tanner crabs. It seemed like one crab would move out and another bunch would move in. And we used to throw our tanners away by the hundreds. Then someone started processing them, and some people did very well with them. And dungeness, they started small and then become a big industry. A lot of people today have million-dollar boats just solely from dungeness fishing. They'd fish in the great bays, like on Sitkalidak Island, and the huge bays there, and off of Cape Alitak. Where the great basins were the water was shallow for miles and miles and just ideal for dungeness. And over on the mainland in all the places too. A lot of boats [went] out dungeness fishing. Some Ouzinkie boats tried it too, but I guess they didn't like the dungeness. They were so quick, and they bit so hard. [laughs] King crab were easier to handle.

And then shrimp. Did you ever fish shrimp?

I worked on a shrimp processor down in Jap Bay, and shrimp was a big industry for a while too, on the south end of the island especially. And there was an abundant amount of shrimp. But the local canneries here didn't go in for it much. It was mostly the processors on big ships. Kodiak, of course, had shrimp processing.

I wondered whether the Old Harbor boys ever got into shrimp. I never heard that they did.

No, no. They did go into king crab and eventually tanner crab, but the Old Harbor boys were big for herring too. They went in after herring.

Still do.

Cod was a big industry here before salmon even.

I guess the market isn't as high for cod now as it used to be, huh?

No. I don't know why. Codfish to me is more delicious than a salmon. Maybe it's the Scandinavian in me. [laughs] Well the Scandinavians they were more or less the epitome of modern fishermen, and they knew how to split fish right away, salt fish. They learned quickly about smoking fish, curing fish, and all the other ways that they brought from their home countries that they learned there.

They [the Scandinavians] must have brought in the pickling too.

They had a pickling, and the huge salteries that they had. I remember down in Old Harbor and in Trap Point—huge warehouses just filled with huge barrels where they put in their salt-fish products and then have them shipped out by steamer to the lower forty-eight. I don't know what they were paid for them then.

And did your family use a lot of seal and sea lion?

Oh yeah. My father too, even though he was from Denmark really enjoyed sea lion and seal liver. To my way of thinking it tastes even better than that taken from a cow. A seal or sea lion liver is just pure, and it's really good. Seal liver, I don't know, it has to be soaked out quite a bit before you can eat it. A seal itself is so rich in blood, 'cause it tries to get used to the cold water, I guess, that it's meat is actually dark. But if you run it, and run it under a faucet or in a creek or stream, you'll notice that it'll turn red like any other meat.

Then we have our seagull eggs, which it being May fourteenth now, fifteenth, so the seagull eggs will start showing up. They're probably already down there by Red River and Old Harbor. The center parts of the island seem to get 'em first. We're here in the northern part here.

Is that one of your favorites, seagull eggs?

Not really. The women say they make good baking, better baking than chicken eggs. That's their opinion. I don't know.

And kittiwake eggs too?

All kinds of eggs. We've got the Triplets out here with hundreds of thousands of birds. One of the great sanctuaries in Alaska for birds. It belongs to the Ouzinkie Native Corporation. There are birds of every kind of species imaginable out there. Should you go out there in a skiff or something, the sky would turn black with the birds flying all over from the Triplets around you, curious. There would be kittiwakes and puffins and a mingling of seagulls and whatnot, the common shag, and every other kind of ducks, birds of all description.

Yeah. That old man Anakenti Zeedar, you knew him? He told me how they used to go along the cliffs and reach in and grab the eggs out of the puffin nests. Sometimes they got bit.

In Aleut we call the puffin the *amagaq*, and the seagulls are *kadayaks*, and the ducks are *shaguuliks*. The seagulls are *kadayaks*, and we all have names for the different things around here. The weasels are *amidaduuqs*. Everything has a different name.

Did you grow up speaking Aleut [Alutiiq] from your mother?

No. She never wanted me to learn it. I guess when she was going to some school there, they didn't want to teach Aleut. They were against the Aleut language. They were doing this in a lot of places. It seems ironic now that they have schools teaching Aleut [i.e. Alutiiq], that are set by the government, which was totally against the speaking of Native tongues.

You guys have done better than any place I know, as far as dividends go. It looks like to me that people are depending on the dividends so much that they've stopped fishing.

But they're not getting no money for their fish. Even guys that come in and say, "Don't have dividends." They can't afford to fish. The fuel is too high. The groceries are too high. You think our prices are high. Old Harbor's is higher. Port Lions is not so bad, but the communities, the farther away they are from the central point of Kodiak, the higher the groceries are.

You don't think the dividends from the [Ouzinkie Native] Corporation have discouraged people from working?

No. Whenever we have work, jobs, and public health service has work to do, upgrading and renovating, and sewer lines and this and that, housing developments, Danger Bay projects over there where our people are sent every other week almost to work, there's always an abundant bunch of workers ready to work and willing to work. It's just that they're not interested in fishing. This is mainly because the boat owners can't afford it.

Well, this has been a good interview. I don't know if you have anything else you want to say, but I think I've run out of questions. Thank you very much—good interview.

That's about all. Yeah. We did cover a lot.

Fig. App. A1. *Crab pots and buoys, Old Harbor lagoon, 1992. Photo by Craig Mishler.*

APPENDIX B

BARABARA COVE OIL SPILL JOURNAL

by Theodore Squartsoff Sr., Ouzinkie, Alaska

[***Editor's Note:*** Barabara Cove is shaped by a sandy reef and promontory which juts out into Kizhuyak Bay south of the community of Port Lions, on Kodiak Island. It is here, at a site passed on to them by their father and grandfather, that fisherman Theodore Squartsoff and his brothers, Martin and Pete, have cabins and do much of their subsistence hunting, fishing, and gathering. The journal is included here because it is the only journal we know of that was kept by an Alaska Native living in an oil spill community following the oil spill. Theodore and Toni Squartsoff's experience may not be typical in that they were volunteers and did

Fig. App. B1. *Squartsoff family cabins at Barabara Cove, Kizhuyak Bay, October 1996. Photo by Craig Mishler.*

not work for wages on VECO cleanup crews, but this document nevertheless illustrates the vigilant efforts of local people in protecting their environment. The journal has been edited only for spelling and punctuation.]

May 30, 1989

First oil spill to hit Barabara Cove. Two big rafts of kelp drifted into the cove about 9:00 A.M., spent about three hours trying to tow them out of cove till S.E wind started to come up. Saw it was a losing battle, so went to Port Lions and reported it to the *Summer Gale* (took some samples); they sent three boats and five skiffs to try to clean it up, but most of it got on the beach. My wife Toni and I worked till 9:00 P.M. picking it up; as it came ashore we filled thirty bags. Lots of oil on kelp so had to pick up all the kelp also. (9:00 A.M. to 9:00 P.M.)

May 31, 1989

The *Tasha* came to pick up bags and bring more empties. Oil trapped between log booms and Pom-Pom's. No one cleans it up—so small amounts keep coming ashore. Toni and I pick it up as it comes ashore. Get about six bags. (6:00 A.M. till 9:00 P.M.)

June 1, 1989

Toni and I started early again at 6:00 A.M. You have to pick it up before the sun gets it or it melts. Get some help about 8:00 A.M. Evelyn Mullen, George Squartsoff, and Robin Boskofsky give us a hand. A good S.E. blew it all off the Pom-Pom's last night, so we shoveled the whole tide line. Filled twenty-nine bags. Got done at 5:00 P.M. (6:00 A.M. till 5:00 P.M.)

June 2, 1989

Big N.E. storm last night, fifty knots or better. Oil boom no longer a threat to our beach. It was broken up into about eight pieces. The tipar broke into about four pieces. One large chunk starts drifting ashore, so I tow it across to the other beach so it doesn't get buried in the sand. Toni and me. (9:00 A.M. till 12:00 Noon) No VECO skiffs show up.

June 3, 1989

With oil booms gone, no more oil comes ashore. Take a ride around Bay with Toni—do not find any more oil in water—do not check any beaches. VECO skiffs finally show up again. (8:00 A.M. till 10:00 A.M.)

June 4, 1989

Toni and I take short ride around Bay (still nothing). (8:00 A.M. till 9:30 A.M.)

June 5, 1989

Take two rides around Bay today with Toni 7:00 A.M. till 9:00 A.M. and 4:00 P.M. till 6:30 P.M. Then I help Sonny on the *Tasha* tow logs off the beach. Started at 10:00 P.M. and got done at 1:30 A.M. Had to work with the tides. High tide at 3:00 A.M.—long day today. (7:00 A.M. till 1:30 A.M.)

June 6, 1989

Running low on gas, had to go to Port Bailey to get gas today; left at 11:00 A.M., got back at 1:30 P.M. (224 gal. gas)

June 7, 1989

Heard rumors of oil in Bay today, spent three hours looking. Didn't find anything. VECO skiffs tow excess logs to Port Lions. (1:00 P.M. till 4:00 P.M.)

June 8, 1989
Blow day, take day off.

June 9, 1989
Had to go to Kodiak today to get more supplies. Went on a cab No. 80 through Anton's [Anton Larsen Bay road] left at 10:00 A.M. and got back at 4:00 P.M.

June 10, 1989
Day off. Lots of oil in Izhut [Izhut Bay, Afognak Island].

June 11, 1989
Got call from the *Shanee* that they were bringing me a gill net monitor, and I was supposed to know all about it—but I sure didn't. Then we took another ride around the Bay. Still no oil. Lots of oil reported along Afognak shore, Hog Island, and all the way to Port Lions. Also all around Ouzinkie Island. So oil is on the way. Expect some here tomorrow. (3:00 P.M. till 6:00 P.M.)

June 12, 1989
Helicopter lands here below the cabin and gives me more info on oil monitor. Plan on going to Ouzinkie tomorrow to set it. Check beaches hourly, still no oil. Skimmer and boats picking it up about two miles from Barabara. Wind dies down, so threat is over again for another day. (6:00 A.M. till 10:00 P.M.)

June 13, 1989
Toni checks beaches—no oil. Set monitor today; went to check it twice and took a ride to check a few tide streaks, lots of oil—no oil on monitor. (10:00 A.M. till 9:00 P.M.)

June 14, 1989
Toni checks beaches—no oil. Checked monitor, then made two scoops and went out to pick up the elusive oil—picked up eighteen bags in six hours (two five-gal. cans per bag, straight oil, no kelp). No oil on monitor. Carl and Kevin Smith. (9:00 A.M. till 6:00 P.M.)

June 15, 1989
Called D.E.C. and got O.K. to leave monitor. Left Ouzinkie at 3:00 P.M. Took Guy Bartelson (VPSO) back to Port Lions. Got back to Barabara at around 4:30 P.M. Toni checked beaches all day (still no oil). (3:00 P.M. till 4:30 P.M.)

June 16, 1989
Started checking back beach at 6:00 A.M. (nothing). Checked again at 9:00 A.M., found about twelve mousse pieces. It kept coming in all day. Toni and I picked up about ten gal. of straight mousse. We quit at 8:00 P.M. I reported it to the *Peril Cape* and they put more boom up in Barabara. Winds switching to N.W. tomorrow. Don't expect much. Checked Ursin's beach with skiff (nothing). (6:00 A.M. till 8:00 P.M.)

June 17, 1989
Winds switch to N. and die down. Make first check at 6:30 A.M. As expected don't find too many; hopefully that will be all for the day. We worked for about three hours to fill five gal. of mousse. The pieces were a lot smaller today. Still a few more coming in. Winds switch to S.W. (offshore) at 12:30 P.M.—no more oil—hopefully that's the end of it. (6:30 A.M. till 6:00 P.M.)

June 18, 1989

"Fathers Day." Take walk with kids at 8:00 A.M. and find a few mousse pieces on beach below Cabin. Work till noon to clean up whole tide line. Take ride around Bay with brother Peter in Melvin's skiff—nothing. (8:00 A.M. till 6:00 P.M.)

June 19, 1989

Very long day today. Started at 7:00 A.M. and filled a bucket by 9:00 A.M.—lots of very small pieces. VECO skiff comes and picks up our oil—about twenty gal.—two very heavy bags. Brian Beinly and two other people. Wind picks up to about thirty knots at noon N.E. and mousse starts coming again. Benny, Maras and Liz show up at 3:00 P.M.—mousse starts coming in pretty good by then. They help us pick it up for one hour till 4:00 P.M., then they leave. Toni and I work till 9:30 P.M. It starts to rain so we quit. We get about thirty gal. of straight mousse. Stuff still coming in. Some even shows up below the smokehouse. (7:00 A.M. till 9:30 P.M.)

June 20, 1989

Toni and I start at 7:00 A.M. Mousse on both sides. Not too much on the front but plenty on the back beach. Pick twenty gal. of straight mousse till 9:00 A.M.—then have to call for help—too much coming in. VECO Port Lions sends a beach crew on the *KFC 5*. They work from 11:00 A.M. till 4:30 P.M. and get eighty-five bags. They pick up all the kelp, that's why they fill up so many bags. They only get half of the big kelp patch. Say they'll be back tomorrow. After they leave, Toni and I go work till 9:00 P.M. and get thirty more gal. of straight mousse. When we quit there is still a lot on the beach. (7:00 A.M. till 9:00 P.M.)

June 21, 1989

Every day gets busier. Start at 6:00 A.M. The whole back beach is covered with oil from the high tide mark down to the low tide mark. We picked 5 bags of straight mousse by the time Ducky on the *Arlene Louise* arrives. They come to pick up the bags. We get 5 more by the time they leave. They came at 10:00 A.M and leave at 1:00 P.M. They take about 110 bags. Peter [Squartsoff] arrives at noon to give us a hand. We work till 3:00 P.M., then take an hour break to give our backs a rest. We go for skiff ride to check the beaches in the Bay up to Herman's cabin, not very much oil. Peter leaves at 5:00 P.M. We picked up 10 bags of straight mousse while he was here. After supper wind switches to S.E., so we work till 11:00 P.M. to try to get as much off the back beach as possible before it drifts away. We get 25 more bags. Each bag contains two to five gal. cans of oil. Nice sunny day. We clean about three-fourths of beach—no beach crew from Port Lions shows up today. We sure could have used help. Hope we are able to get up tomorrow. Very tired. Expect oil on front beach tomorrow. Winds are S.E. thirty knots. Ninety five-gal. cans of mousse picked up today. (6:00 A.M. till 11:00 P.M.)

June 22, 1989

Go take a ride at 7:00 A.M.—no oil on front beach—wind switches back to N.E.—The S.E. blew most of the stuff off the back beach—still quite a bit on the north end of beach. Got our rain back. Have to work between squalls—no rain gear. Sun comes out at 9:00 A.M. *KFC 5* and *Windigo* come help us. Get all done at noon. Finally get a break. Winds N.E. fifteen to twenty, should get some more as tide comes in. Martin gets here at noon. More help. Winds go back to S.E. at 2:30. *Windigo* and *KFC 5* have to leave. Getting too rough. Get only one more bucket of mousse from tide line on back beach. Get one more bucket from front beach—real small pieces. Very slow work. After supper Martin, Toni, Marv, Maria, and myself go over both beaches real careful and slow and pick up every speck.

We get done at 8:30. Get two more buckets. Beach is very clean. (7:00 A.M. till 8:30 P.M.)

June 23, 1989

Martin starts at 6:00 A.M. Toni and I get to sleep in till 7:30; we start at 8:00. Martin has a bucket full by 8:00 A.M.. Small amounts are coming in on both beaches. Dax and I take a skiff ride and try to pick it off the water before it hits the beach but it's too scattered; we only get one-fourth of a bucket. A chopper lands at 6:15 P.M. I guess two Exxon or VECO guys to see what's happening. (Oil still coming in while they are here.) We trade smoked salmon for a couple of short chopper rides. Four people each trip. We take turns picking it up. It slows right down by 8:00 P.M. as the wind switches to S.W. We only get three bags (six buckets). Today finally getting caught up. Quit at 9:00 P.M. (8:00 A.M. till 9:00 P.M.)

June 24, 1989

Start at 7:00 A.M. Only get one-fourth bucket between both beaches, check again at noon then 6:00 P.M., only get three-fourths bucket all day. Winds S.W. (7:00 A.M. till 6:00 P.M.)

June 25, 1989

Start at 7:00 A.M. Check beaches—no new oil. Go over beaches very careful and get about three-fourths bucket of old mousse. Beaches are now "very clean." VECO crew picks up tipar. (7:00 A.M. till 10:00 A.M.)

June 26, 1989

Make check every four hours: 8:00 A.M., 12:00 Noon, 4:00 P.M., 8:00 P.M. Only get twelve mousse pieces all day. (8:00 A.M. till 8:00 P.M.)

June 27, 1989

No oil, winds S.W.

June 28, 1989

No oil, winds S.W.

June 29, 1989

No oil. Heading home for two days.

June 30, 1989

N.E. wind. Martin gets five gal. mousse. Small pieces coming in all day.

July 1, 1989

No oil, wind S.W.

July 2, 1989

No oil, winds S.W.

July 3, 1989

Winds N.E. Mousse coming in again—very small pieces. Fill five-gal. can by noon. High tide at 4:00 P.M. Quite a bit comes in; we fill two five-gal. cans. (8:00 A.M. till 8:00 P.M.)

July 4, 1989

Holiday today sleep till 10:00 A.M. Start at 11:00 A.M.and work till 2:00 P.M. Finish three-fourths beach. Fill five-gal. can of very small pieces. Work for two more hours, 4:00 to 6:00 P.M. Fill one-fourth bucket very small pieces; still not more hours, 4:00 to 6:00 P.M. Fill one-fourth bucket very small pieces; still not done. (11:00 A.M. till 6:00 P.M.)

July 5, 1989

Sleep in again. Take first check of beach at 10:00 A.M. About same as yesterday came in. Also a few pieces on the front beach. Did final pickup at 9:00 P.M., beach pretty clean again. (10:00 A.M. till 9:00 P.M.)

July 6, 1989

Did check at 9:00 A.M., not too much came in. Although winds picking up N.E., so expect more today. Got one more five-gal. can by 9:00 P.M. Martin made last check and got fifty-eight tar balls. Heading for Ouzinkie to take care of business. Martin will take over. (9:00 A.M. till 9:00 P.M.)

July 7, 1989

Martin makes three picks today, gets two five-gal. cans. (6:00 A.M. till 6:00 P.M.)

July 8, 1989

Martin checks beach at 6:00 A.M., beach pretty clean. Picks six tar balls from front beach. Doesn't do back beach. We get back at 12:00 Noon. Martin found a dead bird yesterday and gave it to the *Sea Pride*; it was on the back beach. *Tasha* comes and picks up our bags today. Martin, Toni, and I do final pickup at 9:00 P.M., one-third bucket. Peter and Ann get twelve tar balls in mouth of river. (12:00 Noon till 9:00 P.M.)

July 9, 1989

Get about twelve mousse pieces only this morning (9:00 A.M.). Winds flat, calm, so junk slows down again. Fish and Game chopper lands at 10:00 this morning to check out the beach. Expect slow day—no winds. Do last check at 8:00 P.M.—no more comes in. (9:00 A.M. till 8:00 P.M.)

July 10, 1989

Chopper wakes us up at 8:30 A.M. We finally get some rain gear we ordered on June 23. Flat calm sunny day (no oil at 9:00 A.M.), not one piece today.

July 11, 1989

Check at 9:00 A.M., get only three tar balls. (S.E. breeze) 6:00 P.M. check (nothing).

July 12, 1989

Wake up to a N.E. breeze; check at 9:00 A.M., get about twelve pieces. If wind picks up, expect more today. The *KFC 5* and the *New Morning* have beach crews and are cleaning Ursin's beach and working their way in bay. Winds stay pretty calm, ten to fifteen. Only get eight more pieces at noon and five more at 8:00 P.M. Pretty slow day. Port Lions beach crew gets 170 bags in next bight in from Barabara. Kizhuyak is finally getting cleaned up. That much less to drift around. (9:00 A.M. till 8:00 P.M.)

July 13, 1989

Start at 9:00 A.M. and get a pretty good pick—about one hundred pieces or one-third bucket. Winds still N.E. ten to fifteen. Hope that shit would quit coming in now. Sure getting tired of it. Can't do very much—it takes up so much of our time. Winds switch to S.E. by noon—oil quits again—only twenty more pieces by 6:00 P.M. (9:00 A.M. till 6:00 P.M.)

July 14, 1989

N.E. wind again today. Martin and his crew do morning pickup at 8:00 A.M. They get seventy-five pieces from the back beach and eight from the front beach. Get about twenty more at noon and only sixteen at 6:00 P.M. The oil that's been coming in the last four or five days has been a lot softer; it gives off a lot of sheen. There is a lot more sheen coming in the Bay lately. It might be the water temp. is warming up. (8:00 A.M. till 6:00 P.M.)

July 15, 1989

Very windy and raining this morning, N.E. twenty-five—Martin starts morning pick at 8:00 A.M.; he gets over two hundred pieces (five-gal. can almost full) straight mousse. We join him at 10:00 A.M.(rain quits); mousse coming in steady. It keeps coming in all day; we get two more five-gal. cans full 8:00 P.M. Wind gets flat calm and it quits again. Very long day today, had to keep sifting through the kelp so it wouldn't get buried. (8:00 A.M. till 8:00 P.M.)

July 16, 1989

Start at 8:00 A.M. again. Beach pretty clean this morning. Winds light S.W., listening to the boats talk. There is a lot of mousse on the water again. Sounds like Izhut Bay got hit real hard again, so every N.E. we should get some more. Sonny on the *Tasha* came and picked up our bags today; also we got one dead bird today (herring gull). Offshore wind, no more oil. Left for Ouzinkie at 8:00 P.M. for a few days to take care of some business and bills. (8:00 A.M. till 8:00 P.M.)

July 17, 1989

Winds S.W.—no oil—Martin checks.

July 18, 1989

Winds S.W.—no oil.

July 19, 1989

Port Lions skiff (Jeff Lukin), one-fourth can—winds light northerly. Martin also picked one-fourth of a can.

July 20, 1989

Winds S.W.—no oil.

July 21, 1989

Chopper lands, drops off two more rolls of bags. Martin gets about a shovel full of tar balls.

July 22, 1989

Winds go to N.E. Martin gets two shovels full today.

July 23, 1989

Pretty good N.E. wind last night, but Martin only gets one-fourth can of mousse pieces today. Expected a lot more.

July 24, 1989

We got back at 12:00 Noon today. Winds S.W. Toni makes a check and gets a few pieces.

July 25, 1989

We start at 9:00 A.M. and do a real good cleaning, get about half a can—beach is real clean again. At 8:00 P.M. winds are N.E. again.

July 26, 1989
　　Get only about ten pieces.

July 27, 1989
　　No oil—winds S.W.

July 28, 1989
　　No oil—winds N.N.W.

July 29, 1989
　　Winds S.E. at twenty to thirty knots, get five-gal. bucket from front beach.

July 30, 1989
　　No new oil today. We start digging on the ten-foot tide line and fill a bucket. The kelp is rotting so some is getting exposed. There only is some on the ten-foot tide line. The rest of the beach crews came for about an hour this evening 5:30 to 6:30, they get about a five-gal. bucket. They call it four bags.

July 31, 1989
　　The *KFC 5* came to pick up the oil they left yesterday and took ours also. Three bags (six five-gal. cans). No oil came in today—flat calm.

August 1, 1989
　　Another flat calm day—no oil—less than ten pieces.

August 2, 1989
　　No new oil.

August 3, 1989
　　No new oil—a few new pieces.

August 4, 1989
　　No oil—still flat calm.

August 5, 1989
　　No oil—calm.

August 6, 1989
　　Pretty good N.E. wind, only one piece of oil. It must be getting all picked up.

August 7, 1989
　　About ten pieces today.

August 8, 1989
　　Winds still N.E. about same as yesterday, ten to fifteen pieces.

August 9, 1989
　　Heading for Ouzinkie.

REFERENCES CITED

A. Written Sources

Alaska Commercial Company
1881   Kaguiak [Kaguyak] Station Log Book, April 1, 1881, to April 1, 1882. Alaska Commercial Company Records, 1868–1913. Box 15, Folder 196. Alaska and Polar Regions Department, University of Alaska, Fairbanks.

1884–1885   Kodiak District Accounts, Sea Otter Parties. Box 15 Oversize. Alaska Commercial Company Records. Alaska and Polar Regions Department, University of Alaska, Fairbanks.

1894–1898   Ousinka [Ouzinkie] Station Accounts, Individual and Assorted and Inventories of Merchandise. Alaska Commercial Company Records. Box 135, Folders 1272 and 1273. Alaska and Polar Regions Department, University of Alaska, Fairbanks.

Alaska Department of Fish and Game
1897–1996   Kodiak Management Area Commercial Salmon Annual Reports. Division of Commercial Fisheries. Kodiak.

1999   *Whiskers!* Marine mammals multimedia database. CD-ROM. Division of Subsistence, with the Alaska Native Harbor Seal Commission. Anchorage.

Alaska Limited Entry Commission
1998   Internet on-line database. Address: www.cfec.state.ak.us

Anonymous
1887   "The Russian Marriage." *The Alaskan*, August 27, pp. 1–2.

1888   "*Albatross* Report: Voyage from San Francisco to Unalaska." Unpublished manuscript. RG 22, Box No. 2 of 7, Entry 63. National Archives, Washington, D.C.

1992   "Military Buildup on Kodiak." *Alaska Geographic* 19(3):45–47.

1995   "Kodiak village corporations paid $60 million for land inholdings." *Alaska Economic Report* 1995 No. 10 (25 May 1995): 8.

2002 "Kodiak Village Corporation Gives Big Distribution." *Alaska Business Monthly* (November 2002): 9.

Bailey, Marie
1949 "Old Harbor." pp. 6ff. *Alaska Sportsman* (April).

Befu, Harumi
1970 "An Ethnographic Sketch of Old Harbor, Kodiak: An Eskimo Village." *Arctic Anthropology* VI(2):29–42.

Berger, Michael
1993 "Ouzinkie Native Corporation." *Alaska Business Monthly* 9(11):26–27.

Bernsten, Ron
1991 "Give It Back to the Indians." *Tundra Times*, December 16, p. 2.

Black, Lydia
1977 "The Konyag (The Inhabitants of the Island of Kodiak)," by Iosaf [Bolotov] (1794–1799) and by Gideon (1804–1807). *Arctic Anthropology* 14(2):79–108.

1992 "The Russian Conquest of Kodiak." *Anthropological Papers of the University of Alaska* 24:165–182.

Buckley, Mark
1998 "Bulk of Kodiak's Halibut Fleet in Port." *Kodiak Daily Mirror*, March 25, p. 1.

Bureau of the Census, U.S. Department of Commerce
1920 Fourteenth U.S. Census. Household enumeration sheets. Microfilm T625, Roll 2031. Anchorage: National Archives.

Bureau of Indian Affairs (BIA)
1934 Alaskan Village Census Rolls, Old Harbor. Microfilm P2286, Cabinet 46, Roll 46. National Archives, Anchorage.

Chaffin, Yule, Trisha Hampton Krieger, and Michael Rostad
1983 *Alaska's Konyag Country*. n.p.: Pratt Publishing.

Chernikoff, Mike
1982 Interviewed by Anna Rae Bent and Jo Ann Torsen. *Ukulahā* II, pp. 14–19. Ouzinkie High School.

Clark, Donald W.
1984a "Prehistory of the Pacific Eskimo Region." Pp. 136–148. In: David Damas, ed., *Handbook of North American Indians, Vol. 5: Arctic.* Washington: Smithsonian Institution.

1984b "Pacific Eskimo: Historical Ethnography." Pp. 185–197. In: David Damas, ed., *Handbook of North American Indians, Vol. 5: Arctic.* Washington: Smithsonian Institution.

1987 "On a Misty Day You Can See Back to 1805: Ethnohistory and Historical Archaeology on the Southeastern Side of Kodiak Island, Alaska." *Anthropological Papers of the University of Alaska* 21(1–2):105–132.

Crowell, Aron
1992 "Postcontact Koniag Ceremonialism on Kodiak Island and the Alaska Peninsula: Evidence from the Fisher Collection." *Arctic Anthropology* 29(1):18–37.

1994a "Archaeology and the Capitalist World System: The View from Three Saints Harbor: An 18th Century Russian Fur Trade Site on Kodiak Island." Ph.D. dissertation, University of California at Berkeley.

1994b "Koniag Eskimo Poisoned-Dart Whaling." Pp. 117–142. In: W. Fitzhugh and V. Chaussonnet, eds., *Anthropology of the North Pacific Rim*. Washington: Smithsonian Institution Press.

1997 *Archaeology and the Capitalist World System: A Study from Russian America*. New York and London: Plenum Press.

Crowell, Aron, Amy Steffian, and Gordon Pullar, eds.
2001 *Looking Both Ways: Heritage and Identity of the Alutiiq People*. Fairbanks: University of Alaska Press.

Curtis, Marion
1948 "Stricken Village." *Public Health Nursing* 40:578–582.

Davis, Nancy Yaw
1970 "The Role of the Russian Orthodox Church in Five Pacific Eskimo Villages as Revealed by the Earthquake." Pp. 125–146. In: *The Great Alaskan Earthquake of 1964*. Washington, D.C.: National Academy of Sciences.

1971 "The Effects of the 1964 Alaska Earthquake, Tsunami, and Resettlement on Two Koniag Eskimo Villages." Ph.D. thesis, University of Washington. Ann Arbor: UMI Press.

1979 *Kodiak Native Sociocultural Impacts*. Southwest Gulf of Alaska Petroleum Development Scenarios. Social and Economic Studies Program, Minerals Management Service. Alaska OCS Region. Technical Report No. 41. Anchorage: U.S. Department of the Interior.

1984 "Contemporary Pacific Eskimo." Pp. 198–204. In: David Damas, ed., *Handbook of North American Indians, Vol. 5: Arctic*. Washington: Smithsonian Institution.

1986a *A Sociocultural Description of Small Communities in the Kodiak-Shumagin Region*. Technical Report No. 121. Anchorage: U.S. Minerals Management Service.

1986b "Earthquake, Tsunami, Resettlement, and Survival in Two North Pacific Alaskan Native Villages [Kaguyak and Old Harbor]." Pp. 123–154. In: A. Oliver-Smith, ed., *Natural Disasters and Cultural Responses*. Williamsburg, Va.: College of William and Mary, Dept. of Anthropology.

Davydov, G. I.
1977 *Two Voyages to Russian America, 1802–1807.* C. Bearne, transl., R. A. Pierce, ed. Kingston, Ont.: Limestone Press.

Department of Community and Regional Affairs (DCRA)
1998 DCRA Community Database. State of Alaska Internet Web site: www.comregaf.state.ak.us/CF_BLOCK.cfm

Dobbyn, Paula
2000 "Ouzinkie Invests in Tourism." *Anchorage Daily News.* January 21, pp. D-1 ff.

Eliel, R. Monk Gerasim
1989 *Father Gerasim of New Valaam.* Ouzinkie, Alaska, and Platina, Calif.: St. Herman Press.

Eliot, John
1993 "Kodiak, Alaska's Island Refuge." *National Geographic Magazine.* November. pp. 34–59.

Ellanak, Larry
1982 Interviewed by James Anderson. *Ukulahā* II, pp. 32–35. Ouzinkie High School.

Fall, James A. and L. Jay Field
1996 "Subsistence Uses of Fish and Wildlife before and after the *Exxon Valdez* Oil Spill." In Proceedings of the *Exxon Valdez* Oil Spill Symposium, S. D. Rice, R.B. Spies, D. A. Wolfe, and B. A. Wright, eds., pp. 819–836. American Fisheries Society Symposium 18. Bethesda, Maryland: American Fisheries Society.

Federova, Svetlana
1975 *Ethnic Processes in Russian America.* Occasional Paper No. 1. Anchorage: Anchorage Historical and Fine Arts Museum.

Fitzhugh, Ben
1998 "Community Archaeology on the Kodiak Archipelago, or, On the Importance of Getting One's (Sod) House in Order." Paper presented at the Alaska Anthropological Association Annual Meeting, Anchorage.

Fortuine, Robert
1989 *Chills and Fever: Health and Disease in the Early History of Alaska.* Fairbanks: University of Alaska Press.

Gibbs, Jim
1968 *West Coast Windjammers.* New York: Bonanza Books.

Gibson, James R.
1976 *Imperial Russia in Frontier America.* New York: Oxford University Press.

Golder, Frank
1968 *Father Herman, Alaska's Saint.* San Francisco: Orthodox Christian Books and Icons.

Graham, Frances Kelso
1985   *Plant Lore of an Alaskan Island.* Anchorage: Alaska Northwest Publishing Company.

Gregory, Bishop (Afonsky)
1977   *A History of the Orthodox Church in Alaska, 1794–1917.* Kodiak: St. Herman's Theological Seminary.

Haakanson, Sven Sr.
1984   Transcript of Proceedings, Village Meeting. Volume 49: Larsen Bay. November 20. Fairbanks: Alaska Native Review Commission, Elmer Rasmuson Library, University of Alaska.

Hall, Andy
1993   "Spraznikom—Orthodox Christmas." *Kodiak Daily Mirror*, January 7, p. 1.

Harvey, Lola
1991   *Derevnia's Daughters: Saga of an Alaskan Village.* Manhattan, Kansas: Sunflower University Press.

Helmig, Katherine
1992   "Interview with an Aleut Woman from Ouzinkie, Alaska." Interviewed by Sandra Camp. *Tundra Times*, November 11. Pp.1ff.

Herman, Father
1989   Letter to Abbot Jonathan of Valaam, December 13, 1819. In: *Little Russian Philokalia, Vol. 3: St. Herman.* Ouzinkie, Alaska, and Platina, Calif.: St. Herman Press.

Holmberg, Heinrich Johan
1985   *Holmberg's Ethnographic Sketches.* F. Jaensch, transl., W. Falk, ed. Fairbanks: University of Alaska Press.

Hooks, Bell
1989   *Talking Back: Thinking Feminist, Thinking Black.* Boston: South End Press.

Huggins, Eli
1981   *Kodiak and Afognak Life, 1868–1870.* Kingston, Ont.: The Limestone Press.

Hunter, Kathy
1979   "Priest [Fr. Michael Oleksa] Acts to Save Native Language." *Alaska Magazine* 45(June):a31.

Impact Assessment, Inc.
1990a   *Public and Private Sector Economic Impacts of the* Exxon Valdez *Oil Spill.* Interim Report No. 2. Prepared by the Oiled Mayors Subcommittee, Alaska Conference of Mayors. Anchorage and La Jolla, Calif.

1990b   *Social and Psychological Impacts of the Exxon Valdez Oil Spill.* Interim Report No. 3. Prepared by the Oiled Mayors Subcommittee, Alaska Conference of Mayors. Anchorage and La Jolla, Calif.

Jeffrey, Sue
1998   "St. Herman's Seminary Dean Claims Monks 'Imposters.'" *Kodiak Daily Mirror*, January 28, pp. 1 and 3.

Jerry, Danielle
1998   Letter to Craig Mishler from the United States Department of the Interior, Fish and Wildlife Service, Division of Realty, April 10.

Johnson, Dennis
1979   "Alaska's Early Cod Fishery." *The Alaska Journal* 9(2):75–80.

Katelnikoff, Philip
1981   "The Crow and the Goose." As told to Jo Ann Torsen and Fred Shanagin. *Ukulahā* I, pp. 17–18. Ouzinkie High School.

Khlebnikov, Kiril
1835   "Life of Aleksandr Andreevich Baranov." 65 pp. In: Melvin Ricks, ed., *The Earliest History of Alaska*. Anchorage: Cook Inlet Historical Society, 1970.

Klouda, Naomi
1996a   "Elder Inspires Kodiak Island Youth to Embrace Culture, Challenges." *Anchorage Daily News*, October 13. pp. J1ff.

1996b   "Old Harbor." In: Susan F. Rogers, ed., *Alaska Passages*. Pp. 103–113. Seattle: Sasquatch Books.

1997   "Defending Old Harbor." In: "We Alaskans." *Anchorage Daily News*, July 20. pp. H8–H14.

1999   Letter to the author. October 26.

2000   "Walt's Store: The Essence of Old Harbor." *Kodiak Daily Mirror*, March 22, pp. 2ff.

Kodiak Area Native Association (KANA)
1997   Kodiak Island Spirit Camp, Grants Progress Report to the Department of Community and Regional Affairs, Division of Administrative Services, State of Alaska. September 1997. 5 pp.

Kozely, Lado
1963   "Ouzinkie." Anchorage: Bureau of Indian Affairs. Mimeographed copy at the ARLIS Library, Anchorage.

Kreta, Father [Joseph]
1983   "The Story of St. Herman of Alaska." pp. 8–9. In: Ann Vick, ed., *The Cama-i Book*. Garden City, N.Y.: Anchor Books.

Langsdorff, Georg Heinrich
1993   *Remarks and Observations on a Voyage Around the World from 1803 to 1807*. Transl. by Victoria Moessner. Ed. by Richard A. Pierce. Fairbanks: The Limestone Press.

Leer, Jeff
1989   *A Conversational Dictionary of Kodiak Alutiiq.* Preliminary Edition. Fairbanks: University of Alaska, Alaska Native Language Center.

1990   *Classroom Grammar of Koniag Alutiiq, Kodiak Island Dialect.* Preliminary Edition, Vol. I. Fairbanks: Alaska Native Language Center, Univ. of Alaska.

Liapunova, Roza
1994   "Eskimo Masks from Kodiak Island in the Collections of the Peter the Great Museum of Anthropology and Ethnography in St. Petersburg." Pp. 175–204. In: W. Fitzhugh and V. Chaussonnet, eds., *Anthropology of the North Pacific Rim.* Washington: Smithsonian Institution Press.

Llanos, Dora
1981   Interviewed by Carl Smith, Kevin Smith, and Jo Ann Torsen. *Ukulahā* I, pp. 21–23. Ouzinkie High School.

Lund, Jean
1946   "Letter to friends from the Ouzinkie Baptist Mission, February 12." Unpublished typescript, in private collection of Joyce Smith, Ouzinkie.

Mason, Rachel
1998   "Intermarriage and Migrations among Kodiak Island Villages in the Twentieth Century." Paper presented at the Alaska Anthropological Association Annual Meeting in Anchorage, March 21.

Mishler, Craig
1988   "The Nuta'aq: Musical Folk Drama in Nanwalek, Alaska." Paper presented at the Alaska Anthropological Association Annual Meeting, Fairbanks.

1991   "From Quantitative to Qualitative: Subsistence Food Harvests and Alutiiq Cultural Traditions." Paper presented at the Alaska Anthropological Association Annual Meeting, Anchorage.

1995   "Head Lice in a Match Box: Some Notes on Kodiak Alutiiq Weather Lore." Paper presented at the American Folklore Society Annual Meeting, Lafayette, Louisiana.

1997   "Aurcaq: Interruption, Distraction, and Reversal in an Alutiiq Men's Dart Game." *Journal of American Folklore* 110(436):189–202.

Mishler, Craig, and Rachel Mason
1996   "Alutiiq Vikings: Kinship and Fishing in Old Harbor, Alaska." *Human Organization* 55(3):263–269.

Morehead, Albert, Richard Frey, and Geoffrey Mott-Smith
1964   *The New Complete Hoyle.* New York: Doubleday & Company.

Morrison, Dorothy
1981   Interviewed by Anna Rae Bent. *Ukulahā* I, pp. 24–26. Ouzinkie High School.

Moss, Brigette
1998a　"Spirit Camp: Living in Alutiiq Culture." *Kodiak Daily Mirror*, July 24, p. 6.

1998b　"Pilgrims Journey to Monk's Shrine." *Kodiak Daily Mirror*, August 12, p. 6.

Mousalimas, Soterios
1995　*The Transition from Shamanism to Russian Orthodoxy in Alaska*. Providence, R.I.: Berghahn Books.

Mulcahy, Laurie
1987　*Adaq'wy: The Time Has Come*. Kodiak: Kodiak Area Native Association.

Muller, Fred
1982　"Katmai Eruption." *Ukulahā* II, pp. 37–38. Ouzinkie High School.

Muller, Jackie
1982　Interviewed by Anna Rae Bent, Sheila Anderson, and JoAnn Torsen. *Ukulahā* II, pp. 30–31. Ouzinkie High School.

Murkowski, Carol
1989　"Ouzinkie: No Place Like Home." *Alaska Magazine* 55(5):20ff (May).

1990　"Stars over Old Harbor." *Alaska Magazine* 56(1):22ff (January).

Murray, Martha G. and Peter L. Corey
1997　"Aleut Weavers." *Concepts*. Technical Paper No. 8, Alaska State Museums. Juneau.

Oleksa, Michael
1990　*Orthodox Alaska: A Theology of Mission*. Crestwood, N.J.: St. Vladimir's Seminary.

Opheim, Edward N., Sr.
1994　*The Memoirs and Saga of a Cod Fisherman's Son: Ten Years of Dory-Fishing Cod (1923–1933) at Sunny Cove, Spruce Island, Alaska*. New York: Vantage Press.

Ouzinkie Government School
1946　*Spruce Bough*. (Mimeograph yearbook) Copy in possession of Joyce Smith, Ouzinkie. 40 pp.

1947　*Spruce Bough*. (Mimeograph yearbook) Copy in possession of Joyce Smith, Ouzinkie. 32 pp.

Ouzinkie Native Corporation (ONC)
1998　"Ouzinkie Native Corporation Explains Eviction of Native Monks." *Kodiak Daily Mirror*, March 4, p. 5.

Panamarioff, Johnny
1982　Interviewed by Sheila Anderson and Lisa Bent. *Ukulahā* II, pp. 25–29. Ouzinkie High School.

Parker, Nell
1997 "Salmon on Schedule." *Kodiak Daily Mirror*, June 6, p. 1.

Pestrikoff, Geri
1997 "Old Harbor Students Find Ties to Heritage During Alutiiq Week." *Kodiak Daily Mirror*, May 14, p. 19.

Phillips, Natalie
1997 "Cash Windfall Divides Natives." *Anchorage Daily News,* November 3, pp. 1ff.

Porter, Robert
1893 *Report on the Population and Resources of Alaska at the Eleventh Census: 1890.* Washington: U.S. Bureau of the Census.

Pullar, Gordon
1992 "Ethnic Identity, Cultural Pride, and Generations of Baggage: A Personal Experience." *Arctic Anthropology* 29(2):182–191.

Reeves, Randall, Stephen Leatherwood, Stephen Karl, and Evelyn Yohe
1985 "Whaling Results at Akutan (1912–1939) and Port Hobron (1926–1937)." In: *Thirty-fifth Report of the International Whaling Commission*, pp. 441–457.

Richardson, Jeff
1997 "Cruise Ships Plan Old Harbor Stops This Summer." *Kodiak Daily Mirror*, January 21, p. 3.

Robinson, Deborah B.
1996 "Changing Relationships to Marine Resources: The Commercial Salmon Fishery in Old Harbor, Alaska." M.A. thesis, Dept. of Geography, McGill University, Montreal. Ann Arbor: UMI.

Roppel, Patricia
1994 *Salmon from Kodiak: An History of the Salmon Fishery of Kodiak Island, Alaska.* 2nd edition. Anchorage: Alaska Historical Commission. Originally 1986.

Roscoe, Fred
1992 *From Humboldt to Kodiak, 1886–1895.* Fairbanks and Kingston: The Limestone Press.

Rostad, Mike
1988 *Time to Dance: Life of an Alaska Native.* Anchorage: A.T. Publishing.

1992 "Bad Weather Doesn't Stop Ouzinkie from Starring." *Kodiak Daily Mirror*, January 13, page 16.

1997a "Old Harbor Youth Join Elders at AFN Conference." *Kodiak Daily Mirror*, October 22, p. 11.

1997b "Traditional Knowledge Can Be Important Part of School Curriculum." *Kodiak Daily Mirror*, December 8, p. 6.

1998   "Priest Helps Rebuild Village Church." *Kodiak Daily Mirror*, May 6, page 14.

2000   "Obituary: Old Harbor's Walt Erickson Dead at 75." *Kodiak Daily Mirror*, March 22, p. 2.

Russian Orthodox Church of America
1905   Confessional Records for Theotokos Church at Afognak. Translated from the Russian. St. Herman's Seminary Archives, Kodiak.

Salisbury, Richard F.
1984   "Affluence and Cultural Survival: An Introduction." Pp. 1–11. In: Richard Salisbury and Elizabeth Tucker, eds., *Affluence and Cultural Survival*. Washington: American Ethnological Society.

Setzkorn, Mary
1946   "Letter to friends from the Ouzinkie Baptist Mission, January 23." Unpublished typescript, in possession of Joyce Smith, Ouzinkie.

Shugak, Tom
1992   "Tom Shugak, Uncle Principal." *Alaska Geographic* 19(3):49–53.

Simeone, Bill
1997   Unpublished Kodiak Trip Report, September 16–19. Alaska Department of Fish and Game, Division of Subsistence, Anchorage.

Smith, Barbara, David Goa, and Dennis Bell
1994   *Heaven on Earth: Orthodox Treasures of Siberia and North America*. Anchorage: Anchorage Museum of History and Art.

Sturgeon, John
1994   "Forest Management on Alaska Native Lands." *Journal of Forestry* 92(5):10–13.

Taylor, Kenneth
1966   "A Demographic Study of Karluk, Kodiak Island, Alaska, 1962–1964." *Arctic Anthropology* 3(2):211–44.

Tennessen, Karen
1983   "Egg Trading." *Alaska Magazine* 49(April):6–7.

Tikhmenev, P. A.
1978   *A History of the Russian-American Company*. Transl. and edited by R. A. Pierce and A. S. Donnelly. Orig. 1861–1863. Seattle: University of Washington Press.

Toomey, Sheila
1997   "Shellfish Warnings Follow Death." *Anchorage Daily News*, June 10, p. A1; A8.

U.S. Department of the Interior
1995   Agreement for the Sale, Purchase, and Donation of Lands and Interests in Lands between Old Harbor Native Corporation and the United States of America. Anchorage: U.S. Fish and Wildlife Service, Division of Realty, Document 0137.

Williams, Ann Elizabeth
1993   "Father Herman: Syncretic Symbol of Divine Legitimation." Unpublished M.A. thesis, University of Alaska, Fairbanks.

Wolfe, Robert J. and Craig Mishler
1997   *The Subsistence Harvest of Harbor Seal and Sea Lion by Alaska Natives in 1996.* Technical Paper No. 241. Juneau: Alaska Department of Fish and Game, Division of Subsistence.

B: Oral Interviews

** Tapes and typed transcripts are on file at the Alaska Department of Fish and Game, Division of Subsistence, Anchorage.
* Notes only, no tape.
~~ Tapes only, no transcripts.

Alexanderoff, Wilfred
N.d.   Interviewed by Linda Finn Yarborough. ACSA 14(h)(1) oral history, Tape 7_KON004. Bureau of Indian Affairs, Anchorage.

Anderson, Martha*
1997   Interviewed by Craig Mishler in Anchorage, January 17.

Bernsten, Ron**
1997   Interviewed by Craig Mishler in Old Harbor, February 7.

Chernikoff, Fred and Esther*
1998   Interviewed by Craig Mishler in Ouzinkie, May 26.

Christiansen, Freddy**
1997   Interviewed by Craig Mishler in Old Harbor, September 11, dubbed from videotape.

Erickson, Walt**
1996   Interviewed by Craig Mishler in Kodiak, November 21.

Haakanson, Arthur**
1997   Interviewed by Craig Mishler in Ouzinkie, May 15.

Haakanson, Sven Sr. and Mary**
1997   Interviewed by Craig Mishler in Old Harbor, February 2.

Inga, George Sr.
1987   Interviewed by Laurie Mulcahy in Old Harbor, September 18. Kodiak Area Native Association Collection. Typed transcript. Alutiiq Museum, Kodiak.

1996** Interviewed by Craig Mishler in Old Harbor, September 10, dubbed from videotape.

1998* Interviewed by Craig Mishler in Old Harbor, September 25.

Kahutak, Paul
1987 Interviewed by Laurie Mulcahy in Kodiak City, August 11. Typed transcript. Alutiiq Museum, Kodiak.

1997a** Interviewed by Craig Mishler in Anchorage, March 12.

1997b** Interviewed on videotape by Craig Mishler in Old Harbor, September 11.

Kvasnikoff, Christine*
1997 Interviewed by Craig Mishler in Ouzinkie, May 15.

Nelson, John Sr.
1994 Interviewed by Craig Mishler in Port Lions, December 10.

Opheim, Ed Sr.**
1997 Interviewed by Craig Mishler in Kodiak, February 26.

Oswalt, Reed**
1997 Interviewed by Craig Mishler in Kodiak, February 25. Comments focused on photograph collection.

Pestrikoff, Nick Sr.**
1996 Interviewed by Craig Mishler in Kodiak, November 21.

Smith, Joyce~~
1997 Interviewed by Craig Mishler in Ouzinkie, January 21.

Toms, Hender**
1997 Interviewed by Craig Mishler in Seattle, March 9.

Zeedar, Anakenti and George Inga Sr.~~
1991 Interviewed by Craig Mishler in Old Harbor on September 18.

1994 Interviewed by Craig Mishler in Old Harbor on December 7.

C: Video Sources

Bayer, Wolfgang, director
1994 *Giant Bears of Kodiak Island.* 60 minutes. Washington: National Geographic Society.

Mishler, Craig, editor and director
1991 *Alaskan Subsistence: The Kodiak Connection.* 30 minutes. Anchorage.

INDEX

A
Abalik. See Kahutak, Paul
Adonga, Albert, 45
Afgonak Lake, 157
Afognak Island, 14, 19, 50–51, 54, 60, 74, 131–132, 155–157, 211, 214–215, 219, 222, 225–226, 234
Afognak Joint Ventures, 211
Afognak, 21, 31–33, 41–42, 48, 51, 57, 59, 73–74, 96, 154, 219
Agnot, Ephraim, Sr., 80, 84, 100
Agnot, Miney, 84
Agnot, Simeon, 84
Agusha, Jacob, 84
Ahulaq (Bigfoot), 129, 131
Aiaktalik, 73, 75, 84
airstrips, 42, 47, 65, 204
Akademik Shokalskiy (cruise ship), 207
Akhiok, 18, 22, 24–25, 31, 42, 51, 66, 73, 80–85, 96, 100, 113, 136, 161, 163, 193, 208, 214, 219, 226
Akhiok-Kaguyak Corporation, 210–211
Alaska Commercial Company, 31–34, 50, 112, 126
Alaska Department of Fish and Game, 12, 66
Alaska Federation of Natives, 16
Alaska Native Claims Settlement Act (ANCSA), 18, 65–66, 89, 90, 209
Alaska Packers cannery, 223
Albatross (sailing ship), 32, 34–35
Alexanderoff family, 69
Alexanderoff, Betty, 14
Alexanderoff, Peter, 84
Alexanderoff, Sergie, 169–171
Alexanderoff, Wilfred, 84, 129, 139
Alitak, 114, 225
Alokli, Eliza, 84
Alutiiq Heritage Week, 13, 126, 135, 137, 217
Alutiiq Museum, 12–14, 25, 135, 215, 219
Ambrosia, Alex, 12
Aminak, Arsentii, 31
Anchorage Daily News, 210
Anchorage, 12, 16–18, 21, 25, 42, 44, 76, 77, 90, 139, 147, 194
Anderson family, 51, 69
Anderson, Alice, 55

Anderson, Andy, 12, 91–92, 214, 222
Anderson, Herman, 11, 17, 62
Anderson, Johnny, 74
Anderson, Martha, 17, 51, 53, 57, 118, 126, 138, 145
Andrewvitch family, 69
Andrewvitch, Herman, 84
Andrewvitch, Marra, 135
Andrewvitch, Wilmer, 113
Anton Larsen Bay. *See* Larsen Bay
Arlene Louise (ship), 235
Armstrong, Karl, 35
Arndt, Katherine, 34
Ashouwak family, 72
Askoak, Wasilly, Father, 46
Aurcaq (dart game), 76, 136–138
Azuyak family, 72
Azuyak, Arthur, 128
Azuyak, Gavrilla, 84
Azuyak, Tony, 12, 84, 114, 139

B
baidarkas, 31–33
Bailey, Marie, 131
Baker House, 57
Ban Island, 74
banyas, 47, 112, 120, 141–147, 153, 219
Baptist Mission, 18, 20, 57, 59, 62, 72
Barabara Cove, 19, 26, 66, 74, 158, 159, 221, 232–239
barabaras, 29, 30, 32, 33, 34, 38, 75, 142–143, 217–219, 234
Baranof, Alexander, 48
Baranov Museum, 12
Barling Bay, 38, 177, 186–187
Barletson, Guy, 234
basketball, 48
basketry, 112, 133–135
beach seines, 35
bears, 40, 118, 155, 157, 170–171, 173–176, 208, 225
Beinly, Brian, 235
Berger Commission, 65
Berns, Rick, 12, 16, 90–92, 115, 145, 169, 204
Berns, Wilma, 115, 181, 204
Bernsten, Darryl, 14
Bernsten, Ron, 14–15, 101–102, 145, 201–202
berries, 155, 191, 225
bidarkis. *See* chitons
Big Creek, 38, 170, 181, 218

Bigioli, Emily, 116
bingo, 18, 25, 47, 90, 121, 124, 138–139, 153
bird eggs, 155, 161, 172–173, 229
Bligh Reef, 66
boat building, 62
boat captains (skippers), 100–102, 114, 144, 203
Bolotov, Iosaf, 103
Boskofsky family, 73
Boskofsky, Mike, 12
Boskofsky, Robin, 233
Boskofsky, Waska, 62, 116, 128
boxing, 123
Bristol Bay, 77
buoy bouncing (game), 153
Bush Point, 159

C
Camel's Rock, 51, 74, 165
Campfield, Angeline, 12, 91–92
Canadian geese, 160
canneries, 41–42, 54–57, 59, 61–63, 195, 223, 225–226, 228
Cape Alitak, 228
Cape Barnabas, 168–169
Capjohn, Kalumpi, 84
Capjohn, Whitey, 92, 115
Carla Rae C. (purse seiner), 196
Carmel (Halibut Bay), 16
Cat Island, 51, 165
Charlotte B. (mail boat), 41
Chenega Bay, 24, 193, 214
Chenega Corporation, 214
Chernikoff family, 51, 69
Chernikoff, Doc, 62
Chernikoff, Esther, 21, 126, 130
Chernikoff, Fred, Sr., 21, 62, 126, 130
Chernikoff, Jenny, 21, 50, 72, 130, 154, 191
Chernikoff, Mike, 21, 54, 56–57, 66, 89, 154
Chichenoff family, 69, 73
Chichenoff, Roy, 125
Chichenoff, Zack, 12, 90–92
Chignik Bay, 24
Chignik Lagoon, 24
Chignik Lake, 24
Chigniks, 15
Chinese, 54
Chiniak, 33
chitons, 164–165
Christiansen family, 69, 180
Christiansen, Carl, 44, 116, 144–145

Christiansen, Emil, 12, 91, 114, 123
Christiansen, Freddy, 16–17, 101, 145, 154, 172, 203–204, 208
Christiansen, Glenna, 17
Christiansen, Harold, 181
Christiansen, Jack, 145, 164
Christiansen, Nels, 41
Christiansen, Oscar, 181
Christiansen, Randy, 208
Christiansen, Rocky, 145
Christiansen, Rolf, 37
Christmas, 38, 112–116
Christofferson, Andy, 207
Chya, Connie, 125–126, 216
City of Old Harbor, 90
City of Ouzinkie, 64, 90
clams, 67, 163–166
Clark, Donald, 30
Clough, Glenn, 159
Clough, Phyllis, 220
cockles, 165
codfish, 38, 53, 69, 73, 186–189
commercial fishing, 47, 51, 54, 62, 66, 67, 73, 76–77, 102, 109, 195–196, 200, 203–204, 206, 208–210, 215, 225
commercial hunting, 50
Cook Inlet, 24, 66, 209
Cordova, 220–221
crab, 55, 114–115, 124, 164, 195–196, 199, 227–228, 231
Cratty, Al, 209
Cratty, Al, Jr., 12
Cratty, Johnetta, 209
Crimson Beauty (boat), 123
Crowell, Aron, 122–123, 154
Curtis, Marion, 41

D
dances and dance halls, 21, 37, 42, 49, 60, 69, 112, 117–118, 120, 125–129, 138, 153, 216–217, 219–220
Danger Bay, 60, 74, 102, 109, 157, 200–201
Davis, Nancy Yaw, 13, 220
Davydov, Gavriil, 103, 135
Dayton, Jim, 42, 44
Deadman's Bay, 18, 40, 225
deer, 67, 154–157, 177, 204, 206
Delphin (sailing ship), 48
Denali, S.S. (freighter), 53–54
Devoe, Pete, 228
Dog Bay, 177

dolphin (manaq), 137
Downtown (Old Harbor), 46–47, 91, 113–114, 116, 220
Duchess (fish tender), 36
ducks, 154, 157–158, 163, 191, 203–204, 206, 217–218, 225–226

E

Eagle Harbor, 16, 18, 31, 33, 72, 74, 81, 84–85, 88
earthquake (1964). *See* Great Alaskan Earthquake
Easter, 41, 83, 87, 121–122, 137, 151–152
ecotourism, 203–204, 215
Egegik, 24
Eleventh Air Force, 15
elk, 154–155, 157
Ellanak family, 72
Ellanak, Larry, 50
Erickson family, 116
Erickson, Jenny, 45, 183
Erickson, Walt, 15, 18, 47, 129, 146, 163, 166, 183, 185, 206–207, 220, 224
Ethnicity, 22, 68–69, 72
Exxon Valdez oil spill, 15, 20, 22, 25–26, 31, 50, 63, 66–67, 76–77, 91–92, 125, 129, 164–165, 186, 194, 209, 213, 215, 219, 226, 232–239

F

Fairbanks, 16
Fall, Jim, 12, 66
False Pass, 14
family territories, 74–75
Farsovitch, Evon, 84
Fawn (seine boat), 17
Federal Subsistence Management Program, 40
Filipinos, 54, 57, 189
Fitzhugh, Ben, 217
flu epidemic, 41, 51, 75
folk speech, 112, 140–141, 153
folklore, 112, 129–133
Fortune (seine boat), 17
Fourth of July, 122–125
Fox Lagoon, 30, 131–132, 159–160
foxes, 30, 38, 51, 74, 118, 176
fur trade, 69

G

games, 112, 123–124, 135–140, 153, 194, 216–217
Garden Point, 51
Gatter, George, Jr., 204, 206
Gerken, Sergio, Father, 46, 113, 115
Gideon, Father, 107, 144
gill nets, 19, 178-180, 196, 200, 219, 227, 234

Glennette C. (purse seiner), 202
gold rush, 34
Grant, George, 228
graves, 112, 122, 130, 148–153
Great Alaskan Earthquake, 42, 45–47, 61–62, 66, 73, 75, 80, 83, 89, 128, 160, 181. *See also* tsunami
Gregory, Leroy, 200, 203, 219
Grimes Packing Company cannery, 17, 20, 52, 54, 55, 57, 60, 62–63, 75, 225
Grimes, Ella, 54
Grimes, Oscar, 54, 62
grocers, 226

H

Haakanson family, 69, 116
Haakanson, Arthur, 60, 78, 90, 215, 225–230
Haakanson, Arthur, Jr., 90
Haakanson, Arthur, Sr., 18, 37, 227
Haakanson, Herman, 90, 227
Haakanson, Mary, 13–14, 95, 116, 120, 125, 144, 172, 181, 217
Haakanson, Phyllis, 123
Haakanson, Sven, Jr., 13–14, 116, 219
Haakanson, Sven, Sr., 13–14, 18, 42, 60, 65, 90, 92, 95, 116, 119–120, 122–123, 144, 172, 182, 189, 217
Haakanson, Wanda, 115
halibut, 41, 186–188, 190, 199–200, 207, 209
Hammerly, Frank, 126
Hansen, William, Jr., 40
Harvey, Lola, 132
health clinic, 47
Herman, Abbot, 222
Herman, Father, 31, 48–49, 59, 113, 124, 130, 222
Herman, Saint, 49, 59, 113, 124, 222
herring, 35, 53–54, 69, 73, 124, 199–201, 204, 226–227
Holmberg, Heinrich, 142
Huggins, Eli, 49
hunting partnerships, 157

I

IFQs (individual fishing quotas), 199
Igatsky, Orlov, 31
Ignatin, Christine, 135
Ignatin, Nickolas, 40
Ignatin, Sophie, 134
Ignatin, Thomas, 136
Ignatin, William, 84, 174–176
Inga family, 72
Inga, Alexis, 83–84
Inga, Costia, 45, 84
Inga, Fedosia, 133–135

Inga, George, Sr., 14, 17, 35, 38, 40, 44–45, 72, 74–75, 80, 113, 121, 134, 139, 159, 171–172, 174, 176, 178, 182, 185–186, 190, 194, 203, 221
Inga, Innokenti, 84
Inga, Jennie, 16
Inga, Mike, 15, 40
Inga, Sasha, 35
Inga, Simmy, 84
Inga, Sophie, 15, 121, 139, 194
Iosaph, Father, 222
Italians, 226
Ivanof Bay, 24, 193
Izhut Bay, 74, 234

J

Jap Bay, 228
Japanese, 38, 40, 59–60
Johanssen family, 69
Johnson, Phil, 216
Juneau, 44
Juvenali, Father, 31

K

Kadiak Fisheries cannery, 35, 75, 81, 225
Kaguiak, Barris, 84
Kaguyak, 31–33, 42, 45, 73, 81, 84, 226
Kahutak family, 72
Kahutak, Martha, 16–17, 147
Kahutak, Paul (Abalik), 13, 16, 41, 44, 74, 79, 80, 128–129, 131–133, 144, 147, 174–175, 182–183, 185–186, 190, 206, 220
Kaiuganak Bay, 160
Kalakala (processor), 63
Kaliuda Bay, 35
Karakin, Ivan, 167–168
Karakin, Keratina, 168
Karluk, 18, 22, 24, 26, 31, 33, 42, 50, 66, 86, 122, 166, 193, 218, 225–226
Karluk River, 211
Katelnikoff family, 69
Katelnikoff, Aleck, 51
Katelnikoff, Freddy, 11, 62, 128
Katelnikoff, Irene, 51
Katelnikoff, John, 51, 118
Katelnikoff, Nick, 57, 62, 118, 126, 128
Katelnikoff, Nick, Jr., 51
Katelnikoff, Paul, 33
Katelnikoff, Peter, 128
Katelnikoff, Philip, 11, 62, 74, 130
Katelnikoff, Steve, 74
Katelnikoff, Zack, 118, 128
Katmai, 19
Katmai Bay, 208
Katmai Creek, 48, 58, 177
Katmai Packing Company, 54
Katmai Wilderness Lodge, 208

kayaks, 30, 32, 34, 167
Kazhuyak Bay, 19, 26, 66, 74, 227
Kazhuyak Point, 60
Kelly, Caroline, 126, 128
Kelly, Joe, 135, 137, 216, 219
Kelly, Sasha, 37
KFC5 (ship), 235, 239
Kichak, Pasha, 84
Kiliuda, 33
Kiliuda Bay, 29, 35, 175, 177, 213
King Cove, 14
kinship, 94–110, 153, 217
Kizhuyak Bay, 19, 66, 89, 158, 232, 237
Klouda, Naomi, 13, 107, 129, 208, 209
Kodiak Alutiiq Dancers, 125, 128
Kodiak Area Native Association, 13, 25, 77, 92, 110, 135, 216, 218
Kodiak Baptist Mission, 18
Kodiak City, 12–15, 20, 24–26, 28, 31, 34, 40–41, 47, 55, 59–60, 62–63, 65, 78–79, 90, 92, 118, 126, 134–135, 194, 209, 215–216, 220, 222–223, 228, 234
Kodiak Daily Mirror, 78
Kodiak Elders Advisory Group, 16, 18
Kodiak Historical Society, 12
Kodiak Island, 16, 19, 21–23, 28-31, 35, 38, 40–42, 45, 48, 50, 59, 64–66, 74, 81, 89, 95, 107, 109, 112, 118–119, 124–125, 141–142, 147, 154–157, 160, 163, 165–166, 167, 172–173, 176, 186, 199, 209, 216, 219, 221–222, 224–227, 232
Kodiak Mirror, 20, 125, 210, 215, 223
Kodiak National Wildlife Refuge, 40, 209–211
Kodiak Soonaq dancers, 126, 141
Koniag, 22, 24, 28, 30, 65, 68, 92, 135, 140, 142–143, 154, 194
Koniaq Corporation, 13, 17, 22, 211
Koowaq (bow-and-arrow game), 137
Korean War, 125
Krauten, Raymond, 41
Kreta, Joseph, Father, 120
Kreta, Peter, Father, 124
Krumrey, Roy, 209, 216
Krumrey, Stella, 92, 209
kulich (Easter bread), 121–122
Kvasnikoff, Christine, 19–20, 51, 53, 74, 132
Kvasnikoff, Ponto, 20

Index   253

L

Laetnikoff, Alex, 113
Lam, Carla, 216
land buybacks, 209–214
land otters, 30, 38, 51
Langsdorff, Georg, 30
Larionoff family, 69, 73
Larionoff, Kalumpi, 171
Larionoff, Moses, 129
Larsen Bay, 21–22, 24, 26, 42, 50, 59, 65–66, 74, 122, 124, 147, 163, 173, 193, 208, 225–226, 234
Lent, 83, 120–121, 137, 185
Levine, Arthur, 126–127
Lisianskii, 29
Litnik, 219
Little Afognak, 56, 73
logging, 67, 102, 200–201, 214–215
Long Island, 155
long lines, 199
loptuq (Aleut baseball), 137–138

M

mail boats, 41–42
Makarii, Father, 31
Malina Bay, 226
Malutin, Denise, 219
Malutin, Moses, 128
Marmot Bay, 19
Marmot Bay Excursions, 207
masking, 116-120
Mason, Rachel, 13, 97
masqarataq whistle, 117–118
Matfay, Arthur, 127–128, 220
Matfay, Larry, 12, 44, 84, 125–126, 128–129, 131, 135, 138, 191
Matfay, Martha, 135, 191
matrilocality, 72, 103
Mazhlinik (Mardi Gras), 120
McCord, Jack, 35
McCormick, Phil, 122
McDonald Lagoon, 30, 132, 159–160
meetings, 82
Melissa Rae (purse seiner), 169
Melovedoff family, 45, 69
Memorial Day, 122
Michener, Ken, 220
Middle Town (Old Harbor), 46–47, 91, 113–114, 220
Midway Bay, 170
Mishler, Clark, 13
Mishler, Susanna, 12, 26, 144, 147, 182, 186
Monashka Bay, 66, 89
Monk's Lagoon, 31, 48–50, 59–60, 73, 124–125
mortality, 77–79
Moser Bay, 225
Mt. Katmai, 50, 73
Mulcahy, Laurie, 13, 25, 130
Mullen, Evelyn, 233
Muller, Julian, 128

Muller, Walt, 228
music: accordion, 42, 126, 128–129; balalaikas, 49; banjo, 129; guitar, 42, 49, 126, 128–129; harmonica, 129; mandolin, 42, 126, 128; piano, 128–129; skin drum, 128; steel pedal guitar, 128; ukulele, 128; Unuguu song, 131; violin, 42, 126, 129

N

namesake (alukaq), 100
Nanwalek, 24, 119, 193, 213
Natalia Bay, 160
Natives of Kodiak, Inc., 214
Native Heritage Weeks, 216, 218–220
Naumoff, Alfred, 44
Nelson Island, 223
Nelson, John, Sr., 155
New Town (Old Harbor), 46–47, 113
New Valaam Monastery, 222
Newman's Bay, 160
Ninilchik, 20
North Cape, 51
Norwegians, 20, 37, 53, 188
Nuta'aq (New Year's play), 119

O

octopus (devil fish), 166–167, 186
olaqs (short hairy men), 131
Old Harbor Native Heritage Week, 216–217
Old Harbor City Council, 12, 80
Old Harbor family territories, 74
Old Harbor Narrows, 31
Old Harbor Native Corporation, 12–13, 15–16, 40, 65, 90–91, 209–211, 214, 220
Old Harbor Native families, 70
Old Harbor school, 13, 15, 27, 218, 221
Old Harbor Tribal Council, 12, 16, 80, 82, 90–91
Oleksa, Michael, Father, 46, 141, 223
Olga (ship), 48
Olga Bay, 225
Opheim, Chris, 20, 53
Opheim, Ed, Sr., 20, 25–26, 51, 53, 62, 74, 127, 155, 188, 222, 224
Oswalt, Marion "Jake," 20
Oswalt, Reed, 20, 25–26, 51, 55–56, 69, 74, 127
Ouzinkie City Council, 12, 91
Ouzinkie Community Hall, 64, 110, 121
Ouzinkie family territories, 74

Ouzinkie Narrows, 59, 66, 74, 166
Ouzinkie Native Corporation, 12, 18, 64–65, 90–92, 125, 208, 214, 222–223, 230
Ouzinkie Native families, 71
Ouzinkie school, 60
Ouzinkie Seafood Cannery, 62
Ouzinkie Trading Company, 62
Ouzinkie Tribal Council, 12, 64, 66, 77, 89–91

P

Pacific American Fishery Company, 226
Pacific cod (codfish), 38
Pan (Panguingue) card game, 139–140, 153
Panamarioff, Nicky, 128
Panamarioff, Paul, 12, 53, 91
Panamarioff, Sergei, 58
Panamarioff, Stan, 62
Panamarioff, Teddy, 62, 128
Panamarioff, Tim, 66, 89, 127
paralytic shellfish poisoning (PSP), 166
Paramanof Bay, 227
Pascha (Russian Easter), 83, 121–122
Pauline Collins (schooner), 32
Perenosa Bay, 19, 74
Peril Cape (ship), 234
Perryville, 24, 193
Pestrikoff Beach, 50
Pestrikoff family, 64, 223
Pestrikoff, Buddy, 159, 209
Pestrikoff, Charlie, 129
Pestrikoff, David, 59
Pestrikoff, Dorothy, 91–92
Pestrikoff, Ed, Sr., 40, 129
Pestrikoff, Geri, 217
Pestrikoff, John, 120
Pestrikoff, Johnny, 62
Pestrikoff, Lilly Ellanak, 18, 55
Pestrikoff, Michael, 84
Pestrikoff, Nick (Kolya), 11
Pestrikoff, Nick, Sr., 18, 25, 52–53, 59–60, 63, 102, 116, 125, 129, 131, 146, 203, 223–224
Pestrikoff, Peter, 11, 62
Pestrikoff, Sergei, 40
Pestrikoff, Vasilli, 49–50, 69, 128
Peterson family, 69
Peterson, Loren, 221
Peterson, Jeff, 12, 159, 173–174, 203, 206–208, 218
Petorochin, Peter, 72, 84
Petroff, Ivan, 35
Pewtress, Rick, 145
Phyllis S., (Mail boat), 41

Pilgrimage to Monk's Lagoon, 124–125
Pilot Point, 24
Pinochle (card game), 139–140
pirok (fish pie), 189–190, 193
Pleasant Harbor, 20, 59, 155, 223
pneumonia, 41
Ponti, Libby, 219
population trends, 75–76
porpoises, 154
Port Bailey, 233
Port Graham, 24, 119, 193
Port Heiden, 24
Port Hobron, 35, 133
Port Iron Creek, 226
Port Lions, 19, 22, 24, 26, 66, 73, 90, 96, 109, 116, 120, 122, 147, 155, 157, 161–162, 193, 200, 232–235, 237
Port Otto, 41, 160
Port Vida, 226
Port Wakefield, 226
Port Williams, 53
power dories, 56
Powers, Charlie, 204
Price, Gary, 159, 204
Price, Shawn Michael, 95
Price, Wanda, 95, 135, 204
Prince William Sound, 24, 66, 141, 143, 209
Protestant missionaries, 47
ptarmigan, 163
Pullar, Gordon, 28, 216, 223
purse seiners, 13, 18, 47, 62, 101–102, 114, 122, 149, 157, 164, 169, 172, 195–196, 200, 202, 204, 227
Pyles, Bill, 92

R

rain, 48, 181
Raspberry Island, 155–157
Raspberry Straits, 226
Rathburn, Robert, 24
Reft, Alfred, 62
Refuge Rock, 30–31, 132
regional migrations, 72–74
Renshaw, Tommy, 127
Roberts, Margaret, 125
Rogers, A. L., 59
Rolling Bay, 16, 74, 159
Ruf Ryder (mail boat), 41
Russian Christmas, 25, 112–116, 118, 122
Russian Easter, 121–122
Russian New Year's, 116–120
Russian Orthodox, 15–17, 24–25, 31, 39, 42, 46–47, 49, 56, 59, 67, 72, 86–87, 92, 107–109, 112, 120–121, 126, 137, 141, 148, 150, 152, 189–190, 222
Russian-American Company, 31, 48, 69

S

Salisbury, Richard, 215
salmon, 13, 35, 37, 45, 48, 53–54, 62, 66, 73, 75–76, 113–114, 132, 134, 141, 154–155, 176–179, 180–186, 189, 190–191, 196–198, 200–201, 204, 208–209, 217, 225–226
Saltonstall, Patrick, 219
Sargent, Fred, 54
Scandinavians, 13, 68–69, 72–73, 93, 95–96, 103, 125, 137, 141, 229
Schmaltz, Gerasim, Father, 11, 46, 56, 59, 122, 124–125, 222
Scroll, Miss, 59
sea lions, 103, 154, 167–172, 229
sea otters, 30, 32–34, 69, 194
Sea Pride (ship), 237
Seal Bay, 19, 74, 160
seal oil, 29, 50, 172
seals, 33, 154, 167, 169, 171, 176, 217, 219, 225–226, 229
Seldovia, 213
Setsicorn, Miss, 59
Settlers Cove, 161
Seward, 38
Shakmanoff Point, 74
Shanee (ship), 234
Shanigan, Trefim, 74
Shearwater Bay cannery, 35, 42, 62, 75, 81
Shearwater Bay, 35–36, 75, 159
Sheep Island, 159, 164
Shelikhof Strait, 66
Shelikhov, Gregorii, 28–29, 31
Shellfish, 155, 163, 166
Sheratine Bay, 74
Shields, Mr., 48
shrimp, 228
Shugak family, 72, 74, 84
Shugak, Alex, 209
Shugak, Roselissa, 37
Shugak, Tom, 195, 221
Shugak, Willie, 129
Shumagin Islands, 20
Shuyak (mail boat), 41
Shuyak Island, 54, 225
sikiaq (half-smoked salmon), 190, 217
Simeonoff, Judy, 219
Simeonoff, June, 135
Simeonoff, Mitch, 208, 219
Simeonoff, Speridon, 219
Simeonoff, Teacon, 219
Sitka, 16, 20, 50, 108, 135
Sitkalidak Straits (excursion boat), 17, 204–205
Sitkalidak Island, 16, 29–30, 35, 40, 45, 74, 129, 132–133, 159, 169, 204, 210, 219, 228
Sitkalidak Lodge, 47, 113, 169, 204–205, 206
Sitkalidak Straits, 28, 35, 37, 45, 159, 213
skiff man, 101
skiffs, 47, 56, 59, 62, 65, 132, 156, 158, 165, 170–171, 173, 175, 177–181, 186, 209, 222, 233–235
Skonberg family, 69
smallpox, 31
Smith, Carl, 234
Smith, Kevin, 234
Smith, Joyce, 20, 59
Smith, Norman, 20, 59
Smith, Sasha, 191
smokehouses, 177, 181–183
social mobility, 76–77
Soldier's Bay, 40, 60
Sonja (processor), 46
Sourdough Beach, 165
Sourdough Flats, 51, 53, 90, 131
Spirit Camps, 216, 218–220
sport fishing, 203–204, 206, 209
sport hunting, 156, 206
Spruce Bough (newspaper), 20, 118
Spruce Cape (boat), 62
Spruce Cape, 62
Spruce Island Charters, 207–208
Spruce Island, 19–21, 48–49, 51, 59–60, 66, 73–74, 89, 124, 173, 222
Squartsoff family, 51, 69, 74, 232
Squartsoff, Billy, 62
Squartsoff, Fred, 62, 177
Squartsoff, George, 233
Squartsoff, Herman, 92, 125, 190, 207–208
Squartsoff, Ivan, 33
Squartsoff, John, 33
Squartsoff, Martin, 19, 158, 165, 232, 235–238
Squartsoff, Melvin, 161
Squartsoff, Peter, 19, 33, 74, 116, 158, 161, 232–235, 237
Squartsoff, Theodore "J. R.," Jr., 158, 186, 191, 221
Squartsoff, Theodore, Sr., 19, 26, 129–130, 132, 157–159, 161, 163, 165–166, 177, 180, 182, 186, 189–191, 208, 232–239
Squartsoff, Toni, 19, 132, 177, 182, 186, 189–190, 208, 232
Squartsoff, Verna, 19
Squartsoff, Wasilly, 50, 58, 62, 74
St. Herman's Sisterhood of Holy Resurrection Orthodox Church, 118
St. Herman's Sisterhood, 222
St. Paul Harbor, 31
Stanley, George, 84
staristaq (church warden), 16, 80, 84, 86–87, 92
starring, 113–116
Steffian, Amy, 12, 219
storytelling, 112
Sturgeon River, 211
subsistence, 14–15, 17, 25, 40, 50, 66, 76, 81, 91, 112–114, 137, 154–192, 194, 206, 215, 218–219, 225–226, 232
suicides, 78–79
sukashiq (second chief), 80, 84, 86
Summer Gale (ship), 233
Sunny Cove, 20, 53
susekas (house mascots), 130–131
Svendsen, Charlie, 53

T

Table Island, 170
taboos, 174
Tanganak, 160
tariqs (banya scrubbers), 144
Tarissa Jean C. (fishing boat), 17
Tasha (ship), 233, 237–238
Tatitlek, 24, 141, 143, 193, 221
Taylor, Kenneth, 96
Thanksgiving, 125
Three Saints (ship), 31
Three Saints Bay, 28–29, 31, 35, 122, 129, 160, 213
tides, 31, 66, 156, 164–166, 173, 179, 226, 233, 236
Togiak, 77
Toms, Hender, 20, 26, 56–57
Tonki Bay, 74
Torsen family, 69
Torsen, Albert, 128
Torsen, Fred, 62, 74
Toshwak, Ana, 131
Toshwak, John, 131–132
tourism, 67, 206–209
toyuq (chief), 80, 84–86
Trap Point, 229
Trinity Islands, 32
tsunami (tidal wave), 42–43, 45, 61–63, 73, 75, 147, 160, 226. See also Great Alaska Earthquake
tuberculosis (TB), 38, 41
Tugidak Island, 33
Tundra Times, 14
Tunohun family, 84
Tunohun, Polly, 134
Two-Headed Island, 168, 172

U

U.S. Army, 15, 40, 49
U.S. Department of the Interior, 66, 89
U.S. Fish and Wildlife Service, 40, 173, 213
U.S. Navy Seabees, 60
Ugak Bay, 29, 31, 72, 160
Uptown (Old Harbor), *See* New Town

V

Vanek, Vicki, 219
VECO, 67, 233, 235–236
Veterans Day, 122, 125
Vietnam War, 125
village governance, 80–89
volleyball, 48, 144, 216
von Scheele, Robert, 41
VPSOs (Village Public Safety Officers), 92, 113, 234

W

Ward, Columbia, 62
Wasbikoff, Mike, 74
Washington Fish and Oyster Company, 225
weasels, 30, 38, 74, 176
weddings, 108–109, 144
welfare, 44, 202
Whale Pass, 74
whales, 29, 35, 133, 137, 154, 167
Windigo (ship), 235
winds, 35, 47–48, 51, 65–66, 158–159, 161, 165–166, 233–239
Wolkoff, Peter, 20, 62
Women's Bay, 40
Woody Island, 16, 31, 33, 50, 59, 72–73, 81
World War II, 15, 17, 20, 38, 59, 62, 109, 118, 129, 138
wrestling, 25, 216

Y

Yakanak, Anton, 84
Yakoff, Jacob, 62
Yak-Tat-Kwan, 214
Yakutat, 214
Yinchuns (dwarves), 130
Youth-Elder Conferences, 126, 216, 220–221

Z

Zeedar family, 45
Zeedar, Anakenti, 17, 80, 84, 92, 142, 159, 171, 181, 186–187, 229
Zeedar, Nina, 17
Zeedar, Senafont, 80
Zeedar, James, 171, 181

Index   255

ABOUT THE AUTHOR

Craig Mishler has been doing field work in Alaskan folklore and anthropology since 1972. He received a doctorate in folklore and anthropology at the University of Texas at Austin in 1981. From 1982 through 1986 he worked as a historian with the Alaska Department of Natural Resources, Division of Geological and Geophysical Surveys.

For ten years, he was a subsistence resource specialist with the Alaska Department of Fish and Game, Division of Subsistence, where he served as lead researcher on Kodiak Island and as the statewide marine mammal coordinator. Now retired from government service, he runs a private consulting business, Vadzaih Unlimited, and is affiliate assistant professor of anthropology at the University of Alaska, Anchorage.

Dr. Mishler has published several articles on Alutiiq culture in scholarly journals and is a contributor to *Looking Both Ways: Heritage and Identity of the Alutiiq People* (University of Alaska Press, 2001). In 1993 he published his first book, *The Crooked Stovepipe: Athapaskan Fiddle Music and Square Dancing in Northeast Alaska and Northwest Canada* (University of Illinois Press). In 1995 he edited a bilingual volume of Gwich'in folklore, oral history, and autobiography, *Neerihiinjìk: We Traveled from Place to Place: The Gwich'in Stories of Johnny and Sarah Frank* (Alaska Native Language Center, University of Alaska, Fairbanks), now in its second edition. Current projects include an ethnography and ethnohistory of the Han Indians, co-authored with William Simeone, to be published in 2003 by the University of Alaska Press, and an oral life history of Tanacross elder Kenny Thomas Sr.

Craig Mishler with a silver salmon in Old Harbor, September 1997. Photo by Paul Kahutak (Abalik).